Jacks on Tax
Your Do-It-Yourself Guide
to Filing Taxes Online

Evelyn Jacks

KNOWLEDGE BUREAU
NEWSBOOKS

WINNIPEG, MANITOBA, CANADA

Evelyn Jacks

JACKS ON TAX
Your Do-It-Yourself Guide to Filing Taxes Online

Printed and bound in Canada

ISBN No. 978-1-897526-97-2

Published by:
Knowledge Bureau, Inc. www.knowledgebureau.com
187 St. Mary's Road, Winnipeg, Manitoba R2H 1J2
204-953-4769
Email: reception@knowledgebureau.com

Research and Editorial Assistance: Walter Harder and Associates, Deanne Gage
Cover Design: Walter Harder and Associates
Page Design: Typeworks

Acknowledgements

A book of this size and scope takes a village: people who believe in the vision that Canadians will be able to find financial freedom faster if they understand how to do a better tax return.

I wish to thank the contributions of my long time tax research assistant, Walter Harder, who is dedicated both to the cause and the detail. He seems to love modelling tax case studies and new tax software tools with me (☺) and in general, is just wonderful to "think taxes" with. It's a pleasure to continue to work with you, Walter. Can't wait to see what we'll dream up next!

Deanne Gage has been an outstanding editor on this project, a respected and prolific financial writer in her own right. Sharon Jones does consistently pristine work in laying out our books, all with complete professionalism—so appreciated as we run up against tight deadlines.

Al Gordon and all the staff at the Knowledge Bureau are the "work family" supports who make it fun to go to work every day. Thanks for believing in our dream.

To three outstanding MFA designates—Alan Rowell, Doug Nelson and Kevin Gebert— thank you for your sage advice on how taxpayers can work smarter with Master Financial Advisors like you.

My sons, Cordell and Don, inspire me to aim higher and do my personal best always, because they do.

Hubby Al, thank you for being funny and loving at all the right times… my love for life soars daily, because you are such a big part of it.

Finally, to the many readers of this book across the miles and over the years, thank you for making the many hours worthwhile… we all do this just for you!

Sincerely,
Evelyn

Table of Contents

Introduction 7

Part 1 Getting Started 9
1   It All Begins With Hard Copy 11
2   Forget the Math: Rely on Your Software 16
3   Forget the Stamp: You Can NETFILE! 20
4   A Tax Return in 30 Seconds! 24
5   For CRA: It's About the Income 29
6   For You: It's About Tax Deductions and Credits 34
7   No Income Credit Filers 39
8   Avoid Common Errors 44
9   Know What You Don't Know: When to See a Pro 46

Part 2 Reporting Employment Income 53
10   Employment Income 56
11   RPP Contributions 62
12   What About Your RRSP? 65
13   Employment Expenses 69
14   Auto Expenses and Home Office 73
15   Claiming Child Care Expenses 79
16   Claiming Moving Expenses 84
17   Special Situations: Truckers and Others 88
18   Schedule 1 Tax Credits: The Costs of Going to Work 95
19   Severance and Unemployment 98
20   Your T4 Slip Entry Guide 102

Part 3 Families and Children 107
21   Conjugal Relationships: Filing With Your Spouse 109
22   Claiming the Kids: Yours, Mine and Ours 120
23   Students in the Family 130
24   Medical Expenses 137
25   Caring for the Sick and Disabled 141
26   Charitable Donations 149
27   Attribution Rules 153
28   Relationship Breakdown 159

Part 4   Reporting Investment Income..167
  29   Reporting Dividends, Interest and Other Investment Income 169
  30   Reporting Gains and Losses..180
  31   Personal Residences 200
  32   Rental Property...205
  33   Deducting Carrying Charges..209
  34   T-Slip Entry Guide 212

Part 5   Pensioners—Where the Action is! 219
  36   OAS Pension Reforms...221
  37   The New Canada Pension Plan Benefits.................................226
  38   Benefits From Private Pensions 230
  39   Splitting Pension Income With Your Spouse 238
  40   T-Slip Guide for Seniors...243

Part 6   Special Situations 255
  41   Immigration and Emigration...258
  42   Death of a Taxpayer...267

Part 7   Be Sure 275
  43   Double Check 276
  44   Avoid Penalties..278
  45   Exercise Your Rights: It's About What You Keep 282

Appendices 285
  1   Tax Filing Milestones...286
  2   Carry Forward Information 287
  3   Refundable and Non-Refundable Tax Credits Summary.............288
  4   T1 Line-By-Line Tax Guide..292
  5   Additional Resources..315

Index...316

Introduction

This book is about filing a better tax return in an electronic world. You'll find value if you use a paper process, or a combo—software preparation and paper printing and filing.

Regardless of your filing preference, you file your returns annually for three key reasons: to avoid penalties by filing on time, to tap into social benefits available from government, and to set yourself and your family up for better financial results, after tax. For many Canadians, the tax return is the single most significant financial document in the year. That's because it involves a lot of money.

The *Jacks on Tax* books I have written over the years have evolved with the changes at Canada Revenue Agency (CRA), which was previously known as Revenue Canada and Canada Customs and Revenue Agency. Today, the way Canadians file their returns is remarkably different.

We now file and transmit tax returns within a wired world. Each one of us may use a different tax software program and the screens we work on may look completely different. Some of us will print our returns and drop them into a mailbox or at the local Tax Services Office. Others will avoid the paper altogether and NETFILE.

In fact, over five million people file their tax returns electronically through CRA's NETFILE service. Another 11 million have their tax pros file their returns using EFILE. Starting in 2012, EFILING is mandatory for tax preparers: if filing more than 10 returns, tax pros must use EFILE or face a penalty of $25 per paper-filed return.

This is a great way to take better care of Mother Earth, given that there are over 26 million tax filers in Canada. But electronic filing also makes the work of CRA—collecting and redistributing tax across many government departments and then to millions of social benefit recipients—much easier. It's more accurate and cost efficient and it's also easier for auditors to spot unusual trends and even fraudulent filing practices.

If you don't consider yourself a tax or math whiz, using tax software will make compliance with CRA easier. The software does the math and automatically calculates and recalculates the complicated federal and provincial tax calculations. It adds and subtracts when it's supposed to and figures out your refund or amount owed with instant precision. If you use NETFILE, you don't even need to put a stamp on an envelope to deliver your return to CRA anymore.

But, here's where you do come in: you need to make it your business to know that you have filed the *most correct* tax return for your situation. Don't be among those tax filers who are leaving a small fortune on the table, not because tax software isn't doing a great job, but because they aren't fully using its power to reclaim for themselves the most money possible.

That's why you need this book. It can help you better understand:

- what documents to collect;
- what tax deductions and credits you can claim to reduce your income; and
- how you can plan your financial affairs over a period of years to pay the least amount of taxes.

You'll also learn how to have a more confident working relationship with the tax department and the financial professionals you may consult to help you build your personal net worth. That's important because today, indebted governments expect you to take care of your own future. Using tax software to do "what if" scenarios will make it easier to understand your opportunities to build, grow and accumulate savings with tax-efficient investment strategies.

When I wrote my first tax book, people were interested in understanding, line by line, what number to add to their paper-filed returns. To be honest, the framework of the tax return itself not changed much; neither has the importance of understanding the tax rules behind those lines. It's just a lot easier now to connect the dots between the changes in the economy, tax law and your family's life events because we have the power and convenience of tax software to help us.

Just by reading this book, I know there's an opportunity for you to discover many things you didn't know about your money. I'm betting you'll find at least one golden nugget that saves you money time and again for many years.

So, join me in this year's tax filing journey… especially important if you plan to use tax software or work with a tax pro who does.

Yours in tax savings,
Evelyn Jacks

PART 1

Getting Started

What's New

Millions of Canadians are using their computers to prepare tax returns and millions more are using CRA's electronic transmission services to file them. This will continue as CRA is encouraging those who print returns to avoid the paper process.

However, this doesn't eliminate the need to start with the hard copy and retain it for CRA's audit purposes if required. Today the news about filing a tax return is about online processes, but, make no mistake, CRA is very active in post-season audit activities. Your responsibilities haven't changed much in that regard: it's still as much about retrieval of hard or soft copy to back up your numbers as it is about the filings themselves.

Hard Copy

Before you enter any data into your tax software you'll need to gather source documents. But what do you need to find? Print out a copy of the tax return itself as well as Schedule 1. Use these as a checklist. Gather and sort T-slips as they arrive, and find receipts for out-of-pocket expenses—everything from medical costs to safety deposit boxes. Check last year's returns to make sure you don't forget one of the employers you worked for, various bank accounts or educational institutions attended. Arrange all documents in "data entry" to cut errors and omissions.

Software Tips

Finding the right tax software package is important for tax preparation and tax planning purposes. It's also your ticket to filing your return without a stamp. Get it early, so you can enter data from your hard copy as it arrives throughout the spring.

Tax Sleuthing

In filing a tax return, you're really trying to nail a couple of moving targets: annual changes in tax forms and rules, plus changes in your family's life events and financial milestones. Taking the time to update yourself on all the tax changes that could apply to you—with the help of the Appendices at the back of this book—will save you time and money. Then update yourself to the changes within your tax software as a final primer.

Tax Pro Alert

Your relationship with a tax professional is important even if you file your own tax return. Throughout various life events, the services of a trusted financial educator, advocate and steward will pay off.

1

It All Begins With Hard Copy

Despite all the help computers and software will provide in filing an accurate tax return, you can't escape the paperwork. Sorry, that's the bad news ☹.

It still all begins with the hard copy: gathering and sorting your tax documentation. This is the most difficult part of the job for most, but it will pay off to do it consistently, all year long. Three reasons:

- Data entry will be easier, and more importantly, faster.
- You will then focus more time on the various tax rules that will reduce taxes or increase refunds for every family member.
- A future tax audit, ever a reality, will be a breeze.

What should you keep? File the various T-slips you get in the mail. I like to enter the data into my tax software as they come in, then file them. But many more documents that can reduce your taxes or increase your tax credits and social benefits.

Not sure what to keep? Err on the side of everything! This includes all investment statements, and purchase, sale or maintenance details regarding your non-financial assets like cars and real estate. Personal expenses, like medical expenses, transit passes and children's extracurricular activities count, too. And, if you are required to work from a home office, use your car for work, or pay your own expenses, your "mixed use expenses," that is, the expenses for your car, home office and entertainment, may be deductible, as long as you deduct the personal use component in them. Keep a log of your business-related travel and an appointment log if you see clients or employees in your home office.

How long do you keep records? When it comes to tax compliance, it's all about retrieval! CRA won't want most of your receipts now, but be prepared to send supporting documents if required. That's true even if you have a scanning system. The record retention period is six years after the end of the year in which you file your tax return. Storing, sorting and filing hard copy properly, therefore, is an important part of the job.

How do you keep track of everything? I carry a wallet designed for receipt saving. I sort the chits once a week and store them in ever-ready tax files in a nearby file cabinet. It's pretty foolproof—it's a rare receipt that goes missing. My personal electronic devices help me keep an exact calendar of activities and appointments, including driving to and from appointments. Google Maps help me keep a level of precision to my business/personal travel logs so calculating auto expense claims are easy. Whatever storage and retrieval system works for you, use it consistently, all year long, is the way to go. But, if this is new to you, start three working files:

1. The Permanent Data File

This file carries information you'll use from one year to the next:

- Changes in names, address, marital status, date of immigration/emigration or date of death
- Employment contracts or severance package details
- Information about employer-sponsored pension plans, group benefits or stock options, private savings like RRSP or TFSA deposits
- Purchase price and/or proceeds of disposition of business assets, or non-registered investments
- Capital and non-capital loss carry-forwards
- Capital gains deductions or elections previously claimed
- Unclaimed moving, charitable, medical or tuition expenses
- Adjustments made to prior filed returns

While some of these tax terms may be foreign to you now, don't worry, you'll get to know them better throughout this book. Start this file now and have it handy so you can add some notes, definitions and questions as you learn more. This is also the place for questions for your tax, legal and financial advisors.

Carry Forward Summaries. Because this Permanent Data File is carried forward for use every year, enclose a copy of the carry forward statements printed from your software.

Some tax software packages also have a multi-year summary of your prior filed returns. Drop a copy of this into your permanent file for quick review. If you have switched software vendors or are using software for the first time, check to be sure that all the prior year information required to reduce your taxes this year has been carried forward. Having hard copy of prior filed tax returns and their significant schedules and forms is a good plan B.

2. The Working Copy File

Label this file prominently with the current tax year and the taxpayer's name; then place copies of last year's Notice of Assessment or Reassessment from CRA at the front, followed by all T-slips (Check the data entry framework in your tax software for the order it requires and sort slips accordingly—T4A, T4A(P), T4 OAS, T3, T5, etc.)

Behind this, keep a hard copy of the summary of the final return and all significant supporting schedules and working papers you may wish to refer to. This file may contain additional notes and calculations that explain how you prepared the return, and why, in case of audit.

 CHECK IT OUT | **What's the date on your N of A?** The date on your Notice of Assessment or Reassessment will determine deadlines for your appeal rights.

Print Out the T1 Tax Return. This is your roadmap and will act as your "anchor document" if you get lost in your tax software. Put it at the very back of your working copy file. This exercise provides a good way to test out the print functions as you set up your software. (If your software doesn't allow you to print out a certain blank form, you may want to download the forms in pdf format from CRA's website.) Printing the tax forms will also help you better understand that your tax software may be calculating certain figures as well as your refund or balance due in the background.

Basic Elements of the T1 Return. When you know the basic elements of the tax return, you'll be better able to "drive" your tax software. You'll find many tax filer profiles discussed in this book will refer to these elements:

- **Identification Area:** The information here must be precise. From birthdate to marital status to address and dependant information, it determines the size of income-tested social benefits and tax refunds/balances due, when the return is finished and how to deposit them (by cheque or direct deposit).
- **Line 150: Total income**
- **Line 236: Net income** (your tax credits are based on this number)
- **Line 260: Taxable income** (used to compute your taxes payable, if any)
- **Line 350 on Schedule 1**: (Federal Tax and Non-Refundable Tax Credits)
- **Line 484/485: Refund or balance owing**

Provincial Returns. While all Canadian resident filers complete a federal tax return, in every province, except Quebec where a separate tax return is filed, all provincial tax calculations are conjoined with the federal results. You'll look for Line 428 for provincial taxes payable and Line 479 for provincial tax credits on page 4 of the T1 tax return.

Auxiliary Tax Forms. This is also a good time to print out some of the additional forms CRA provides. This can include statements for Rental Income (T776), Income from

Self-Employment (T2125) or Moving Expenses (T1M). Often your software will ask you to select these as you set up your tax files. Printing them can help you to chase down the information you need to complete the return and attach the audit-required calculations and notes.

The first such form to address on the return is important, although largely ignored, despite the fact that similar filings for U.S. citizens made national news last year:

Form T1135 Foreign Asset Disclosure. Canadian residents who own assets abroad, must submit this form to CRA to disclose whether they had specified foreign assets held during the year if their value at any time exceeded $100,000 Canadian. You will find reference to this on page two of the T1 General Return and is, generally, in the identification areas of the software you may be using. Don't miss this step.

Non-compliance comes with big penalties. Fines as high as $12,000, $500 a month for up to 24 months, plus an additional penalty of 5% of the total cost of the foreign holdings, can be charged.

The foreign disclosure rules also apply to taxpayers who have transferred assets to active foreign affiliates controlled by the taxpayer, who has an interest in a foreign trust, who has transferred or loaned money to a foreign trust, or who has received distributions from a foreign trust. In this case an annual tax return as well as Forms T1141 and T1142, are filed, as required.

Excluded from the foreign disclosure requirements are personal use properties like a vacation home used exclusively for personal use, property used exclusively in an active business, property in an RRSP, RRIF and a registered pension plan, mutual funds that include foreign investments, property of immigrants (those who file a return for the first time in Canada) and shares in a foreign affiliate.

3. The CRA Audit File

This is the audit copy of all your back-up documents, which you may have to forward to the CRA if they request it. This might include medical expenses, babysitting, charitable donations, business expenses, utilities, etc. Always keep a copy of all information sent to CRA when they do ask for it.

 CHECK IT OUT | **Did you miss gold on prior-filed returns?** Professionals have systems that allow for continual review of prior filed returns and that's important for you to do as well, because you can reach back and correct errors and omissions on most federal tax provisions for 10 years under the Taxpayer Relief Provisions.

A taxpayer has 10 years from the end of a relevant tax year to request relief from penalties, request a refund or payment reduction beyond the normal three year period, or to ask the Minister to accept late filed, amended or revoked elections. This includes elections to have assets transferred to a spouse at fair market value for tax purposes (an important planning tool) and certain elections to roll assets over to family members when a taxpayer dies. There are also rules that allow a taxpayer to defer a capital gain when a replacement property is acquired.

This 10-year adjustment period rolls forward every January 1, so for the 2012 tax-filing year, for example, you have until December 31, 2022 to request taxpayer relief for most provisions.

CRA will be able to cancel penalties or interest when there are factors beyond your control: illness, death, disaster, civil disturbances and so on. When interest or penalties result from errors or omissions in public documents or delays in providing information to the taxpayer, it is possible to apply for relief.

When you request taxpayer relief for refunds beyond the normal three-year limitation, do know that "permissive deductions" are not included. You will not be allowed to request adjustments to Capital Cost Allowances (CCA) where less than the maximum claims were made, for example. In this case, you must make adjustments within 90 days on the date of the Notice of Assessment or Reassessment. Other permissive deductions include deductions that reduce business or rental income.

Provincial Tax Adjustments. Provinces usually offer a Statute of Limitations of three years. You need to keep track of this too. Always adjust your returns for any errors or omissions, bearing in mind that CRA will want to see back-up documentation and that such a request can initiate a review of your returns as a whole.

Voluntary Compliance. If you think you may have understated your income or overstated deductions or credits, it's important to adjust your returns (or file omitted returns) before you are asked by CRA to do so. That way, you can avoid gross negligence and tax evasion penalties.

Formal Appeals. Taxpayers who cannot get relief as described above may appeal formally to the Chief of Appeals at CRA or through the court system, by filing a Notice of Objection; 90 days after your Notice of Assessment or Reassessment and one year after the filing due date of your return.

 The Bottom Line | Address the six major sections of the tax return in order, for a consistent tax preparation experience. If you do tax returns for your whole family, this will save you time and money as you transfer provisions from one to another or split income.

2

Forget the Math:
Rely on Your Software

Tax software can help your family benefit from your tax filing rights in many ways. And you can largely forget about the difficult tax computations.

In fact, because the federal and provincial tax calculations are automatically working in the background, recalculating your results with every new number you enter, you'll be amazed to see the end game change with every keystroke. Your tax refund can change instantly, depending on what data is entered and how it is manipulated to give you the best results. So you can largely forget about the math!

Advantages of Software-Prepared Returns. Your goal is to take advantage of all the tax provisions available to reduce the income taxes you pay, or to get the most from social benefits available through the tax system. Using tax software can help with this. It can also help you be more compliant with the tax department. Remember, you are only required to pay the correct amount of tax. It is your legal right and duty to arrange your affairs within the framework of the law to pay the least taxes legally possible.

Optimization. Tax software can assist with the optimization of provisions that help you split income between family members, maximize transfers and carry forwards. This puts you in better control of your finances as an individual but also as a family unit. When you do a more correct tax return for your family situation, it increases your income and your capital. The financial decisions you need to make also become more obvious. When you see the tax savings, for example, you might find it difficult to give up contributing to your RRSP to go on the bus trip to the casino next month.

Maximize Investments. Tax software calculates and stores vital data you need to make important financial decisions, like how much money to put into that RRSP, for example, or what your capital loss balance is so you can take that into account when selling your rental property this year, so you don't pay more tax than you need to on those dispositions. Together with your three-step filing system described earlier, you will have all the information you need in your software, at your fingertips, all year long.

Maximize Income and Income Supplements. Your software will combine net income results on family tax returns to help you get the most from refundable tax credits like the Canada Child Tax Benefit, or non-refundable credits like the tuition, education and textbook amount and medical expenses. Software often provides the best solution automatically, but you will want to work that back… see all the numbers on the appropriate forms… to make sure.

Therefore, choosing the right software for your situation is important.

 CHECK IT OUT | **How do you choose the right tax software?** You can buy tax software at the store or download it from the internet. But how do you choose the right one for you. Here are some tips:

- What tax filer profiles can the software do? (Make sure it can do the six profiles discussed in Chapter 4).
- What is the cost per return?
- How does this compare in cost to using a tax preparation service which guarantees its work and represents you in case of audit?
- Can you NETFILE with this software package? (see next chapter for details)
- Can you print and file on paper if you don't have a NETFILE code?
- Where is the data stored? (In the "cloud" [a remote server] or on your computer?) Which is the best option for you?
- Are there educational tutorials in the software?
- Is there service and support if you run into a problem?
- Look for a free trial—so you can check out the environment for ease of use.
- Are there tax planning screens—opportunities to do "what if" scenarios all year long?

Setting Up Your Tax Software. Because there are so many tax software packages available, the comments in this book cannot be specific to all of their features. We will give you a good overview of how most tax software packages "think" but part of the software set-up instructions for each new tax year is to do the following:

- Familiarize yourself with the new features of the software.
- Familiarize yourself with the changes in tax law and how they may affect the returns you will be filing. (See the Appendices in the back of this book.)

- Import your data from prior-filed returns and update the identification sections and the "carry forward screens," that show important information from prior years that will be applied to this year's tax computations and/or used in other returns.

Importing Last Year's Data. If you used tax software last year, set up your current year return in the program. What a tremendous asset this is—all of your "carry forward" information is entered into your current year return, including all personal contact and birthdate details, and specific tax provisions that may be available to you from one year to the next.

Do this by opening the current year version of the software and then looking for tax return carry-forward command. Some tax software companies refer to this as importing a prior-year return, transferring a prior year return or converting a prior-year return if you've changed software products. Note that conversions between software products is not always available and may not convert all information. If you change software products and import or convert your prior-year return, be sure to check over the converted information carefully.

Carry Forward Information: Your Notice of Assessment or Reassessment. When you received your tax refund or balance due last year, you also received an explanatory note with important information about what changes were made to your tax return, how that affected various lines on your tax return, your current RRSP contribution room, amounts owed to CRA or whether you paid any interest to, your unused capital loss balances and so on. It's important to dig out that documentation now to see if any information needs to be added into your "carry forward" screens.

New Software Users. If you are new to filing your return with software this year, enter all the personal data for each family member on the head person's return. Some software may have a screen for entering family members and other software may require that you create a return for each family member and link the returns together based on each family member's relationship to the head person. Make sure all birthdates and address information is correct.

Then, enter any carry forward information from prior years into the program. If you are switching to a different type of software this year, you will need to import the data from last year's software. Not all software can import data from other software brands and where import is available, be sure to check the imported data for accuracy.

Take a Basic Tax Course. If you would like to take a tax course to help you with "what if" scenarios to better use the full potential of your tax software, do contact Knowledge Bureau at www.knowledgebureau.com. We also offer some free course trials that can help you get started using selected tax software options. The beauty of the trial scenarios is you can become familiar with both your tax software and changes in tax law.

Working With Hard and Soft Copy. Developing a consistent process for tax filing is important because you are dealing with several moving parts: the changes in tax law and administrative procedures from government, and the changes in your own life. How you work in entering data is important when you are using software. Most tax software makes the entry of data from T-slips very easy. Just follow along plotting information from the boxes on the slips into the matching info boxes in the software.

However, after this, when the supporting schedules, auxiliary tax forms, worksheets, notes or any other relevant documents saved throughout the year in support of other provisions come into play, you need to follow a consistent data entry plan.

I like to deal with the supporting documents and life events together, addressing them in the order of the line numbers on the actual tax return to make sure nothing is forgotten. This is also how we teach professionals at the Knowledge Bureau. They start by understanding the T1 return and its supporting schedules first. It's a good idea for you to do the same and keep it by your side as a checklist or guide.

 The Bottom Line | Tax software is an important tool in filing your tax returns and in developing a strategic income and capital investment plan. You will do your return more quickly and easily. It can also help you understand the T1 and your supporting hard copy better too, so you can plan to take better control of your after-tax dollars.

3

Forget the Stamp:
You Can NETFILE!

It's true, the stamp is out; electronic filing is in. Did you know that of the 26 million tax returns filed in Canada, only about a third of them still are sent to CRA on paper?

> ✓ **CHECK IT OUT** | **How many returns are filed electronically?** Here are the facts, based on the 2011 tax-filing year:

- Just under nine million tax returns in Canada are filed on paper. Some are prepared by individuals using tax software, but then the returns are printed and delivered to CRA.
- Over five million people NETFILE—they complete their returns on software and then electronically transmit them to CRA—no postage stamp required!
- Professionals using tax software also print to submit returns but that's no longer allowed for 2012 if your pro prepares 10 or more returns.
- Over 11 million returns are electronically filed by tax pros using EFILE.

CRA is very interested in reducing the paper delivery methods. Electronic transmissions of tax returns can have several advantages, including a faster turn around time for refunds and greater accuracy, as the information is only keyed in once—by the filer or his/her preparer. No need for CRA to have their data entry people do it again. The information is safe, encrypted along the way to ensure your information stays protected and confidential.

What's Required? You can use NETFILE if you have a 4-digit access code. You'll find it on the information sheet that CRA sends you. Keep this in a safe place to guard against identity theft. If you've lost it you can call in to receive a new one (1-800-714-7257) or go online to this link: http://www.netfile.gc.ca/ccsscd-eng.html.

Next, choose software with a NETFILE option. You can find a listing of approved vendors at this CRA weblink: http://www.netfile.gc.ca/sftwr-eng.html. The software packages we reviewed all printed returns, either directly or by creating a pdf file, which is important especially if you are doing returns for first time filers who don't have a NETFILE access code or others for whom a paper return is required.

Costs. For some tax filers this will be free. For others, costs begin around $10 per return and up. Some software programs or web applications for these purposes, charged by the return but others charged for the tax software, which included, at no extra charge, the opportunity to file a number of returns (up to 20, for example). If your tax return doesn't qualify for free service, you will have to pay whether you print or NETFILE. Transmission is always via the internet using your browser and no transmission fee is involved.

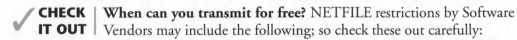

CHECK IT OUT | **When can you transmit for free?** NETFILE restrictions by Software Vendors may include the following; so check these out carefully:

- For free transmission services, net income on Line 236 is generally low. For some packages it must be less than $25,000, in others, $20,000 or $10,000.
- Several of the software products support only certain provinces.
- For the self-employed and investors, note that many of the choices do not support rental or self-employment income, limited partnerships or tax shelters and non-business foreign tax credits.
- Farmers note that many of the free offerings do not support the forms needed to report income under the AgriStability/AgriInvest programs.

NETFILE Restrictions. CRA also has its own restrictions: you cannot NETFILE if you wish to transmit an amended tax return, a tax return for any year except the current tax year; or a tax return for another person. Also, you're not eligible if:

- You or one of your dependants is claiming the disability tax credit for the first time or a new Disability Tax Credit form is required by CRA.
- There are several restrictions if you qualify to claim the foreign tax credit. You must use the full foreign tax credit available or you can't NETFILE, nor can you use the service if you are claiming a non-business foreign tax credit for more than three countries or a business foreign tax credit.
- Don't use it if you are filing a tax return for someone who died during the tax year or if you suffered a bankruptcy in the current or immediately preceding tax year.

- Immigrants, emigrants, non-residents or a deemed resident of Canada may not NETFILE.
- Don't use NETFILE if you are reporting income from a business which has its permanent residence outside your province or territory of residence.

There are other more obscure restrictions on the list, as well. Check it out at this link: http://www.netfile.gc.ca/rstrctns-eng.html#other.

The CRA Transmission Instructions. When you are ready to transmit your return to CRA, you will find yourself in a series of screens which require the following:

- You certify that the electronic return you are about to transmit is complete, reports all your income sources and is accurate. It must be original, eligible for the service and if you file more than one, you can be denied.
- Your Social Insurance Number, date of birth and access code.
- The path and name of the file that contains your electronic tax return. These programs will download a **.TAX** file to your hard drive. This is the file that contains the individual's tax return. You must find and select this and then transmit it to CRA.
- CRA will do a preliminary check of the file and if it meets these tests, you will receive a confirmation number, which means your return has been accepted.
- Rejected returns will be accompanied by a list of errors or corrections required. Corrected returns can be resubmitted.
- Remember: you cannot change your name, address, date of birth or direct deposit information through NETFILE; a paper filed return is required.
- Supporting documentations must be retained for six years after the end of the year you filed, in case CRA wants to see them.

Data Storage. As mentioned, there are applications for Windows, MAC and web products. If you choose a web-based product, you should be aware that, in most cases, your data will be stored online and you won't be able to convert your return for use on another tax program in a future year. If you choose an application for Windows or Mac that you download, your data will be stored on your own hard drive allowing you to review it at any time and possibly switch to a different product next year and convert your data.

 CHECK IT OUT | **Can you use EFILE?** If you are restricted by CRA from NETFILING, your choices are to use a third party transmitter registered for EFILING, or print and mail in your return.

Who Can EFILE? EFILE can be selected by those who file tax returns for others, generally tax professionals. However, any member of the public can qualify, but you must complete an application form and meet suitability testing by CRA first. The qualification process normally takes up to 30 days. If you have a history of tax fraud or evasion, have been previously rejected or are delinquent in complying with the *Income Tax Act*, *Excise Tax Act* or *Tax Rebate Discounting Act*, don't expect to receive your EFILE number or password.

Pros Must EFILE. Starting in 2013, for the filing of 2012 tax returns, those who file more than 10 tax returns for compensation must use EFILE—they may no longer process more than 10 returns on paper, unless the return falls under the various EFILE restrictions.

To EFILE, the tax preparer must be registered with CRA to provide the service and deal directly with the client. They must see all the source documents and enter the information on software that includes electronic filing as an option. Most tax pros will offer tax preparation and EFILE for a bundled price.

There are two ways to EFILE. Using *EFILE Online*, electronic filers are able to transmit a single return using the internet—a system much like NETFILE but available to registered EFILE service providers. The taxpayer's personal access code is not needed for EFILE in that case. *EFILE Online Plus* allows preparers to transmit batches of tax returns to CRA.

EFILE service providers enjoy an enhanced relationship with CRA. Like all electronic filers, it is possible to get immediate notification of debt owed by the taxpayer which could result in a reduction of the tax refund. The EFILE provider, with taxpayer consent can also act on behalf of the taxpayer, answering questions CRA may have regarding the tax return.

If you decide to become an EFILE provider because you transmit returns you prepare on behalf of others, it is a good idea to go through the registration or renewal process before December 31. EFILE is available through CRA from mid February until the end of November.

 The Bottom Line | Depending on the various tax filing profiles in your family, you may wish to choose tax software that has few filing or transmission restrictions. The more comprehensive, the better. Most reputable tax software companies will allow you a free demo; many also prepare tax software for professionals to use, so they are certified by CRA for all types of filing scenarios. Take advantage of the opportunity to try out several. Start early, as you wait for the various T-slips and other documents to arrive.

4

A Tax Return
in 30 Seconds!

Guess what? You can do a federal T1 Income Tax and Benefit Return (T1 for short) in 30 seconds. It's a fun demonstration for novice tax preparers and a sense of accomplishment to do your first one. With tax software, there are just a few simple steps, once you have loaded it and know your way around:

1. Enter all the identification information for the tax filer, address, spouse, dependants and birthdates.
2. Ask CRA to compute and forward GST/HST Credits when the tax filer turned 19 and let CRA know about foreign assets.
3. Enter the T-slip information.

Voila! The software effortlessly calculates the federal T1. Unless your province of residence offers refundable tax credits, chances are good that the provincial tax calculations have been done as well. Refundable tax credits in various provinces will have to be addressed separately. A brief synopsis can be seen in *Appendix 2 The Tax Forms—What's New Behind the Lines?*

You should be able to see it all on the tax return itself, as most tax software programs will let you print a one-page summary screen, which may look something like this:

Knowledge Bureau · Income Tax Estimator

Tax Year: 2012

Province	Ontario		John Student	
Children:	0	Single	Age:	18 to 65

Total income

Employment Income		$2,400.00
	Total Income	$2,400.00

Net income

	Net Income	$2,400.00
	Taxable Income	$2,400.00

Refund or Balance owing

Federal tax		$360.00

Federal non-refundable tax credits

Basic personal amount	$10,822.00	
EI premiums	$43.92	
Canada employment amount	$1,095.00	
Total	$11,960.92	
x Credit rate:	15.00%	
Total federal non-refundable credits		$1,794.14
Net federal tax		$0.00
Provincial tax		$121.20

Provincial non-refundable tax credits

Basic personal amount	$9,405.00	
EI premiums	$43.92	
Total	$9,448.42	
x Credit rate:	5.05%	
Total Provincial non-refundable credits		$477.17
Net provincial tax		$0.00
Total Payable		$0.00
Tax deducted, Instalments, or Provincial or other refundable credits		$240.00
Refund		$240.00

Estimated GSTC: $267.00

Your Tax Summary: Know the Benchmarks. Because the tax software will calculate a new refund or balance due with every number you enter, you will soon become familiar with tax filing benchmarks that are meaningful. For example, circle the important income lines:

- Line 150 Total Income,
- Line 236 Net Income,
- Line 260 Taxable Income,
- Line 350 Total Non-Refundable Tax Credits,
- Line 484/485 Refund or Balance Due.

You will find Line 350 amounts on Schedule 1; the rest of the lines on pages 2 to 4 of the T1 return.

CHECK IT OUT | **What's the most important line on the T1?** Arguably, Line 236, the figure used in income-testing for the purposes of refundable and non-refundable tax credits, because it is used extensively in tax planning.

When you reduce net income with an RRSP deduction, for example, you'll end up with more federal refundable tax credits like Child Tax Benefits or the GST/HST Credit. For seniors, keeping net income below certain "clawback zones," which are also determined at Line 236, will generate more Old Age Security. That helps in planning retirement income. There are several case studies throughout this book to illustrate. Also see *Appendix 3*.

Data Entry Approaches. As you become more confident in using your tax software and get to know the components and lines on the T1, you will note the data entry process may differ for different tax filing profiles discussed below. Software will usually account for this by allowing several data entry approaches. For example:

- **Line-by-Line Approach.** If your software allows you to use the T1 as an option for entering data, start at Line 101 and work in order of the line numbers, entering data from the line to any required schedules, auxiliary tax forms (e.g. T778 *Child Care Expense*), or worksheets (e.g. Auto Expense calculations).
- **Questionnaire Approach.** If your software has a data entry tab only, or a questionnaire it leads you through, you will need to follow this pre-defined order, at least at the start. Most programs will have you enter all the T-slips first, and you will want to do that carefully, as described below. Once you're done, ask the software to show you a copy of the completed return and review it line by line to make sure nothing was missed. At this point, you may be able to change your data entry approach to be more "profile oriented."

Carefully Enter T-slips first. Most tax returns are simple, requiring no more than a half dozen or so entries which originate from boxes on the T-slips. It's a good idea to enter these first, as you will immediately get a sense of the tax bracket this taxpayer will fall into and whether the withholding taxes deducted at "source" were enough. Common examples are:

- T4 Slips for Employment Income
- T4A Slips for Superannuation and Other Pension Income
- T5 Slips for Investment Income
- T3 Slips for Trust Income allocations

 CHECK IT OUT | **What should you do with all those boxes?** *See Appendix 4 Line-by-Line Tax Guide* for quick instructions on where to put information from every box on the most common T-slips.

CRA will have received one copy of these slips from the employer or financial institution and will cross-check your figures when they run their matching program in the summer. In the province of Quebec, some taxpayers will receive a tax return that already has the information from those slips on it so the tax filer simply verifies the amounts and then claims other provisions unique to their financial situation.

Tax Filer Profiles: Most tax filers will fall into one of these six tax filing profiles, depending on their primary source of income.

1. Credit Filers (these are income-tested; software will calculate allowable sums)
2. Employees
3. Investors
4. Pensioners
5. Self-Employed
6. Income Supplements (Worker's Compensation, Social Assistance, Spouse's Allowance and Guaranteed Income Supplement)

The opportunity is to understand what deductions and credits link to each income profile. This will help you to maximize those you are entitled to. In addition, you may not be aware that your software is in fact calculating some of these claims automatically in the background. Most people find this quite mind-boggling, as they are at a loss to explain how a number appeared on the return. Understanding what tax filing profile you fit into helps.

Line Linking. Every January, Knowledge Bureau leads a workshop for professional advisors called the T1 Line-by-Line Tax Update. Anyone can attend so let us know if you are interested. The most fun part of the day is when we do the "line linking" exercise. We essentially work through each income line of the tax return and indicate what deduction and credit lines link to it.

The object is to do a more complete tax return, faster and to the ultimate best benefit of the household. This happens because when you know the line numbers that link with each tax filing profile, you'll think of assembling all the possible information up front. I'd like to share the method with you.

 CHECK IT OUT | **Line Links.** Take a moment to discover some of the basic "line links" that will appear when you enter an income number on your return, on the chart that follows at the end of this chapter. It will help you familiarize yourself with your software. You will note that the income line that links to the most other lines on the return is employment income. That means your "simple" return may qualify for more tax savings than you may think.

The Bottom Line | Every tax filer has a primary tax filing "profile" but for most, this will be a hybrid. For example, you may be an employee with investment income who qualifies for the Child Tax Benefit. Knowing the deductions and credits that belong to your primary profile will help you do a tax return very quickly—often in less than a minute in simple cases—but more accurately. This will create new money for spending and savings.

5

For CRA: It's About the Income

What's the definition of income for tax filing purposes? It's an important question, first because there are many definitions, as you have already discovered in the basic elements on the tax return. But second, CRA will penalize you if you understate your income. If you do so intentionally, it's fraud and it could land you in jail.

Income. The word "income" has a broad meaning in the eyes of CRA. It covers most income receipts (see exempt list below) that is received in cash or in kind within the calendar year for most people. The calendar year is January 1 to December 31. In a very few cases, certain businesses and compounding investments, for example, a different fiscal year is possible for income reporting.

Income in kind can include something that has a commercial value, such as a bushel of grain, a gaggle of geese, gold, shares or a variety of services. To record such income receipts requires valuation. The onus of proof for fair market value is on the taxpayer. Therefore, do keep all indicators (appraisals, newspaper clippings, etc.) to justify the price you put on those items.

When is income considered to be received? For most taxpayers, income will be reported when received. This is called the cash basis. It doesn't have to be received in your own hands. It can come through an agent, be deposited in your bank account and so on. In the case of a cheque, it is considered to be received when it is deposited at the post office (i.e. it leaves the hands of the sender). This gives important guidance when you are trying to decide when to report that December-dated cheque received on January 3.

Cash vs. Accrual. The accrual method of reporting income is used by most businesses and for compounding investments. Notable exceptions are farming and fishing enterprises where the cash method is acceptable. Under the accrual method, income is reported when earned (whether or not received) and expenses are deducted when incurred (whether or not paid).

Income Definitions on the T1. In the previous chapter you have had a good look at the lines that relate to income sources. Take a moment now to better understand the various definitions of "income" on the tax return:

Total Income. Total income is Line 150 of the tax return, and includes income from all sources:

- Employment Income
- Commissions Earned By An Employee
- Other Employment Income including tips, wage loss replacement benefits that were jointly funded by employer and employee, and net research grants
- Pension Income (Canadian and foreign)
- Employment Insurance and Universal Child Tax Benefits
- Investment Income from taxable dividends, interest and rental properties
- Net Taxable Capital Gains (net of current year losses)
- Other Income Sources, including support payments, RDSP, RESP payments
- Self-Employment
- Income Supplements like Worker's compensation, social assistance and Guaranteed Income Supplements paid to seniors

Non-Taxable Income Supplements. You will note that income supplements are taxable and form part of income on Line 150, but in fact, they do not form part of taxable income. That's because there is a full offsetting deduction for these sources on Line 250. Your tax software will automatically calculate that, but do know that in between is Line 236, Net Income. The effect of these calculations is that the income supplements will decrease refundable tax credits.

Net Income. This is Line 236 of the tax return. It is total income less the deductions on Lines 206 to 235 of the tax return and is the income used for income-tested tax credits and social benefits in Canada.

Taxable Income. This is the income that is used to compute federal and provincial taxes (except in Quebec). It goes to Schedule 1 for computation of federal taxes, after which non-refundable tax credits are used to reduce the taxes payable.

Earned Income—for RRSP Purposes. This is the income that qualifies for building RRSP contribution room. This includes employment income, self-employment profits, rental income, CPP disability pension, taxable support payments received as well as a few more uncommon income sources.

Earned Income—for the purposes of claiming Child Care Expenses. This is the income that is used as a limit for your claim for child care expenses. This includes employment income, self-employment profits, CPP disability pension, training allowances, the taxable portion of scholarships received as well as a few more uncommon income sources.

Earned Income—for the purposes of claiming Moving Expenses. This income, if earned at the new location, is used as one of the limits for your claim for moving expenses. It includes employment income, amounts received under the WEPP program in respect of your employment at the new work location, self-employment profits, and the portion of scholarships and research grants that must be included in your income.

Exempt Income—very important—these sources will not be taxable:

- Income earned within a Tax Free Savings Account (TFSA)
- Income exempt by virtue of a statute, including the *Indian Act*
- Canada Child Tax Benefits
- Canadian Service Pensions, War Veterans Allowance Act Allowances
- Compensation by Federal Republic of Germany to a victim of National Socialist persecution
- Capital gains on publicly traded shares donated to a registered charity or private foundation
- Foster Care payments
- GST/HST Credit
- Income of Canadian Forces Personnel and Police on High-Risk International Missions
- Inheritance or gifts
- Lottery winnings
- Military Disability pensions and dependant's pensions
- MLA and Municipal Officers Expense Allowances
- Proceeds from accident, disability, sickness or income maintenance plans
- Payments for Volunteer Emergency Services—up to $1,000
- Refundable provincial or federal tax credits
- RCMP Disability Pension or Compensation
- Service Pensions from Other Countries, as well as NATO official's income
- Tax-free benefits of employment, including transportation to a special worksite, certain transportation passes, uniforms supplied to the employee, etc.

Working With Income Definitions. There certainly is a lot to know about your different sources of income. You'll want to understand how to earn and "layer" your income to be taxed by understanding what effective and marginal tax rates apply.

Effective and Marginal Tax Rates. When you divide total income by the taxes payable on Line 435, you will understand the taxpayer's *effective tax rate*—the amount of tax paid on total income.

CHECK IT OUT | **What's your effective tax rate?** Let's say a taxpayer's total income on Line 150 is $100,000 and total taxes paid (federal and provincial) are $35,000. This taxpayer's effective tax rate, therefore is 35%.

Your *marginal tax rate* is something different. It is linked to your tax bracket and analyzes how much you'll pay on the next dollar you earn from various income sources. This is an important concept too—not all income sources are taxed alike.

A taxpayer's MTR (Marginal Tax Rate) is a useful tool in measuring tax-efficiency of both actively and passively earned income sources. It will tell you how much tax you'll pay on the next dollar you plan to earn, while measuring the effect of that income on your eligibility for tax credits and social benefits delivered through the tax system.

This is different from the effective tax rate, which reflects the actual tax rate applied to your income after "progressivity" is taken into account. In Canada we have a progressive tax system, which means, the more you earn the more you pay and the less you receive from income-tested social benefits.

To compute your marginal tax rate, you need to understand that your income sources will be classified into several broad categories for tax purposes. For example:

1. **Ordinary income** is fully taxable and includes income from employment, pensions and interest. It may also include pensions, alimony and certain social benefits like Employment Insurance, and net rental income—what's left after allowable deductions.
2. **Income from self-employment** is reported on a *net* basis—what's left after revenues are reduced by allowable deductions.
3. **Capital gains** are reported upon the disposition (sale or transfer) of an asset. Only half those gains, net of losses, are reported on the return. Sometimes, gains can be avoided when certain properties are donated to charity. Other gains may qualify for specific exemptions from tax (the Capital Gains Deduction, for example).
4. **Dividends** are the after-tax distribution of profits from private or public corporations to shareholders. Reporting them involves an integration of the corporate and personal tax systems, the end result of which is a preferential tax rate.

When you know your marginal tax rate on the next dollars you earn, you can make better choices about your income sources and tax-preferred investments to get the after tax results you want on both income and capital. These results will vary by province, as illustrated below[1].

---

[1] Updates are posted regularly in ***Knowledge Bureau Report***, available free of charge at www.knowledgebureau.com.

Federal and Provincial Marginal Tax Rates for 2012

	Taxable Income Range	Ordinary Income	Capital Gains	Small Bus. Corp. Dividends	Eligible Dividends Large Corps.
BC	Up to $10,822	0%	0%	0%	0%
	$10,823 to $11,354	15.00%	7.50%	2.08%	-2.03%
	$11,355 to $37,013	20.06%	10.03%	4.16%	-6.84%
	$37,014 to $42,707	22.70%	11.35%	7.46%	-3.20%
	$42,708 to $74,028	29.70%	14.85%	16.21%	6.46%
	$74,029 to $84,993	32.50%	16.25%	19.71%	10.32%
	$84,994 to $85,414	34.29%	17.15%	21.95%	12.79%
	$85,415 to $103,205	38.29%	19.15%	26.95%	18.31%
	$103,206 to $132,406	40.70%	20.35%	29.96%	21.64%
	Over $132,406	43.70%	21.85%	33.71%	25.78%
AB	Up to $10,822	0%	0%	0%	0%
	$10,823 to $17,282	15.00%	7.50%	2.08%	-0.03%
	$17,283 to $42,707	25.00%	12.50%	10.21%	-0.03%
	$42,708 to $85,414	32.00%	16.00%	18.96%	9.63%
	$85,415 to $132,406	36.00%	18.00%	23.96%	15.15%
	Over $132,406	39.00%	19.50%	27.71%	19.29%

The Bottom Line | By understanding CRA's various definitions of income reportable on the tax return, you will be able to avoid tax evasion charges, and plan to "realize" various different income sources for tax purposes at different times that bring you the most advantageous tax results. This can make a big and positive impact, especially if you manage to avoid the next highest tax bracket.

6

For You: It's About
Tax Deductions and Credits

What's the difference between a tax deduction, a non-refundable and a refundable tax credit? You're not alone if these terms confuse you. It's important that you understand them though because the majority of the lines on the return are made up of them and if you are going to miss something, that's likely what it will be.

Deductions and credits work hard for you, so you want to claim them all.

Understanding Tax Deductions. Tax deductions come in two flavours: those which will reduce total income on Line 150 leading to net income on Line 236 and those which reduce net income to arrive at taxable income on Line 260.

Deductions that reduce net income can increase your income-tested credits and benefits. Since all deductions reduce taxable income they reduce your effective tax rate and, if large enough, they may reduce your marginal tax rate. It's especially important to understand that your marginal tax rate increases, not just because you pay more tax as your income grows, but also as you lose income-tested credits and benefits due to "clawbacks." Therefore, maximizing all deductions is a double benefit.

 CHECK IT OUT | **What are the most frequently missed deductions?** The most frequently missed tax deduction is the safety deposit box under carrying charges; the most lucrative is often moving expenses. All deductions reduce effective and marginal tax rates to reduce your taxes payable. What are you missing?

Understanding Tax Credits. Tax software does an outstanding job of allocating the various federal and provincial tax credits, many of which you automatically receive. There are three types of tax credits, and people often find this confusing. Often they can't find them and don't know they are receiving them—or could be. So let's begin there:

Federal Refundable Tax Credits. These credits are income-tested, based on the size of your family (both spouses') net income. This means the more you earn the smaller your credit. Check out the Appendices for current income thresholds. What's important is that even if you have no income, you may be eligible for them so always file a tax return.

- GST/HST Credit (paid quarterly starting at age 19)
- Canada Child Tax Benefit (paid monthly the month after your child's birth until they reach age 18)
- Working Income Tax Benefit (may be paid quarterly in advance to supplement expenses of low income earners who start working)

Provincial Refundable Tax Credits. Administered by the federal government, except in Quebec, these credits are also tied to the federal net family income definition, so it is very important to reduce family net income using all legitimate deductions, including available RRSP room. Programs that produce refundable credits (those that will be paid whether tax is payable or not) include the following:

On the federal tax return, Line 479:

- BC Venture Capital Tax Credit
- BC Mining Exploration Tax credit
- British Columbia Training Tax Credit
- Saskatchewan Graduate Retention Program Tuition Rebate
- Manitoba Personal Tax Credits for Taxpayer, Spouse and Dependants
- Manitoba Active Families Benefit
- Manitoba Education Property Tax Credit
- Manitoba School Tax Credit for Homeowners
- Manitoba Primary Caregiver Tax Credit
- Manitoba Advance Tuition Fee Income Tax Rebate
- Manitoba Fertility Treatment Tax Credit
- Manitoba Co-operative Education and Apprenticeship Tax Credit
- Manitoba Odour-control Tax Credit
- Manitoba Green Energy Equipment Tax Credit
- Manitoba Book Publishing Tax Credit
- Manitoba Cultural Industries Printing Tax Credit
- Ontario Energy and Property Tax Credit*
- Ontario Sales Tax Credit*
- Northern Ontario Energy Credit*

- Ontario Children's Activity Tax Credit
- Ontario Political Contribution Tax Credits
- Ontario Focused Flow-Through Share Tax Credit
- Ontario Apprenticeship Training Tax Credit
- Ontario Cooperative Education Tax Credit
- Nova Scotia Volunteer Firefighters and Ground Search and Rescue Tax Credit
- Yukon Research and Development Tax Credit
- Northwest Territories Cost of Living Tax Credit
- Nunavut Business training Tax Credit

* Ontario refundable tax credits are paid monthly rather than being included in your tax refund.

Off the tax return (sent to you as a result of tax computations on the return)

- Alberta Family Employment Tax Credit
- BC Family Bonus
- BC Basic Family Bonus
- BC Earned Income Benefit
- BC HST Credit
- BC Low Income Climate Action Tax Credit
- New Brunswick Child Tax Benefit
- Newfoundland and Labrador Harmonized Sales Tax Credit
- Newfoundland and Labrador Seniors' Benefit
- Newfoundland and Labrador Child Benefit and Mother Baby Nutrition Supplement
- Northwest Territories Child Benefit
- Nova Scotia Child Benefit
- Nova Scotia Affordable Living Tax Credit
- Nunavut Child Benefit
- Ontario Child Benefit
- Ontario Child Care Supplement for Working Families
- Saskatchewan Low Income Tax Credit
- Yukon Child Benefit

Non-Refundable Tax Credits. These are credits that reduce taxes payable, therefore if you have no taxes to pay, they do you no good. Everyone qualifies for the *Basic Personal Amount (BPA)* which is just under $11,000 this year. This is your "tax-free zone"—income under this amount is not taxable.

Most people who are employed will recognize BPA because they will have seen that number of the TD1 *Personal Tax Credit Return*, used to determine income tax source deductions. The BPA is automatically calculated by your tax software program on Schedule 1. Other non-refundable tax credits, depending on your circumstances, can be claimed to increase your tax free zone.

CHECK IT OUT | **Does your province match federal credits?** While both the federal and provincial government share a common definition of taxable income (except in Quebec), they do not have to offer the same non-refundable tax credits. This can make the tax filing process very complicated. Fortunately the tax software program you use will likely enter some of the credits for you on both returns; others are determined by your expenditures and you'll need to find them and address them. The following chart should help:

Name of Federal Refundable Credit	Automatically Entered by Software	Info you must enter	You must have receipts
Basic Personal Amount	Yes	N/A	No
Age Amount	Yes	Your birthdate	No
Spousal Amount	Yes	Marital status and spouse's income	No
Amount for Child Under 18	Yes	Details of dependants	No
Amount for Eligible Dependants	Yes	Details of dependants	No
Amount for Infirm Dependants Age 18 or Over	Yes	Details of dependants	No
Amount for CPP contributions	Yes	T4 slip	No
Amount for EI Premiums	Yes	T4 slip	No
Volunteer Firefighters Amount	No	Eligibility	Yes
Canada Employment Amount	Yes	T4 Income	No
Public Transit Amount	No	Amount paid	Yes
Children's Fitness Amount	No	Expense details	Yes
Children's Arts Amount	No	Expense details	Yes
Home Buyers' Amount	No	Enter the amount	Yes
Adoption Expenses	No	Expense detail	Yes
Pension Income Amount	Yes	Eligible pension income	Yes (Slips)
Caregiver Amount	Yes	Dependant info	No
Disability Amount (self or dependant)	No	Eligibility	Yes (T2201)
Interest Paid on Student Loans	No	Amount paid	Yes
Tuition, Education and Textbook Amount (self and dependant)	No	T2202 info	Yes
Medical Expenses	No	Expense details	Yes
Charitable Donations	No	Amount donated	Yes

The Bottom Line | Take the time to really dig for every tax deduction, refundable and non-refundable credit you are entitled to. Tax software can claim what it thinks you qualify for, but it won't know about your medical expenses or that you purchased your first home. Don't let that that happen at the expense of lucrative amounts that could reduce your taxes this year or in the future.

7

No Income Credit Filers

A credit filer is someone who has little or no income. This person is not taxable and files to receive income supplements from the government, often paid monthly or quarterly, including federal tax credits like the Canada Child Tax Benefits, GST/HST Credits or the Universal Child Care Benefit. Approximately 35% of all returns filed in Canada are not taxable. Millions of others have net income levels low enough to qualify for full or partial refundable tax credits.

Eligibility for Refundable Tax Credits. Refundable tax credits can be received from the federal government, and in some cases, provincial governments. The following people *may not* claim refundable credits:

- Those confined to a prison at the end of the year and so confined for six months or more.
- Those who died during the year.
- Diplomats who are not taxable in Canada.

Teenagers Should File for GST/HST Credits. Typical first-time credit filers are 18-year-olds who file for the federal GST/HST Credit, which they will receive the quarter after they turn 19, and at-home single mothers who file for the UCCB, the CTB and the GSTC.

Filing a Return is Easy. If a GST/HST Credit filer has no income at all to report, filing a return is as simple as counting to five:

1. Enter the taxpayer identification information.
2. Answer the citizenship and Elections Canada questions and address the foreign property lines.

3. Check yes under the GST/HST Credit application in the last box on Page 1.
4. Your software will enter zeros on the key income lines: 150, 236, 260.
5. Your software will determine the amount of credit available to the taxpayer. This will show up on the tax summary as well.

Credit Filers with Income. Many credit filers do have income of some sort so determining the value of deductions they may be entitled to or non-refundable tax credits is the first step in the process of filing the entire tax return.

Because of the importance of net income on Line 236, consider the advantages of an RRSP contribution and deduction even for low-income earners. The objective is to get net income under the "clawback thresholds" so you can get more credits for your family. Clawbacks reduce your available tax credits.

 What do low earners need to know about credit filing?

- No- or low-income adults in most Canadian families should always file a tax return every year to receive their refundable tax credits like the GSTC and the CCTB.
- Both spouses or common-law partners must split certain income sources.
- Both will want to file to receive social benefits like the Universal Child Care Benefit and the Old Age Security Benefits.

Other Important Issues:

- The "statute of limitations" is shorter for federal refundable credits than for most other provisions. Technically, you can only go back 11 months to recover missed credits. It is possible to apply for a recovery for a period longer than this, where the appeal is based on circumstances of hardship. See "Voluntary Disclosure Programs" below.
- Provinces also offer tax form based credits or monthly income supplements which are paid to low-income Canadians according to the net income reported on their returns. Look for reference to Line 479 specific to each province.
- The money received from these refundable tax credits can provide a way to save for a child's future education and/or to split the investment income earned on the money.

 How do you determine if your income is too high for refundable tax credits? "Family net income" is used to determine the level of refundable tax credits, so you'll need to have your spouse's net income figures from Line 236 of the federal T1 return available to file for refundable tax credits.

If you are using tax software, it will automatically calculate the refundable tax credits you are entitled to, provided you have correctly indicated that you have a spouse or common-law partner and what that person's net income is. For those reasons, families should file together (see Chapter 21 for details). But this is also where many single parents can make an important mistake. You may not know that your "live-in" relationship has tax consequences.

 CHECK IT OUT | **What if my marital status changes?** If your marital status changes, you must tell CRA about this on *Form RC 65 Marital Status Change* by the end of the month following the month of change, so they can adjust your claim for your refundable credits. Both spouses must sign the form and submit their Social Insurance Numbers. However, if you become separated, they don't want to hear from you until you have been separated for more than 90 consecutive days.

Generally, the Canada Child Tax Benefit will be sent to the female parent, in the case of couples of the same sex; although, it is possible for the male parent to apply for this if he is *primarily responsible*, which means that a *Form RC66 Canada Child Tax Benefit Application* must be completed.

There are lots of details that can impact who gets these credits, as you can imagine. We will cover this in more detail in Part 3, but be aware, if you have been filing for credits as a single person, using only your net income for the purposes of applying for your refundable tax credits but you are living common-law, you are offside. To avoid penalties and interest you can voluntarily comply with proper notification to CRA.

Voluntary Disclosures Program. When you voluntarily correct errors or omissions on your tax return, you will avoid penalties and interest. It's easy to do. Simply adjust your tax return using form T1ADJ, which you will find in your tax software. You can go back to recover missed provisions for up to 10 years in many cases.

Try It! Use Software to File For Tax Credits

It's a lot of fun preparing your first tax return! The terms are new but using the power of tax software, you'll be empowered to understand how much of your hard earned money you get to keep, and how the opportunities to apply for refundable tax credits and a refund of any overpaid taxes can help you plan investments, too.

Most tax software packages will give you the option to review a "tax summary" similar to the one that follows, to see if you are getting the tax calculation results you should be, based on your tax documentation. It's a great way to check your work. That summary will then be used to match up to the results CRA sends you back on your Notice of

Assessment. Your tax summary should also tell you about how much you can expect from various refundable tax credits.

Case Study | Filing For Credits and to Create RRSP Room

The following is a tax summary for a tax return filed for an 18-year-old girl who has part-time income from babysitting and working at the local hamburger joint.

You will see Jill has created RRSP room with her "earned income," and she qualifies for a GST/HST Credit next year. Note total, net and taxable income is circled. Recall the definitions of each type of income.

If Jill will turn 19 before June 1, 2014, she should apply for the Ontario Sales Tax Credit by filing form ON-BEN with her return. The credit will be paid monthly beginning the month after her 19th birthday.

Now think about how you will use the information to plan for financial life events and to increase future income potential for this young woman with investment planning?

The Bottom Line | It's important to find ways to reduce the lower earner's net income to generate more credits and deductions. Consider filing a tax return for every family member every year.

Knowledge Bureau® Income Tax Estimator — Tax Year: 2012

Excellence in Financial Education

Province	Ontario			Jill Student	
Children:	0	Single	Age:	18 to 65	

Total income

Employment Income		$5,445.24
	Total Income	$5,445.24

Net income

	Net Income	$5,445.24
	Taxable Income	$5,445.24

Refund or Balance owing

Federal tax		$816.79

Federal non-refundable tax credits

Basic personal amount	$10,822.00		
CPP contributions	$96.29		
EI premiums	$99.65		
Canada employment amount	$1,095.00		
Total	$12,112.94		
x Credit rate:	15.00%		
		Total federal non-refundable credits	$1,816.94
		Net federal tax	$0.00
Provincial tax			$274.98

Provincial non-refundable tax credits

Basic personal amount	$9,405.00		
CPP contributions	$96.29		
EI premiums	$99.65		
Total	$9,600.94		
x Credit rate:	5.05%		
		Total Provincial non-refundable credits	$484.85
		Net provincial tax	$0.00
		Total Payable	$0.00
Tax deducted, Instalments, or Provincial or other refundable credits			$544.52
		Refund	$544.52

Estimated GSTC: $267.00

8

Avoid Common Errors

Tax software does make tax filing and transmission much easier, but you can still make costly errors on your tax return. Most of the software packages will ask you pointed questions about the things you may have forgotten about or bar you from going on unless you enter required information. That's a really good thing!

However there are errors or omissions even your smart tax software can't catch. To avoid them, always follow a process that includes double-checking your data entry to all numbers on the hard copy or other source documents. Pay particular attention to these five "wrap up" principles:

1. **Data entry**: Did you avoid transposition errors (89 instead of 98) and keying information into wrong line or box numbers?
2. **Tax compliance**: Did you report all income—amounts received in cash or in kind— for the calendar year?
3. **Tax theory:** Did you claim all the tax deductions and credits you are entitled to?
4. **Document Assembly**: Did you assemble your Permanent File, Working File and CRA Audit file appropriately to communicate with precision in case of audit or adjustment for errors or omissions?
5. **Logic:** Does the outcome make sense? Did you make $20,000 more this year but find you are paying less tax? The year-to-year tax summary comparisons in many software programs are very helpful in this regard. Be sure to find out why. There may be an error.

CHECK IT OUT | **Have you made a common mistake?** Consider this list as you file your return, then check your return carefully before you deliver it—electronically or otherwise—to CRA. You won't want to hold up your refund, or understate it!

Category	Error or Omission	Line
Income	Taxable Benefits Double Reported—remember, taxable benefits are already included in Box 14 of your T4 slip.	101
Income	Missed Premium Deduction on Wage Loss Replacement Benefits Received—get this info from your payroll department.	104
Income	Failure to Report Tips and Gratuities	104
Income	Failure to Report Taxable Foreign Pension	115
Income	Interest income not reported	121
Income	Missed claiming capital losses or capital gains	127
Deductions	Lost RRSP receipt; claim taken in incorrect tax year	208
Deductions	Missed GST/HST Rebate on employment expenses	457
Deductions	Moving expenses—missed real estate commissions	219
Deductions	Missed safety deposit box fees in carrying charges	221
Deductions	Missed home office and auto claims by eligible employees	229
Deductions	Business loss not carried back or forward using Form T1A	252
Deductions	Prior year capital losses not recorded	253
Credits	Spousal Amount—gross Rather than net income entered	303
Credits	Amount For Eligible Dependants—for single parents	305
Credits	Caregiver Amount—Missed claim for infirm parent	315
Credits	Disability Amount—Missed claim for sick child or spouse	318
Credits	Tuition, Education and Textbook Credits—missed transfer to parents or other supporting individual	324
Credits	Medical expenses—missed claims for self or dependants	330
Credits	Donations—claimed on both spouses' returns instead of one	349
Instalments	Tax instalment payments made missed	476

 The Bottom Line | Take time to prepare an accurate, audit-proof return, starting with the lowest earner in the family and working to the highest. It's time consuming and therefore vexing to have to correct errors later. Even if you use tax software, remember, there are lots of ways to go wrong, so have a consistent process for double-checking your tax returns before sending them in to CRA.

9

Know What You Don't Know: When to See a Pro

Filing a tax return is a life skill everyone should have. Paying taxes will not go away any time soon, and you need to know how to do three things:

1. Keep more of the first dollars you earn.
2. Hold onto them the longest.
3. Make sure they have purchasing power when you need them.

Knowing more about your tax filing rights and opportunities makes you the master of your money. You will earn more and keep more because you are making tax-savvy decisions. However, that knowledge can be significantly enhanced when you work with a professional advisory team, including a tax professional.

That person, if trained well, should not just be able to do the transaction of filing returns for you. He or she should also be your tax educator, an advocate for your tax filing rights and a steward of your family's money by making sure you only pay the correct amount of tax throughout your lifecycle.

When to see a Pro. You should be prepared to speak to a pro when you have a "trigger question," that is, there is a financial decision you feel you need to make about life events, financial events or economic events that may affect you. Tax filing time is a good one to do so. There are three types of triggers you may wish to discuss and the following checklists can help you gather your thoughts:

Life Triggers. These age-related tax milestones indicate a new or changed filing status:

Milestone	Significance for Tax Preparation or Planning
Birth to age 7	• Claim child care expenses and apply for enhanced Child Tax Benefits and Universal Child Care Benefits • Claim non-refundable credits for dependent children under 18 • Children's Fitness Tax Credit and Children's Arts Tax Credit available • Claim Disability Amount for a disabled child • Open bank account and deposit Child Tax Benefit and gifts from non-residents—both are free from the Attribution Rules • Gift investments that produce capital-gains—Attribution Rules do not apply • Open RESP savings accounts to earn up to $500 CESG or CLB Credits
Ages 7-17	• Claim amount for dependent children under 18 • Child care expense claim reduced but still possible • Children's Fitness Tax Credit and Children's Arts Tax Credit available • Canada Child Tax Benefits reduced but still possible • Create RRSP room by reporting all employment/self-employment • Continue to invest in RESP; CESG eligibility ends at end of the year the child turns 17 • Continue to deposit Child Tax Benefits into untainted savings account
Age 18	• File return so child receives GST/HST Credit starting after 19th birthday • CPP premiums become payable the month after the 18th birthday • Child tax benefits end; Eligibility for amount for eligible dependant ends • TFSA contribution room begins to accumulate
Age 19	• GST/HST Credit becomes payable the quarter after turning 19 • Post-secondary school bound: report RESP income, tuition/education/textbook amounts, student loan interest
Ages 20-30	• Conjugal relationships: income splitting, RRSP spousal plans, TFSA • First Time Home Buyers' Tax Credit may be utilized • Use Home Buyers' Plan and Lifelong Learning Plan under RRSP
Ages 31 to 59	• Peak productivity: RRSP and TFSA maximization; tax efficiency in non-registered savings; business start rules important • Tax-wise employment negotiations important • Family issues: consequences on divorce, illness and death • Charitable gift planning: annual updates required • Parental care: Caregiver Amount, medical expenses

Milestone	Significance for Tax Preparation or Planning
Age 60 plus	• CPP early retirement (age 60 – 64); split income with spouse • Retirement income sources change taxpayer profile • Pension withdrawal planning; clawback zones; pension income splitting • Sale of taxable and non-taxable assets • Transfer of property within the family • OAS begins at age 65 (but may be delayed beginning July 2013) • Age Credit Amount starting at age 65 • Pension income splitting for RRSP/RRIF starting at age 65 • Withdrawals from RRSP by age 71; make spousal RRSP contribution if spouse is under age 71 and you have contribution room • Check instalment payment requirements

Financial Triggers. Consider seeing a tax or financial pro (or both) if you aren't sure of the answers to these 12 questions:

1. Have I claimed everything I was entitled to in previous tax years?
2. Have I reported all the capital losses I may be entitled to claim in the future?
3. What are the marginal tax rates on our various source of income?
4. How much should each family member contribute to RRSPs this year?
5. When should I make a $2,000 RRSP over-contribution?
6. How should I structure my employment bonus to pay the least tax?
7. How should I structure my severance package to pay the least tax?
8. Should I defer taking my OAS or CPP pensions or should I begin CPP early?
9. Should I phase into retirement by tapping into my employer-sponsored pension plan early?
10. What is the most tax-efficient way to transfer assets to my spouse or child?
11. Should we be investing in a TFSA?
12. Should we be investing in an RESP or RDSP?

Economic Triggers. A lot is going on in the global economy these days and one of the ways to hedge your investments against the potential of increasing inflation, taxes or volatile economic performance is to make sure you are discussing your tax efficiency strategies today. You may be concerned about how to offset the losses you have in your various investment accounts, or how to shelter your savings from inflation in the future. You may also wonder whether you should remain in equities or bonds. Use the economic circumstances of the day and the following checklist to find a tax and financial advisor to help:

Interview Checklist: Finding A Professional Team

• What are your top three concerns about your taxes?
• What are your top three concerns about your investments?
• Has the professional answered your concerns in plain English?

- Would you consider this person a financial educator?
- How does the professional price his or her services?
- Are they available to help you year round?
- Do they have a "succession" team—juniors they are mentoring so you can get service in case of vacation or illness?
- Is there a guarantee of services—what happens if there is an error or omission that costs you interest, penalties or causes you to lose money?
- Can the professional provide you with three referrals to professionals who have worked with him/her?
- Can the professional provide you with three referrals to clients who have worked with him/her?

You may also wish to go over the "line links" that follow as a way to double check your understanding of what's happening on your returns. Has everything you are entitled to been claimed this year or in the past?

You may also wish to pick up a copy of the companion book to this one: *Essential Tax Facts: Secrets and Strategies for Take-Charge People* will help you to answer economic trigger questions so you can plan your investments and income withdrawal choices with the right professional team. In the meantime, using this book to learn more about filing your own return is an important step in working smarter with tax, investment, retirement and estate planning pros.

 The Bottom Line | Especially if you file your own tax return, a relationship with a financial advisory team, including a tax, investment, retirement, estate and legal advisor, can help you take charge of your wealth and make better decisions about your money. Make sure you deal with competent professionals who can be your financial educator, advocate and steward of your hard earned money. Look for someone who has training as a wealth advisor and can work strategically within a team structure.

Figure 1.1 T1 Line Links

Filing Profile	On T1 (Pages 2 to 4)	On Schedule 1
Employment: Line 101—From Box 14 of T4 Slip 102—Commissions 104—Other Employment Income (e.g. tips)	206 Pension adjustment 207 Registered pension plan deduction 208 RRSP deduction 209 Saskatchewan Pension Plan deduction 212 Annual union, professional, or like dues 214 Child care expenses 215 Disability supports deduction 219 Moving expenses 229 Other employment expenses 244 Canadian Forces personnel and police deduction 248 Employee home relocation loan deduction 249 Security options deductions 255 Northern residents deductions 437 Total income tax deducted 448 CPP overpayment 450 Employment Insurance overpayment 452 Refundable medical expense supplement 453 Working Income Tax Benefit 457 Employee and partner GST/HST rebate	308 CPP or QPP contributions: through employment 312 CPP or QPP contributions: through self-employment and other earnings 330 Medical expenses for self, spouse or common-law partner, and dependent children 332 Allowable amount of medical expenses for other dependants 349 Donations and gifts 363 Canada employment amount 364 Public transit amount 362 Volunteer firefighters' amount 415 Working Income Tax Benefit advance payments received 426 Overseas employment tax credit
Pensioners		
113 OAS Income	235 Social benefits repayment 422 Social benefits repayment 476 Tax paid by instalments	301 Age amount 326 Amounts transferred from spouse or common-law partner 330 Medical expenses for self, spouse or common-law partner, and dependent children 349 Donations and gifts
114 CPP Income	152 Disability benefits 208 RRSP deduction 437 Total income tax deducted	Schedule 1: 301 Age amount 306 Amount for infirm dependants age 18 or older

Filing Profile	On T1 (Pages 2 to 4)	On Schedule 1
115 Periodic Canadian & Foreign Pensions	210 Deduction for elected split-pension amount 256 Additional deductions 437 Total income tax deducted	301 Age amount 303 Spouse or common-law partner amount 314 Pension income amount 326 Amounts transferred from spouse or common-law partner
116 Elected Split Pension Amount	210 Deduction for elected split-pension amount 437 Total income tax deducted 476 Tax paid by instalments	301 Age amount 303 Spouse or common-law partner amount 314 Pension income amount
Social Benefits		
117 UCCB **185**	213 Universal Child Care Benefit repayment 214 Child care expenses	305 Amount for an eligible dependant 318 Disability amount transferred from a dependant 364 Public transit amount 365 Children's fitness amount 367 Amount for children born in 1994 or later 370 Children's arts amount 326 Amounts transferred from spouse or common-law partner 453 Working Income Tax Benefit (WITB)
119 EI	235 Social benefits repayment deduction 422 Social benefits repayment	
Investors		
120 Dividends	221 Carrying charges and interest expenses 476 Tax paid by instalments	303 Spouse or common-law partner amount 424 Federal tax on split income 425 Federal dividend tax credit 427 Minimum tax carryover
121 Interest	221 Carrying charges and interest expenses	
122 Net Partnership Income	221 Carrying charges and interest expenses 251 Limited partnership losses other years	

Filing Profile	On T1 (Pages 2 to 4)	On Schedule 1
125 RDSP Income	215 Disability supports deduction	316 Disability amount (for self)
126 Rental Income	208 RRSP deduction 476 Tax paid by instalments	
127 Capital Gains	253 Net capital losses of other years 254 Capital gains deduction 476 Tax paid by instalments	349 Donations and gifts
128 Support Payments	208 RRSP deduction 437 Total income tax deducted 476 Tax paid by instalments	
129 RRSP Income	208 RRSP deduction 437 Total income tax deducted 476 Tax paid by instalments	
130 Other Income	208 RRSP deduction 418 Additional tax on Registered Education Savings Plan Accumulated Income Payments	319 Interest paid on student loans 323 Tuition, education and textbook amounts
135-143 Self-Employed	208 RRSP deduction 209 Saskatchewan Pension Plan deduction 222 CPP or QPP contributions on self-employment and other earnings 415 Working Income Tax Benefit advance 421 CPP contributions payable on self-employment and other earnings 430 Employment Insurance premiums payable on self-employment and other eligible earnings 452 Refundable medical expense supplement 453 Working Income Tax Benefit 476 Tax paid by instalments	310 CPP or QPP contributions on self-employment and other earnings 317 Employment Insurance premiums on self-employment and other eligible earnings
144, 145, 146 Supplements	250 Other payments deduction	

PART 2

Reporting Employment Income

Tax Fact | Over 16 million tax returns report employment income; and over 15 million tax returns result in an average tax refund of $1,659 per return.

What's New

Most years your paycheque will be affected by changes to "statutory deductions"—Canada Pension Plan (CPP) and Employment Insurance (EI), and Income Taxes due to indexing and changes to rates and credits. This year an important change affects older workers who must continue to contribute to the CPP at least to age 64, even if they are also receiving CPP retirement benefits. Between age 65 and 69, you can choose to opt out.

Hard Copy

Form CPT30 is the new form will be used to opt out of contributing to CPP if you are between age 65 to 69 and receiving a CPP retirement pension. Also, if you work offshore check out Form T626. It calculates the lucrative Overseas Employment Tax Credit, which will be phased out starting in 2013. Contract renegotiations and tax remittance adjustments will be required.

Software Tips

Your tax software will do many calculations automatically for you but you'll need to avoid data entry traps and common errors to help get the results you want:

- *Enter the Numbers on T4 Slips.* It's easy to slip up so take your time. Your T4s have boxes for the majority of your employment-related deductions and credits, as explained in the easy T-Slip guide. If you find another slip after you file, don't file another return. Adjust instead using form T1ADJ.
- *Employment Expenses*. Enter out-of pocket employment expenses on form T777 *Employment Expenses* or the equivalent data entry screens in your software. Make sure *Form T2200 Declaration of Conditions of Employment* signed by the employer accompanies your records in case of audit.
- **Babysitting.** Use form T778 *Child Care Expenses* or equivalent data entry screen.
- **Moving to Take a New Job or Go to School**. Claims for moving expenses are entered on form T1-M or the equivalent data entry screens in your software.
- **Truckers.** Meals and lodging expenses are entered on form TL2.
- **Blue Cross and Charitable Donations at Work?** Be sure to pull these numbers from your cheque stubs to claim them on the medical expense and charitable donation screens. The numbers end up on Schedule 1 and reduce taxes payable.

Tax Sleuthing

The most common errors result from lost receipts; it can pay well to hunt them down:

- Employment expenses, which include costs of auto, use of home, promotional expenses for commission salespeople, tradesperson's tools, expenses of employed musician and artists.
- Child care expenses including the cost of nannies, boarding schools and camps.
- Moving expenses, including your real estate commissions and any hotel costs.
- Public transit passes, including buses, subways and ferries.

Tax Pro Alert

Consider consulting a tax pro if you are:

- Claiming employment expenses for the first time.
- Claiming child care expenses where one spouse is a student or infirm.
- Receiving employee stock options or low-interest loans to make investments.
- Making past service contributions to an employer-sponsored pension plan.
- Negotiating a job termination or new employment agreement.
- Receiving a lump-sum death benefit for a deceased employee.

10

Employment Income

Most Canadians have been employees at some time or another. By definition, you are considered to be an employee if you are in a "master-servant relationship" with a person who

- controls how and where you work;
- supplies the tools you need to do the work; and
- takes the risk of delivering and getting paid for the work.

Employees can be paid in cash, by way of salary, wages, bonuses, vacation pay or director's fees. They may also enjoy receiving taxable benefits. At tax filing time, these various types of remuneration are all included in Box 14 of the T4 slip. That makes tax filing seem simple—just enter the figures from the boxes on the slip in your software. But there is more to it, as we'll explain.

The T4 Slip. The T4 slip is the source document issued by employers to report your employment income and taxable benefits as well as statutory and other deductions withheld by or through the employer. You will receive a T4 slip by the end of February from each of your employers. It's easy to deal with them in your tax software. Just gather them all together and enter the numbers methodically. Yet there are a few circumstances that can trip you up.

 CHECK IT OUT | T4 slip filing errors can delay your return, so be sure to know how to avoid them. (Note: "Check it out" is usually in question form, followed by the answer.)

- **More Than One T4**. If there is more than one T4 slip, your tax software will lead you through a T4 slip summary to better manage the information. If you are missing a slip, contact the employer or take the information from the cheque stubs to estimate the amounts.
- **Late T4 Slips**. If you receive a T4 slip you forgot about after the return has been filed, don't file another return. Just send in a copy of the slip with a *T1 Adjustment Request* Form (Form T1-ADJ—you may or may not find it in your tax software as it cannot be filed electronically). You'll have to mail in the printed form to ask CRA to add the information to the return or you can request an adjustment online at http://www.cra-arc.gc.ca/myaccount/.
- **Employer Errors**. If the employer has made an error on the T4 slip, don't fix it on the return! CRA has been provided with a copy of that slip by the employer and will adjust your return to coincide with the slip they received. Errors on slips, including T4 slips, must be corrected by the company which issued the slip by filing an amended slip.

Perks. The perks of employment can make you wealthier, but don't double-report them on your tax return. Some are taxable; some are not.

 CHECK IT OUT | **What perks of employment are taxable?** Employees may receive taxable or tax free perks, which should form part of every employment negotiation. Look for them in the "Other Information Section" of your T4 Slip.

Figure 2.1 Perks of Employment

Taxable Benefits*	Tax-Free Benefits
Board and lodging	Board and lodging at a remote worksite; limited meals or meal allowances for overtime.
Rent-free and low-rent housing	Discounts on merchandise and subsidized meals; travel passes for the exclusive use of a transit company's employees.
Free or discounted travel passes for a transit employee's family	Transportation to a special worksite or for security reasons, frequent flyer points unless converted to cash
Personal use of employer's vehicle	Recreational facilities, including social or athletic club memberships
Gifts in cash or those that exceed $500	Non-cash gifts under $500; $500 more in cash for birthdays, anniversaries for an annual $1,000 max.
Value of holidays, prizes and awards	Employee counseling services for health, retirement or re-employment

Taxable Benefits*	Tax-Free Benefits
Premiums for a provincial hospital plan	Premiums for a private health plan or lump sum wage loss replacement plan
Tuition paid for courses for personal benefits	Tuition paid for courses for the employer's benefit
Interest-free and low-interest loans	Certain moving expenses if required by the employer
Group sickness, accident or life plans	Employer's required contribution to provincial health and medical plans.
Gains and income under employee stock option plans	Employer-paid costs of attendant for disabled employees or to cover away-from-home education due to work in remote worksites.

* If these amounts include GST/HST, employees who are allowed to claim employment expenses may be able to claim a rebate on Line 457 by filing form GST/HST 370.

Reducing Taxable Benefits. Taxable benefits can be reduced in certain cases. A *T4 Slip Data Entry Guide* follows at the end of this chapter to help you with this. Note two in particular:

- *Personal use of employer-provided vehicle*: This is also known as a "standby" charge. Employees may elect to reduce this taxable income if personal driving is less than 1,667 kilometres per month. Tax-free, however, are reimbursements for supplementary business insurance, parking or ferry/toll charges.
- *Interest-free or low interest loans*—if the loans is used for investment purposes, including investment in an employer's stock, a deduction for the amount shown as a benefit is possible on Schedule 4 under carrying charges.

Statutory Deductions. Employment income is paid periodically—usually every two weeks, by cheque or direct deposit. A pay stub reports the gross and net earnings received, in an envelope or via direct deposit. In either case, keep a hard copy of your pay stubs in your tax files, as sometimes T4 slips get lost in the mail, employers go bankrupt or for any other reason, you may not receive yours. When this happens, you'll need to estimate your earnings and deductions. Tax time will be less frustrating in these cases if you have hard copy.

Statutory source deductions, those required under law, are contributions to the Canada Pension Plan (CPP), premiums for Employment Insurance (EI) and, of course, Income Taxes (IT) withheld to cover the taxes you owe on what you've earned.

It's possible to make an overpayment to CPP, EI and IT, especially if you worked for more than one employer. Your software will automatically calculate those overpayments and show the excess amounts on Line 435 for IT, Line 448 CPP premiums and Line 450 for EI premiums.

Note, if you lived in Quebec, you will receive separate information for the provincial tax withholdings and the Quebec Pension Plan.

CPP Proration. CPP premiums will also be prorated in the year the taxpayer turns 18 or 70, starts receiving CPP disability benefits or turns 65 while receiving CPP retirement benefits. This will also be the case in the year of death. Most tax software will calculate this automatically if you enter the correct year of birth.

✓ **CHECK** | **How have the CPP contribution rules changed?** Beginning in
  IT OUT | 2012, there is some important news for employees age 60 and older.

- Employers of employees who are receiving CPP retirement benefits must withhold contributions to CPP at least until the employee turns 65.
- Those between the ages of 65 to 69 who are receiving a CPP retirement pension must also contribute to the CPP unless they specifically *elect* to stop contributing. Do so by submitting Form CPT30 to your payroll department. Also check out *Knowledge Bureau's CPP Income Calculator* at www.knowledgebureau.com if you need help deciding whether you should do so.

EI Premiums and Exemptions. EI premiums must be paid by employees, regardless of age. The rate applicable for 2012 is 1.83% of insurable earnings to a maximum of $839.97 for the year. If you have more than one employer in the year, you may have more than the maximum deducted. Your software will calculate the overpayment using Form T2204 and apply for a refund of your overpayment for you.

Part-time worker? If your total insurable earnings for the year is $2,000 or less, you are not subject to EI premiums and any amounts withheld from your wages are refundable. The refund of excess premiums deducted is claimed on Line 450 of your tax return. Your software will calculate this automatically for you. This is often the case for students.

Software Tips. Your EI insurable earnings are shown in Box 24 of your T4 slip and most often match Box 14 unless your income exceeds the maximum insurable earnings ($45,900 for 2012). If Box 24 is blank, do not key zero into your software unless you are exempt, which is indicated by an "X" in Box 28 of your T4 slip.

Reduce Income Tax Withholding at Source. While most people are happy to get a refund at tax time, the government makes no interest payments on the use of your money all year long. That makes overpaying your taxes a bad investment. You will want to change that as you become more tax savvy. Here's what you should do to keep more of your money throughout the year:

1. *File your TD1 personal tax credits return.* Most of you will remember these forms—one of the first things you complete when you start a new job. There is both a federal and a provincial form TD1. Your employer will deduct your tax based on your entries.

   Ideally these two forms should be given to you annually for review, because your changing personal circumstances and tax laws can affect your tax withholding rates. The TD1 forms will tell the payroll clerk whether you are able to take advantage of non-refundable tax credits that could reduce your withholdings, like the Age Amount, Pension Income Amount, Tuition, education and textbook Amounts, Disability Amount, Caregiver Amount or Amounts transferred from spouse. Be proactive; it's your money.

2. *File Form T1213 to further reduce tax withholding.* A lesser known form rarely provided by the employer is Form T1213 *Request to Reduce Tax Deductions at Source.* You need to initiate this. It tells CRA that you qualify for deductions that will increase your tax refund like, for example, RRSP contributions, child care expenses, employment expenses, investment carrying charges, rental or business losses, deductible spousal support or non-refundable tax credits like charitable donations and medical expenses. By filing this form, you can get that refund with every pay, instead of waiting until spring.

   Here's what to do: Send the signed T1213 form to CRA, (attach details of your eligibility for the write-offs) who in turn will send the employer permission to reduce your withholding taxes.

   Commission sales employees may also adjust their tax withholdings to take into account their related expenses. The form to use is *TD1X Statement of Commission Income and Expenses for Payroll Tax Deductions.* It must be provided to the employer by January 31 or one month after start date.

   This requires an estimate of net commission earnings for the year and a reduction of those earnings by either last year's expense claim (*Form T777 Statement of Employment Expenses*) or an estimate of this year's expenses. Completing this form gives the employee the benefit of reducing the taxes remitted by the employer all year long, rather than waiting for a refund after filing the return. We will discuss employed commission sales people and their expenses later in this section.

Non-Statutory Deductions. Non-statutory deductions can also be important to the outcomes on your tax return—examples are contributions to your employer-sponsored pension plan (Registered Pension Plan), group health premiums paid by the employer, charitable donations made at work and union dues deducted. Look for these on the T4 slip and report them as described in the *T4 Slip Entry Guide.* More detail on claiming medical expenses and charitable donations follow in Part 3.

Employment Expenses. Most employees are not allowed to claim out-of-pocket expenses for the costs of going to work. Items such as the cost of driving to and from work, eating out at lunch or dry cleaning are not deductible. However, a non-refundable tax credit is provided for these purposes. It's called the Canada Employment Amount (CEC) and it's described in more detail in Chapter 18.

Other Itemized Expenses. Perhaps you're a commissioned salesperson who is required to negotiate contracts on behalf of your employer. Or you are required to work out of the family home and are eligible to claim home office expenses or perhaps, the family pays for child care in order for you to work. If any of these apply to you, they can result in additional deductions on your tax return. These deductions are covered in this part of the book.

 The Bottom Line | Employees have a great opportunity to use their employer's capital to cover current income needs and to save for future income requirements through various perks and benefits. The spending and saving decisions, however, are up to you.

11

RPP Contributions

Your employer can help secure your future income in retirement by offering an employer-sponsored pension plan. This can also be known as a Registered Pension Plan (RPP). In addition, a new type of employer-sponsored pension plan will be offered soon and you may hear of it if you work for a smaller company in the future: the Pooled Retirement Pension Plan (PRPP).

Not only does your employer contribute to the plan with you, the earnings in the plan accumulate on a tax deferred basis, so they grow exponentially. Having an RPP can impact your ability to save separately in a private Registered Retirement Savings Plan (RRSP). By entering the right data in your tax software and then making good decisions about supplementing the employer's plan by contributing to your privately held RRSP, you'll be richer, sooner.

 CHECK IT OUT | **How do I maximize my employer-sponsored pension?** When you contribute to your employer-sponsored RPP, there will be deductions withheld and remitted into the plan for you. You will be able to deduct certain amounts based on your current year services, as shown in Box 20 on the T4 slip. Your software will post this amount to Line 207 of your tax return to claim a deduction.

Past Service Contributions. Sometimes you'll be able to make past service contributions, too. If you make contributions to top up prior years after 1990, those contributions are also deductible in the year and will be included in Box 20.

If you made past service contributions relating to years prior to 1990, those contributions will be shown on your T4 slip in Box 74 (if you were a contributor) or Box 75 (if you were not a contributor). Your claim for such contributions is limited as follows:

- You cannot claim more than $3,500 for past service contributions while you were not a contributor (Box 75).
- For contributions shown in Box 74, you cannot claim more than $3,500 less any other contributions deducted in the current year (current and past service while not a contributor).

Any amount contributed that cannot be deducted in the current year may be carried forward and claimed in a future year according to these same rules.

Software Tips. Each software package will have its own worksheet dealing with past service contributions for years prior to 1990, so follow the worksheet and make sure your claim follows the above rules. Also note any carry-forward amounts because you'll need to know them when you prepare next year's return. Your software may have a carry-forward form or screen that takes care of this for you.

Carry-forward Provisions on Restricted Deductions. While we see fewer of these claims now, it's important to note that if your deduction for past service contributions before 1990 was limited on your prior year return, you may be able to deduct those contributions in the current year. Undeducted contributions from prior years may be deducted following the same rules as outlined above for current year contributions. You'll have to add these amounts to the worksheet in your software for claiming prior-year contributions. This is a complicated process and it may be a good idea to get some professional help in this case to ensure future claims are maximized.

Interest Costs. Any interest you paid because you elected to make those past service contributions in instalments is handled as follows: the interest is deductible for tax purposes as if it were part of the past service contributions and deductions are limited to the rules outlined above for past service contributions.

 CHECK IT OUT | **How do I best manage my RRSP if I have an RPP?** You may not be able to contribute to your own RRSP, depending on how much was contributed to your RPP. You'll need to understand what the PA, PSPA and PAR acronyms are if you want to understand how the RPP and the RRSP provisions interact, so you can maximize contributions to each.

- **What's the PA?** When you contribute to a Registered Pension Plan, your RRSP contribution room for the year is reduced. The amount of the reduction is called a Pension Adjustment (PA). The amount of your pension adjustment is shown in Box 52 or your T4 slip. This will not affect your current-year RRSP contribution limit as it is based on your 2011 income but it will reduce your RRSP contribution room earned in 2012.
- **What's a PSPA?** If you make past service RPP contributions, those contributions will also reduce your RRSP contribution room earned in the year. The reduction is called a Past Service Pension Adjustment (PSPA). You'll receive a T215 slip showing the amount. This will affect your RRSP contribution room for the following year and will be reflected in your RRSP contribution limit as indicated on your Notice of Assessment. Most software does not include the T215 form as it does not affect the current year.
- **What's a PAR?** In some cases, when you cease to be a member of a RPP and the benefits you receive from the plan are less than your accumulated pension adjustments, you'll receive a Pension Adjustment Reversal (PAR). The PAR is reported on a T10 slip and increases your RRSP contribution room for the next year.

The Bottom Line | Becoming wealthier has as much to do with maximizing your take-home pay as it does with negotiating employment benefits to create a future income in retirement. In addition, your employment income level and your contributions to your employer-sponsored pension contributions will affect how much you can contribute to your privately funded RRSP. Tax-astute employees will make sure current and future needs are adequately met with the help of Registered Pension Plans.

12

What About Your RRSP?

Should you contribute to an RRSP even if you have an RPP at work? There are many benefits to doing both, not the least of which is getting a larger tax refund so you can put away the most money possible to work for your own future. You shouldn't miss out. Here are the key benefits:

- RRSP contributions result in an immediate tax deduction for the principal, which reduces your tax bill in the current year, as well as your net income on Line 236.
- By reducing your net income, you will limit reductions of tax credits or social benefits you may be entitled to, including Employment Insurance.
- RRSP deposits accumulate and grow on a tax-deferred basis (that is, earnings within an RRSP are not taxable until they are removed from the plan).
- Withdrawals of RRSP funds in a year when your marginal tax rate is lower will result in a net tax saving.
- Money may be borrowed on a tax-free basis from your RRSP to fund the purchase of a new home under the *Home Buyers' Plan* or to finance post-secondary education under the *Lifelong Learning Plan*.
- Starting at age 65, RRSP withdrawals may be split with your spouse to reduce the taxes payable on the withdrawal.

 CHECK IT OUT | **What are restrictions on RRSP contributions?** There are some rules to follow, as described below.

- **RRSP earned income.** If you earn income from employment, self-employment, net rental income, CPP disability income or taxable support payments last year, you have "earned income" for RRSP purposes this year. Many software packages will show you how this is computed in detail.

How much can you contribute? Each year that you have earned income, you create RRSP contribution room which you can use the following year. The contribution room you generate is the lesser of:

- 18% of your earned income for the year to an indexed annual dollar maximum ($22,970 for 2012 contributions based on 2011 income), less

- any pension adjustments (PA) from your employer-sponsored plans. This is shown on Box 52 of the T4 slip and ends up on Line 206 of the return.

Do you need to use the contribution room? RRSP contribution room is cumulative so if you generate contribution room and don't use it by making your maximum RRSP contribution, the amount carries forward and you can make a larger contribution in a future year.

Maximum RRSP Contributions. Each year your Notice of Assessment or Reassessment from CRA will show the maximum contribution that you can make for the next taxation year. This will include the "unused" room from the past, 18% of your earned income to the current dollar maximum, and adjustments due to changes in your RPP contributions. Your tax software will also keep track of this for you in your carry forward screens, provided you have entered all the numbers properly. You can contribute throughout the year, or within 60 days of the year end to make a tax deduction on this year's return.

Reporting RRSP Contributions. You'll enter the information about the RPP and the PA on your employer-provided T-slips in the appropriate T4 screens; but you'll enter the information about your RRSP contribution receipts on a different screen, which will link to Schedule 7. This screen will vary in name and composition by software. Start by entering your RRSP contribution limit as shown on your Notice of Assessment or Reassessment for the prior year.

Next follow the screen to enter all of your RRSP contribution receipts for the period from March 2, 2012 to March 1, 2013. The contribution date is important and that will be clear as you review the receipts. Any contributions made in the first 60 days after the tax year can be deducted on Line 208 of the T1 in either the prior tax year (2012 in this case) or the year of contribution (2013).

The deductible amounts will show up in two places on your return: Schedule 7, as mentioned and Line 208.

Undeducted RRSP contributions from prior years. If you have undeducted RRSP contributions from prior years, you will need to enter those too. These amounts can be carried forward indefinitely for use in reducing income anytime in the future,

Example: Thomas contributed $5,000 to his RRSP last year because he had some extra money, but it turned out that he didn't need to claim the deduction. He has carried forward the undeducted contributions and plans to deduct them this year.

RRSP Overcontributions. If you are at least age 18 you may overcontribute up to $2,000 above your contribution room to your RRSP. Otherwise, it's best to take overcontributed amounts above this out of the plan as soon as possible to avoid expensive penalties. See a tax professional to help you with this.

RRSP Home Buyers' Plan and Lifelong Learning Plan. If you participated in the Home Buyers' Plan or the Lifelong Learning Plan, you'll need to enter details on the appropriately names screen as well so your RRSP deduction can be claimed. The result will be posted to Schedule 7 for reporting to CRA. This information will be carried forward to assist with proper repayment scheduling as well. If you fail to repay, the unpaid amounts will be added to your income.

Reducing Your Source Deductions: Recall that when you contribute to your RRSP, you can reduce your withholding taxes at source so you essentially get your tax refund with every paycheque.

✓ **CHECK IT OUT** | **How do I figure out what my take-home pay will be?** You can use the *Knowledge Bureau's Take Home Pay Calculator* to figure this out for yourself. Sign up for a free trial at http://www.knowledgebureau.com/calculators. Then figure out how an RRSP deduction can help you put more money in your pocket sooner, using your tax software.

 Case Study | **Plan How an RRSP Can Reduce Your Taxes**

Consider Rupert, who is single and 45 years old. In 2012, his firm closed and he found himself out of a job. His T4 slip shows $65,000 employment income, $2,306.70 in CPP contributions, $839.97 in EI premiums and $15,000 of income tax deducted. He is able to claim $4,500 in employment expenses.

He also has a T4E Slip showing the $10,000 EI in benefits he received. Because Rupert was on EI back in 2003, he is required to repay 30% of the EI he received. But, he may be able to avoid that repayment. How can making an RRSP contribution help?

You will see that by making a $10,000 RRSP contribution, Rupert has changed his $2,143.53 tax bill into a $2,391.50 tax refund. The tax savings of $4,535 represents a 45% immediate return on his RRSP investment! Note, these figures will vary depending on province of residence.

 The Bottom Line | Remember, you're only required to pay the correct amount of tax, no more. Do all you can to minimize over-withholding, then invest the after-tax increases in your net pay in a tax-efficient investment like an RRSP, accelerating your journey to financial freedom. Need help? Ask your tax advisor before you finish with your tax filings for this year.

Knowledge Bureau Excellence in Financial Education **Income Tax Estimator** Tax Year: 2012

Identification: Rupert			W/O RRSP	With RRSP
Province	Ontario			
Children:	0	**Age:**	18 to 65	18 to 65
Total income				
Employment Income			$65,000.00	$65,000.00
Employment insurance benefits			$10,000.00	$10,000.00
		Total Income	$75,000.00	$75,000.00
Net income				
RRSP deduction			$0.00	$10,000.00
Employment expenses			$4,500.00	$4,500.00
Social benefit repayment (EI / OAS)			$3,000.00	$937.50
		Net Income	$67,500.00	$59,562.50
		Taxable Income	$67,500.00	$59,562.50
Refund or Balance owing				
Federal tax			$11,860.51	$10,114.26
Federal non-refundable tax credits				
Basic personal amount	$10,822.00	$10,822.00		
CPP contributions	$2,306.70	$2,306.70		
EI premiums	$839.97	$839.97		
Canada employment amount	$1,095.00	$1,095.00		
Total	$15,063.67	$15,063.67		
x Credit rate:	15.00%	15.00%		
		Total federal non-refundable credits	$2,259.55	$2,259.55
Social benefit repayment (EI / OAS)			$3,000.00	$937.50
		Net federal tax	$12,600.96	$8,792.21
Provincial tax			$4,576.43	$3,850.15
Provincial non-refundable tax credits				
Basic personal amount	$9,405.00	$9,405.00		
CPP contributions	$2,306.70	$2,306.70		
EI premiums	$839.97	$839.97		
Total	$12,551.67	$12,551.67		
x Credit rate:	5.05%	5.05%		
		Total Provincial non-refundable credits	$633.86	$633.86
Provincial surtax (plus OHP)			$600.00	$600.00
		Net provincial tax	$4,542.57	$3,816.29
		Total Payable	$17,143.53	$12,608.50
Tax deducted, Instalments, or Provincial or other refundable credits			$15,000.00	$15,000.00
		Refund		$2,391.50
		Balance Owing	$2,143.53	

13

Employment Expenses

Certain employees may claim out-of-pocket expenses on their tax returns. The *Income Tax Act* is very specific about the expenses that may be claimed however. For most employees, these expenses are claimed on Form T777 *Statement of Employment Expenses* and require the completion of Form T2200 *Declaration of Conditions of Employment,* which is signed by the employer.

The deduction will ultimately show up on Line 229 of the T1 and your tax software should include both forms for your use. It's a good idea to print them; the T777 as a guide to the receipts you need to look for and the T2200 to be signed by your employer.

 CHECK IT OUT | **What out-of-pocket expenses can I claim?** Employees may claim certain specific expenses of employment, depending on whether the employer will verify this was a necessary condition of employment. Commission sales people can claim more expense categories—sales and promotion expenses for example—because they are expected to foster relationships with clients in their negotiation of contracts for their employers. Let's discover who can claim what.

Employees On Salary Only. Those who earn salary only may deduct the following out-of-pocket expenses:

- accounting, but not including income tax preparation, except if you are a commission sales person.

- legal fees may be claimed if incurred to establish a right to collect salary, wages or a retiring allowance or pension benefits, but these costs may not exceed the amount of those sources. Any non-deductible components may then be carried forward and deducted in any of the seven subsequent tax years in which further income from these sources is reported. When pensions or retiring allowances are transferred to an RRSP, the deductible legal expenses must be reduced by the amount of the transfer.
- motor vehicle expenses (including Capital Cost Allowance (CCA)—the tax equivalent of depreciation, interest or leasing costs, as well as operating costs), but only if the employee is not in receipt of a non-taxable allowance for the use of the motor vehicle.
- travel expenses, including rail, air, bus or other travel costs.
- meals, tips and hotel costs, providing the excursion is for at least 12 hours and away from the taxpayer's metropolitan area. Meals and tips are subject to a 50% restriction.
- parking costs (but generally not at the place of employment).
- supplies used up directly in the work (stationery, maps, etc.).
- salaries paid to an assistant (including spouses or children if a salary equivalent to fair market value is paid for work actually performed).
- office rent or certain home office expenses (discussed later).
- Note: the cost of tools acquired by employed mechanics are generally not deductible, however a special rule exists for new tool costs incurred by apprentice vehicle mechanics and tools acquired by tradespersons.

Salary and Commission. Employees who earn their living negotiating contracts for their employers or selling on commission may claim for the expenses itemized above, as well as income tax preparation costs, legal fees incurred to defend charges incurred in the normal course of business, and auto and travel expenses.

This is allowed only if they are required to pay their own expenses and regularly perform their duties away from their employer's place of business. However, the expenses are categorized into two groups: deductible travel and deductible sales expenses. This is because you cannot exceed commissions earned in the year with sales expenses.

A. *Deductible travel expenses* allowed include:

- Auto operating expenses like gas, oil, repairs and fixed costs like licenses, insurance, interest, leasing and capital cost allowance. The latter three expenses are limited to annual maximums if a passenger vehicle is used. See Auto Expenses in the next section.
- Travelling expenses such as the cost of air, bus, rail, taxi or other transportation, which takes the employee outside the employer's metropolitan area. However, travel expenses are claimable only if the employee does not receive a tax-free travel allowance.

Note that when these two types of expenses only are claimed, the amounts may exceed commissions earned (as reported in Box 42 of the T4 slip) and excess expenses may be used to offset other income of the year. Your software will do that automatically for you.

B. *Deductible sales expenses* allowed include the expenses above plus:

- promotional expenses;
- entertainment expenses (subject to a 50% restriction for the personal component of the expense);
- home office expenses.

When you are claiming expenses under category B above, your expenses *may not* exceed commissions earned in the calendar year (Line 102) *except* for interest and capital cost allowance on a motor vehicle.

Because your tax software will calculate this automatically, you may be at a loss to understand why the claimable amounts have been reduced. Worse, any restricted expenses are lost and cannot be claimed in a future year. New sales people are at risk.

Example: Sarah started her career selling real estate as an employed commissioned salesperson in November, and was so excited that she purchased $2,400 in promotional gifts for her future clients and prospects, a new computer and an iPhone. Her first commissions did not materialize until the next spring and to her dismay, her expenditures were not deductible. She could not carry them forward for use next year, either.

 CHECK IT OUT | **What errors do I need to avoid on asset purchases?** Deductible equipment costs are also subject to special rules. Employees are not allowed to make a claim for capital expenditures, like a computer or iPhone at all. However, leasing costs are deductible. In the case of the iPhone, air time is deductible.

The reason is this: the employer is expected to provide those assets for the employee. There are three exceptions: the purchase of vehicles, musical instruments or aircraft used in performing the duties of employment. Therefore, it is wise tax planning to lease computers, cell phones or other equipment.

Artists and Musicians. Artists and musicians may claim expenses for items specific to their profession, including capital cost allowance on musical instruments. These claims are limited to the lesser of $1,000 and 20% of the employee's income from related employment. Claims may be for such items as ballet shoes, body suits, art supplies, computer supplies, home office costs as well as rental, maintenance, insurance and capital cost allowance on musical instruments.

Forestry Workers. Employees working in the forestry industry may claim the actual costs of operating a power saw, including gas, oil, parts and repairs providing an itemized statement is prepared and saved in case of audit requests. The power saws may be written off in full but, in the case of a new saw, the claim must be reduced by trade-in value or sales proceeds received from the disposal of the old saw during the year.

Apprentice Vehicle Mechanics. Apprentice vehicle mechanics may claim expenses incurred in purchasing tools in excess of $1,500. If the taxpayer does not take the maximum deduction in the tax year, the unused portion may be carried forward to apply against income earned in a future year. Apprentice vehicle mechanics may also claim the Tradesperson's Tools deduction.

Tradespersons. Tradespersons are also able to claim a deduction (to a maximum of $500) for the cost of tools in excess of the *Canada Employment Amount* (CEC) for the year. If the cost of tools is less than the CEC, then no deduction is allowed. Electronic communication devices and electronic data processing equipment do not qualify as tools for the purposes of this deduction (i.e., a cell phone, PDA, or laptop is not a "tool").

Your software will likely have a section of the screen for claiming employment expenses dedicated to claims by musicians, artists, apprentice vehicle mechanics and tradespersons. Also see instructions for long distance truck drivers later in this section.

CHECK IT OUT | **Can I get a GST/HST rebate on my employment expenses?** Employees who claim deductible employment expenses may be able to receive a rebate of the GST/HST paid using Form GST370 *Employee and Partner GST/HST Rebate Application* and make the claim at Line 457. Rebates received are added to income in the year received, unless they apply to capital assets, in which case the cost base of the asset may require adjusting. These claims are often missed and can be complicated! Be sure to file an adjustment to prior-filed returns if you have missed it, with the help of a tax pro if necessary.

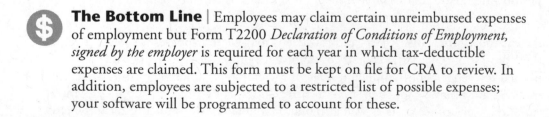

The Bottom Line | Employees may claim certain unreimbursed expenses of employment but Form T2200 *Declaration of Conditions of Employment, signed by the employer* is required for each year in which tax-deductible expenses are claimed. This form must be kept on file for CRA to review. In addition, employees are subjected to a restricted list of possible expenses; your software will be programmed to account for these.

14

Auto Expenses and Home Office

Auto and home office expenses are common deductions for self-employed individuals, and certain employees who work from home offices. They are often audited, however, and the tax filing rules can be complicated. Tax software can do many of the calculations in the background, so you may wish to take some time now to find out how it's done. We'll start with the simpler of the two: the expenses of the home workspace.

Home Workspace Expenses

To qualify to make home workspace expense claims, the space must be

- the place where the individual principally (more than 50% of the time) performs the office or employment duties, or
- used exclusively in the period to earn income from the office or employment and, on a regular and continuous basis, for meeting customers or other persons in the ordinary course of performing the office or employment duties.

The home workspace must be separated from other living areas in the home, but does not need to be a separate room. The home may either be owned by the taxpayer or rented. To determine the amount of deductible home office expenses, total expenses for the costs of maintaining the home are pro-rated by the following fraction:

$$\frac{\text{Square footage of the home workspace}}{\text{Square footage of the entire living area}} \times \text{Total Eligible Expense} = \text{Deductible Expenses}$$

Example: Jona is required to work out of his home as he manages his territory for a manufacturer. His total home expenses are $5,000. The office space is 200 square feet and the entire home is 2000 square feet. Jona can claim 200/2000 x $5,000.

 CHECK IT OUT | **Can employed and self-employed people claim the same expenses?** The answer is no. Whether you are employed or self-employed matters, when claiming home office expenses, as described below:

Employees who do not earn commission may claim:

- utilities;
- maintenance and repairs, including light bulbs and cleaning supplies; and
- rent.

Commission sales employees can claim:

- utilities;
- maintenance and repairs, including light bulbs and cleaning supplies;
- rent;
- insurance; and
- property taxes.

Self-employed people can claim:

- utilities;
- maintenance and repairs, including light bulbs and cleaning supplies;
- rent;
- insurance;
- property taxes;
- interest; and
- capital cost allowance (although this is not a good idea if the home is your principal residence. CCA claims will compromise the principal residence exemption.

Claims are limited to income. An employee may not claim home office expenses that exceed income from the employer. But the good news is that non-deductible home office expenses may be carried forward (indefinitely) to reduce income from that employer in subsequent years.

Example: Marcel is a commission salesman (no salary) who is required to provide his own office space in his home and pay his own expenses. He started his new position in December. He incurred $5,000 in qualifying home expenses, but only earned $200 commission in the tax year: His office comprises of 200 of the 2,000 square feet in his home.

The business use of home expenses are equal to $500 [200 sq ft/2000 sq ft) x $5,000]. As this is more than his employment income from that employer, he may only deduct $200. The remaining $300 may be added to the following year's home office expenses and deducted against income in the following year (if that income exceeds the expenses).

Documentation Requirements. It's important to gather all receipts and print the following from your software and keep on hand for audit:

- A completed *Form T2200 Declaration of Conditions of Employment*, on which the employer certifies that the employee is required to maintain the home office and pay the expenses of operating it.
- Employees' claims for home workspace expenses are made on *Form T777 Statement of Employment Expenses*. It's a good idea to attach receipts in order behind this printed form.

Auto Expenses

The rules of claiming these costs are similar for both employed and self-employed people, and they are also among the most frequently audited. Taxpayers will want to keep proper documentation and make the claims correctly.

Eligibility. Automotive expenses can only be deducted if they are not reimbursed by the employer. An employee who receives a reasonable allowance for the use of the vehicle may not claim the related expenses. Otherwise, employees can deduct auto expenses when they pay their own auto expenses and are required to use their vehicle in carrying out their duties of employment.

For any expenses of employment to be allowed, the employer must sign form T2200 *Declaration of Conditions of Employment,* stating the employee must use the auto for employment and is responsible for paying auto expenses, does not receive a reasonable allowance for auto expenses, and will not be reimbursed for them (if there is a partial reimbursement this must be accounted for).

Business vs. Personal Driving. For those who use their vehicle for both personal and business/employment purposes, it is necessary to keep an auto log that records distance driven for both purposes, for at least one year (the base year). After this you can keep the records for as few as three consecutive months. So long as your driving patterns do not vary on either side by more than 10%, you will be able to claim the ratio determined by your full year log. Your business ration in the current year is determined by the formula:

$$\frac{\text{Current year ratio for log period}}{\text{Base year ratio for same period}} \times \text{Base year full-year ratio}$$

Case Study | Plan Logbook Entries to Calculate Percentage Claimable

June's auto log book for 2011 shows that she drove her car 5,427 kilometres for business use and 3,414 kilometres for personal use (for a total use of 8,841 kilometres). She was able to deduct 61.38% of her auto expenses (5427/8841 x 100%).

For 2012, June must keep a logbook for at least three consecutive months. Her logbook for the months of January, February and March 2011 showed 1,410 km business use and 850 kilometres personal use (total 2,260 km)—62.39% business use.

Her log book for the same three months in 2012 shows 1842 km business use and 945 personal use (2,787 total)—66.09% business use.

Since the difference between the 2011 and 2012 usage was less than 10%, her business use percentage for 2012 is 66.09%/62.39% x 61.38% = 65.02%

Personal use includes vehicle use by other family members, friends, etc. In other words, total personal use of the vehicle is assessed, not just the use by the person using the auto for business or employment.

When there is a "*mixed use*" of the car, the expenses are first totalled. This is based on your actual receipts and a log of cash expenditures, like car washes or parking. Then the total costs are pro-rated by the allowable business use ratio, as calculated above.

Total Allowable Expenses x <u>Allowable business use ratio</u>

Your tax software will have a place for this calculation on an automobile expense screen.

CHECK IT OUT | **What can I claim for my auto expenses?** There are two types of auto expenses that can be claimed: fixed and operating, and this can have an important effect on the type of car you buy or lease and how much money you spend.

A. *Fixed Expenses* include:

- Capital Cost Allowance (subject to a maximum cost of $30,000, plus taxes)
- leasing costs (subject to a maximum of $800 a month, plus taxes)
- interest costs (subject to a maximum of $300 a month)

B. *Operating expenses* include:

- gas and oil, tires, maintenance and repairs
- car washes (keep track of coin operated washes)

- insurance, license fees
- auto club memberships
- parking (generally parking expenses while on business are fully deductible and not subject to a proration for personal component)

In addition, you should know that in general, "cents-per-kilometer" claims are disallowed except in specific instances where a "simplified method" is allowed. This includes a claim for medical travel or certain moving expenses, but not employment expenses.

Cost of Car Matters. How much you can claim for fixed expenses is restricted, as you can see, and this depends on the cost of the car you drive and for what purposes. More complexity here: there are two types of vehicles for tax purposes, which depends on cost and use:

A. *Passenger Vehicles* (sometimes called luxury vehicles) are designed to carry no more than nine passengers and are not on the "specifically excluded" list below. They will cost more than $30,000 plus taxes or $800 a month plus taxes in leasing costs. Interest will be restricted to $300 a month.

B. *Motor vehicles* are vehicles that are not passenger vehicles. They will cost less than $30,000 or if they cost more than this, they may fall into a specifically excluded list:

- ambulances, taxis, busses used in the business of transporting passengers
- hearses and other vehicles used in the transport of passengers in the course of a funeral
- any clearly marked emergency medical vehicle which is used to transport paramedics and their emergency medical equipment
- motor vehicles acquired to be immediately sold, rented or leased
- pick-up trucks that are used more than 50% of the time to transport goods
- vans that are used more than 90% of the time to transport goods
- extended cab pick-up trucks used primarily for the transportation of goods, equipment or passengers in the course of earning or producing income at a work site at least 30 kilometres from any community having a population of at least 40,000

Buying Your Car. Because of the rules above, the first rule to remember when buying a car "for tax purposes" is that you may not be able to write off the full cost if it is a luxury or passenger vehicle.

 CHECK IT OUT | **How do I account for depreciation on my car?** The rules for claiming wear and tear or depreciation on an asset like a car can be complicated, as for tax purposes you will claim a deduction on a Capital Cost Allowance (CCA) Schedule, which applies a specific rate to specific classes of assets. If you're claiming the cost as part of your employment expenses, this CCA schedule will likely be associated with the T777 form. Set up your schedule as follows:

- **Motor vehicles belong to Class 10.** A 30% Capital Cost Allowance (CCA) rate is used. CCA is used at your option, so if your income is not high enough, you can save your *"Undepreciated Capital Cost"* (UCC) balance to make a larger claim next year. Note, in the year that the vehicle is purchased, the claim is limited to 50% of the normal CCA allowed. This is known as the "half-year" rule.

  Things get complicated when you dispose of these assets. If, for example, it was the last asset in the Class 10 pool of assets, the remaining balance must be deducted as a *Terminal Loss*. If other assets exist in the Class 10 pool, then the reduced CCA balance is used to calculate the CCA claim for the year.

  If after removing the amount from the Class 10 pool, the balance in negative, this negative amount is taken into income as *Recapture*. This means you have taken too much for your CCA deduction over the years and must include the over-deducted amounts in income.

- **Passenger vehicles belong in Class 10.1.** If your car cost $30,000 (plus taxes) or more, it is listed in a separate Class 10.1 and again qualifies for a 30% Capital Cost Allowance (CCA) rate, which your software will compute automatically. If your car cost $50,000 claim only $30,000 plus taxes. There is a "half-year rule" on acquisition: only 50% of the normal CCA is claimed in the year you acquire the luxury car.

  Again, it gets more complicated: when you dispose of a Class 10.1 asset, there is another half-year CCA calculation. There is no terminal loss or recapture of capital cost allowance on the disposition of a Class 10.1 vehicle. This restriction reflects the fact that the class never included the full capital cost of the vehicle to begin with.

Change of Use Rules. If the use of a vehicle changes from business to personal use, the CCA pool must be adjusted. The estimated Fair Market Value of the vehicle at the time of the change must be removed from the CCA pool as a deemed disposition and this could cause some of the tax consequences described above (recapture or terminal loss for a motor vehicle or the half-year limitation for a passenger vehicle).

Interest Costs. Remember that interest costs will be restricted to $300 a month if you own a passenger vehicle. In a low-interest rate environment, this shouldn't be a big problem, but your software will be calculating the restriction, and you need to know why.

Leasing Costs. These costs will be restricted to $800 a month plus taxes on your tax return, something to think about before you lease the Bentley.

The Bottom Line | Is it better to own or lease a car for tax purposes? Use your tax software to project forward your after-tax results for at least three years to work out any CCA restrictions, including the "half-year rules."

15

Claiming Child Care Expenses

Child care is expensive. Fortunately, you can look to the tax return for relief. The cost of paying a babysitter or nanny for the care of the children is tax deductible. This works for costs incurred while the parent(s) works in employment or self-employment or attends school, full or part time. Use Form T778 *Child Care Expenses Deduction; then your software will make the claim on* Line 214, usually on the supporting individual·with the lower net income, in the case of couples.

 CHECK IT OUT | **What expenses are deductible for babysitting costs?** Expenses are deductible for the care of dependent children who were under the age of 16 (at any time during the year) or who are physically or mentally infirm. An eligible child must be

- a child of the taxpayer, the taxpayer's spouse or the taxpayer's common-law partner's; or
- a child who was dependent on the taxpayer, or the taxpayer's spouse or common-law partner.

The definition of a child includes an adopted child or the spouse of a child of the taxpayer. If the child is not the child of the taxpayer or the taxpayer's spouse or common-law partner, then the child's net income must be less than the Basic Personal Amount.

Eligible Child Care Providers. Child care must be for services provided in Canada, although deemed residents living abroad qualify as well. The services must be provided by any of the following and receipts must be available to support the claim:

- a day nursery school or daycare centre;
- a day camp or day sports school;
- a boarding school or camp (including a sports school where lodging is involved);
- an educational institution for the purpose of providing child care services; or
- an individual who *is not*
  - the child's father or mother, or a supporting person of the child;
  - a person in respect of whom the taxpayer or a supporting person of the child has claimed a personal amount; or
  - a person who is under 18 years of age and related to the taxpayer.

Note: A deemed or factual resident of Canada who is not physically present in Canada may claim these expenses even though the services are not provided in Canada. There is also an exception to the residency requirements for commuters who live near the Canada-U.S. border as long as the child care expenses were provided at a location that was closer to the taxpayer's place of residence than any place in Canada where such child care services are available.

Eligible Child Care Expenditures. The following are expenses that may be claimed:

- babysitting costs;
- daycare costs;
- costs of a live-in nanny; which may include advertising, salary and benefits including the employer's portion of CPP and EI;
- lodging paid at boarding schools, day camps, overnight sports school and overnight camps to a maximum of:
  - $100 per week for each child age seven to 16 for which the Disability Amount cannot be claimed; plus
  - $175 per week per child under seven for which the disability amount cannot be claimed; plus
  - $250 per week for each disabled child.

Ineligible Child Care Expenditures. The following may not be claimed as child care:

- medical or hospital care;
- clothing, transportation;
- tuition fees;
- board and lodging expenses except when they are included in the total charges for a boarding school, day camp or overnight sports school and do not exceed the weekly limits; and
- expenses which were not actually paid or which were or will be reimbursed.

Earned Income Limitation. The child care deduction is limited to two-thirds of earned income. This includes:

- salaries and wages;
- net profits from self-employment;
- training allowances;
- income received under the Apprentice Grant program;
- the taxable portion of scholarships, bursaries, fellowships and research grants;
- disability pensions under Canada or Quebec Pension Plans;
- apprenticeship incentive grants received under the Apprenticeship Incentive Grant program administered by Human Resources and Social Development Canada; and
- any earnings supplement received under a project sponsored by the Government of Canada to encourage employment or sponsored under Part II of the *Employment Insurance Act* or any similar program.

On EI? No babysitting claimable. Note that Employment Insurance is not listed here. This means that child care cannot be claimed if this is your only income source.

Maximum Child Care Claims. The maximum claim you can make is the least of:

- the eligible child care expenses paid to eligible child care providers,
- two-thirds of earned income, and
- the following limits:
  - $4,000 for each child age seven to age 16 for which the Disability Amount cannot be claimed
  - $7,000 for each child under age seven for which the Disability Amount cannot be claimed
  - $10,000 for each disabled child

Form T778 *Child Care Expenses Deduction* does not apply the limit on a child-by-child basis. Therefore, if the taxpayer has two children under age 7 and pays $10,000 for child care for one and $4,000 for the other, the entire amount may be deducted (if earned income is sufficient).

Students. In addition to the limitations for all taxpayers, students have the following limitations on their child care expense claims. *Full-time students* are limited to:

- $100 for each child age seven to age 16 for which the Disability Amount cannot be claimed, plus
- $175 per child under age seven for which the Disability Amount cannot be claimed, plus
- $250 per disabled child

times the number of **weeks** of full-time attendance.

Part-time students are limited to:

- $100 for each child age 7 to 16 for which the Disability Amount cannot be claimed, plus
- $175 per child under 7 for which the Disability Amount cannot be claimed, plus
- $250 per disabled child

times the number of **months** of part-time attendance.

Who makes the claim? Generally, child care expenses may only be claimed by the supporting person with the lower income. A supporting person includes:

- The child's parent.
- The spouse or common-law partner of the child's parent.
- Anyone making a claim for the *Amount for Eligible Dependants*, Amount for infirm dependants over 18, or Caregiver Amount in respect of the child.

Separated Families. If you were married or living common-law during the year but separated and did not reconcile, each parent may claim child care for the time the expense was incurred and the child lived with the parent. The common law couple will be considered to be separated if they lived apart for a period of 90 days or more during the tax year and did not live together any time during the first 60 days of the new year. Otherwise, if you live together and support the child, you are considered to have a conjugal relationship in which net income levels are compared.

Child Care Claims by Lower Earners. The person who usually makes the claim for child care is the one whose net income, before claiming child care expenses, EI repayments payable or OAS clawbacks, is the lowest. In the unlikely event that two supporting persons have identical incomes, no deduction may be made unless the taxpayers jointly agree which one will make the claim.

Child Care Claims by Higher Earners. The higher income person may only claim child care expenses during periods in which:

- the lower earner was a full- or part-time student.
- the lower earner was incapable of caring for the children because of mental or physical infirmity.
- the lower earner was confined to a prison or similar institution for at least two weeks.
- the higher income spouse was separated from the lower earner due to a breakdown in their relationship for a period of at least 90 days but they have reconciled within the first 60 days after the taxation year.

The claim for babysitting costs when the lower earner is a student will depend on whether you study full or part time:

- When the lower-income taxpayer is a part-time student, the limits to part-time students apply to the claim made by the higher-income taxpayer.
- When the lower-income taxpayer is a full-time student, or was incapable of caring for the children because of the three circumstances above (infirmity, imprisonment or separation), the limits to full-time students apply to claims made by the higher-income taxpayer.

Restrictions to Disability Amounts. Amounts claimed for child care expenses have a negative effect on the Disability Amount. The Disability Amount for a dependant who is under 18 includes a "child supplement" which is reduced by any child care expense claim in excess of an indexed amount. See the Appendices for the current supplement amount and the current child care expense limitation.

Receipts for Expenses. Receipts for child care expenses do not have to be filed with the return but should be maintained for inspection by CRA. These claims are often audited. Receipts for amounts paid to individuals must include the caregiver's social insurance number unless they are paid to individuals who are not Canadian residents.

 The Bottom Line | The child care expense deduction reduces net income and therefore, like Registered Retirement Savings Plan (RRSP) contributions, is a valuable contribution in increasing tax credits, like Child Tax Benefits and the Working Income Tax Benefit. It also reduces taxes payable, so be sure you save all babysitting receipts.

16

Claiming Moving Expenses

The deduction for moving expenses is possibly the most lucrative on the tax return—often in the five figures—so you'll want to be sure you take advantage of it. This deduction is claimed on Line 219 and Form T1-M *Moving Expenses Deduction*. It is available to employees, self-employed persons and students.

To be eligible, the new home must be at least 40 km closer to the new work location than the old home. The distance is measured by the shortest normal route open to the travelling public. Generally the move must be within Canada, although students may claim moving expenses to attend a school outside Canada if they are otherwise eligible.

Expenses may be claimable on moves to Canada if the taxpayer is a full-time student, or a factual or deemed resident. Moves from Canada may also qualify if the student is a full time student, or a deemed or factual resident.

 CHECK IT OUT | **Do I have to earn income at the new location to qualify?** The answer is yes and it must be actively earned. This includes:

- salary, wages (including amounts received under the *Wage Earner Protection Program Act* in respect of work at the new location); or
- self-employment income.

In addition, the taxpayer must stop working or operating a business at the old location, and establish a new home where the taxpayer and family will reside. The following income sources earned at the new location are **not** qualifying income for the purposes of claiming moving expenses:

- investment income
- Employment Insurance benefits
- other income sources, except student awards (see below).

What this means is that if you are unemployed and move to get a job in another province, you'll have to earn qualifying income before moving expenses are claimable. In another example, those who move and retire will need to get a job or start a business, at least for a little while, if they want to have qualifying income against which to deduct moving expenses.

Carryover Periods. If the taxpayer's income at the new location is not sufficient to claim all moving expenses in the year of the move, they may be carried forward and applied against income at the new location in the following year or years.

Since 1997, expenses relating to the move that are not paid until the next taxation year may be deducted in the year paid if income at the new location is sufficient or they may be carried forward to the following years.

Eligible Moving Expenses. Most expenses for moving to the new location are eligible and include the following:

- cost of selling the former residence, including
  - real estate commissions,
  - penalties for paying off a mortgage,
  - legal fees, and
  - advertising costs
- costs of keeping a vacant old residence (to a maximum of $5,000) while actively attempting to sell it, including
  - mortgage interest,
  - property taxes,
  - insurance premiums, and
  - heat and power
- expenses of purchasing the new home (as long as the old home was owned), including
  - transfer taxes, and
  - legal fees
- temporary living expenses, (meals and lodging) for up to 15 days
- removal and storage costs including
  - insurance for household effects
  - costs of moving a boat, trailer, or mobile home (to the extent the costs of moving the mobile do not exceed the costs of moving the contents alone)
- transportation costs

- costs of meals en route (100%—no 50% restriction)
- cost of cancelling an unexpired lease
- cost of revising legal documents to show the new address, replacing driver's licenses and auto permits, cost of utility connections and disconnections

Ineligible Moving Expenses. The following expenses are not deductible moving expenses:

- expenses to make the former property more saleable
- losses on the sale of the former property
- expenses incurred before the move (such as house hunting or job hunting)
- value of items that could not be moved (plants, frozen foods, paint, cleaning products, ammunition, etc.)
- expenses to clean a rented residence
- replacement costs for items not moved such as tool sheds, firewood, drapes, etc.
- mail forwarding costs
- cost of transformers or adaptors for household appliances
- GST on new residence
- expenses that are reimbursed

Home Relocation Loans. Sometimes an employer will require an employee to relocate to another part of the country. In such cases, it is not unusual for a low-interest or interest-free housing loan to be granted to cushion the costs of the move. That benefit (the difference between the *prescribed rate of interest* and the interest rate the employee paid) is a taxable benefit. However a home relocation loan deduction may be taken to offset such a benefit on Line 248. The employee must move at least 40 km. closer to the new work location to qualify.

The maximum annual tax-free benefit is equivalent to the benefits arising from an interest-free housing loan of $25,000 x the prescribed rate of interest, and this will available for the first five years of the loan. The prescribed rate at the time the loan was taken will remain in effect for the full five-year period, so in the current low interest rate environment, it is important to compute the net tax liability being incurred on this arrangement. The amount of the benefit that you are eligible to deduct will be shown in Box 37 of your T4 slip. Your software will post this amount to Line 248 automatically.

The prescribed rate of interest is set quarterly by CRA and is calculated as the average yield on the three-month Treasury Bills sold in the first month of the preceding quarter, rounded up to the nearest percentage point.

Special Rules for Students. Students moving to attend full-time courses at a post-secondary school (or to work as a co-operative student in an industry relating to academic studies), qualifying income against which to claim moving expenses may be the taxable portion of

- research grants, or
- other awards (e.g. prizes for achievement).

Students may also claim moving expenses against income earned at summer jobs or employment/self-employment.

A full-time student is defined as someone who regularly attends college, university or other educational institution at a post-secondary level and is taking at least 60% of the usual course load. Correspondence or a few evening courses will not be sufficient to qualify for these purposes.

Moves Outside Canada. Expenses for moves between two locations outside Canada may be possible if the taxpayer is a deemed resident or factual resident of Canada and the move was taking place from the place the taxpayer ordinarily resided, to a new place where the taxpayer will ordinarily reside.

Simplified Method. Travel expenses may be calculated using a "rate per kilometre" basis rather than claiming the actual amount spent and saving receipts. This method requires a record of the distance traveled during the move. The rate is calculated based on the province in which the move began. The rates allowed for the prior year are announced by CRA in January. Meals en route may also be charged at a flat rate per meal ($17.00 currently) with a maximum of three meals per day (total $51.00). Subscribe to *Knowledge Bureau Report* for a free update at the start of every year, or check the CRA website.

Reimbursements by Employers. Taxpayers who receive reimbursements for moving expenses may only deduct expenses if the amount received as a reimbursement is included in income, or if the amounts claimed are reduced by the amount of the reimbursement.

 The Bottom Line | Moving expenses are very lucrative. Enter your earned income at the new work location in order for your software to calculate the allowable amounts. Be sure to keep a record of the carry forward amount if there is no income at the new work location. You'll need to enter that claim next year, too, unless your software does that for you.

17

Special Situations:
Truckers and Others

In this chapter, we would like to take a closer look at employees for whom there are special tax deductions on the T1:

- Line 229—Transport Employees
- Line 244—Canadian Forces Personnel and Police
- Line 249—Employee Stock Options
- Line 255—Northern Residents

Transport Employees

Transport employees may deduct board and lodging expenses on *Form TL2 Claim for Meals and Lodging Expenses* and report the deductions on Line 229 if they incurred them in the course of their employment. The employer must verify the status of employment and the requirement for the employee to pay expenses by completing the *Employment Information* section and signing the TL2 form and the employee must keep trip logs to support claims for meals and lodging. Qualifying employees must work for:

- Airline, railway, bus and trucking company employees, or
- Be hired as employees whose employer's principal business is to transport goods, passengers, or both.

In the course of their work, they also must:

- regularly travel away from the municipality and, if there is one, the metropolitan area where their home terminal is located,
- use vehicles provided by their employers to transport goods or passengers.

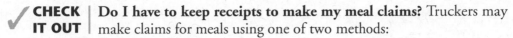

CHECK IT OUT | **Do I have to keep receipts to make my meal claims?** Truckers may make claims for meals using one of two methods:

- *the "simplified method"* which allows one meal every four hours from checkout time, to a maximum of up to three meals per 24-hour period. Claims can be made for a flat rate per meal, without being required to produce receipts. Beginning for 2006, the amount that can be claimed is $17 per meal (maximum $51 per 24-hour period). For trips in Canada, the $17 limit is in Canadian dollars. For trips in the U.S., the amount is $17 U.S.
- *the "detailed method"* whereby claims may be made for the amount shown on actual receipts.

Day Trips. Workers who are regularly required to travel away from their municipality but are occasionally scheduled on runs of 10 hours or less are expected to eat before and after work and therefore may only claim one meal per day on such runs.

Work Crews. Special rules apply for crews of workers who are provided cooking facilities. Under the batching method, receipts are not required but the claim is limited to $34 per day ($30 per day between 2002 and 2005).

Restrictions for Claiming Meals. The 50% meal restriction is modified for long-haul truck drivers who may claim 80% of meal costs, but only for certain qualifying drivers. Your software will do the calculations, but based on your proper theory selections.

The 80% claim is limited to an employee whose principal duty or an individual whose principal business is to drive a long-haul truck in transporting goods, and to employers who pay or reimburse such expenses. In addition, the following criteria must be met:

- a long-haul truck is one with a gross vehicle weight rating in excess of 11,788 kg;
- the enhanced deductibility percentage applies only to eligible travel, which is a period during which the driver is away for at least 24 continuous hours from the employer's municipality or metropolitan area to which the employee reports (employed drivers) or the municipality where the driver resides (self-employed drivers);
- the trip must involve the transport of goods to or from a location at least 160 km from the location described above.

Claiming Lodging Expenses. Claims for lodging must be made using the detailed method—i.e. the actual amounts spent must be claimed. All claims must be supported by receipts.

GST/HST Rebate Possible. There is more good news. Employees who claim deductible expenses such as the Claim for Meals and Lodging Expenses may be able to receive a rebate of the GST/HST paid using Form GST370 *Employee and Partner GST/HST Rebate*

Application and making the claim at Line 457. Rebates received are added to income in the year received.

 The Bottom Line | Long distance truck drivers are in a good position to make lucrative claims for meals and lodging with a variety of filing options. However, these claims are frequently audited; be sure trip logs are available and if the claims are too complicated—especially the GST/HST Rebate, do see a tax pro for help.

Canadian Forces Personnel and Police

Beginning in 2004, certain members of the Canadian Forces or a Canadian police force serving on a deployed operational mission will be entitled to deduct from taxable income the amount of employment earnings from that mission.

The income is reported on Line 101 as usual and is therefore included in the taxpayer's net income, which is used to calculate non-taxable and refundable credits like the Child Tax Benefits (CTB), Goods and Services Tax Credit (GST/HSTC), several provincial credits, etc. The deduction is claimed at Line 244. The income is also included in earned income for RRSP purposes with no adjustment for the deduction.

Software Tips. Your tax software will handle this claim by automatically claiming the deduction when you enter the amount shown in Box 43 of your T4 slip.

 CHECK IT OUT | **Can all military personnel make this claim?** The employee must be serving on a deployed operational mission that is assessed for risk allowance 3 or higher (as determined by the Department of National Defence) or a prescribed mission. The deduction will be limited to the lesser of

- the employment income earned while serving on the mission, and
- the maximum rate of pay earned by a non-commissioned member of the Canadian Forces (approximately $6,000 per month) to the extent that the employment income is included in computing the taxpayer's income for the year.

Selected Canadian Forces missions assessed for risk allowance 2 (as determined by the Department of National Defence) will be "*prescribed missions*" under *Income Tax Regulation* 7400, including the following:

- Operation Calumet (Middle East—Sinai);
- Operation Jade (Middle East—Jerusalem and Damascus);

- Operation Hamlet (Haiti);
- Operation Gladius (Golan Heights); and
- United Nations Mission in the Sudan—Civilian Policing Component (Sudan—Kartoum)

 The Bottom Line | Taxpayers who qualify for this deduction and have other sources of income may want to adjust the tax withholding on that other income or any instalment payments they may have been planning to make as they will likely be in a lower-tax bracket as a result of this deduction.

Employee Stock Options

An employer may provide its employees the opportunity to purchase shares in the employer's corporation at some future date, but at a price that is the current market price when the option is granted (the exercise price). There are no tax consequences when the option is granted.

However, when the employee exercises these security options (also referred to as stock options) it will give rise to a taxable benefit. The benefit is calculated as the difference between the market value of the shares purchased and the exercise price. This benefit is included in income then, but may qualify for a Stock Options Deduction on Line 249.

 CHECK IT OUT | **What can I claim as a deduction?** The amount of the security options deduction is one-half of the taxable benefit and will be detailed in Box 39 (for a CCPC) or Box 41 of the employee's T4 slip. The tax treatment differs, however, depending on whether a Canadian Controlled Private Corporation (CCPC) or a public corporation grants the options.

- *Options Granted by a CCPC.* The taxable benefit included in employment income is deemed to have arisen only when the employee disposes of the shares. The security options deduction is available provided only that the employee held the shares for at least two years before disposing of them.
- *Options Granted by a Public Corporation.* Where the option is granted by a public corporation or by a private corporation that is not Canadian-controlled, the taxable benefit is deemed to have arisen when the employee exercises the option.

For options exercised after February 27, 2000 and before March 5, 2010, employees who would otherwise be taxed on stock option benefits in the year the option is exercised could elect to defer a portion of the security options benefit (up to $100,000) until the shares were disposed of by filing Form T1212 *Statement of Deferred Security Options Benefits* with the tax return each year.

However for options exercised after March 5, 2010, this deferral opportunity is not available. The following rules now apply:

1. When an employee has deferred stock option taxable benefits and subsequently disposes of the securities, the taxable benefits must be reported on Line 101. If the employee is still employed by the same employer, the benefit may be included in Box 14 of the T4 slip. If the employee is no longer employed with the same employer, the amount is calculated on Form T1212.
2. In a year in which a taxpayer is required to include a deferred securities option benefit in income, it will be possible to elect to pay a tax equal to the taxpayer's proceeds of disposition of the optioned shares. (In Quebec the tax is 2/3 of the proceeds.) This election is made on form RC310 *Special Tax On Disposition Of Securities Acquired Under An Employee Securities Option Program* and will make sense when the proceeds are less than the taxes payable on the deferred benefit—that is when the value of the stocks has decreased by more than 80% since the option was exercised.

Software Tips. In all cases except the RC310 election, your software should post the amounts to the proper lines based on your entries for Box 39 or Box 41 on your T4 slip and your entries on Form T1212 if you have deferred benefits.

 The Bottom Line | It's wonderful when an employee can participate in an employee stock option plan. However because of recent complexity, consult with a tax pro to ensure you are claiming your benefits and later, the capital gains and losses on disposition properly.

Northern Residents Deduction

If you lived in a prescribed northern or intermediate zone for a period of at least six consecutive months beginning or ending in a taxation year, you may claim the Northern Residents Deduction on Line 255 by filing Form T2222 *Northern Residents Deductions*. These zones are published in CRA's publication T4039 *Northern Residents Deductions— Places in Prescribed Zones*.

This claim may also be made on the final return of a deceased taxpayer if the deceased lived in a prescribed zone for six months prior to death.

There is no requirement to make income to make this claim; however, because it's a deduction, it will only benefit those with taxable income. It cannot be carried back or forward if you don't use it this year.

 CHECK IT OUT | **What is the amount of the Northern Residents Deduction?** Two types of deductions are available: a residency deduction and a travel deduction, and your software will usually calculate these amounts for you.

The residency deduction is equal to the lesser of:

- 20% of the individual's income for the year, and
- a percentage of:
  - $8.25 for each day in the year in the period in which the individual resided in the prescribed zone (the basic residency amount), plus
  - $8.25 for each day in the year in the period that the individual maintained and resided in a self-contained domestic establishment in the prescribed zone and no other individual residing in that dwelling claimed a residency deduction for that day (the additional residency amount).

For taxpayers who lived in a prescribed northern zone, the percentage applied is 100%. For taxpayers who lived in a prescribed intermediate zone, the percentage applied is 50%. Employees in prescribed zones may also receive a tax-free benefit for the cost of housing. See *Perks* in earlier chapters in this section.

The travel deduction is provided to an employee or a member of the employee's household for travel expenses incurred in connection with:

- any trips made to obtain medical services not available locally, and
- a maximum of two trips per year for other reasons, to the extent that the value of the benefits is included in employment income.

For trips that begin in one year and end in the next, the claim should be made in the year that the taxable benefit appears on the taxpayer's T4 slip. If the amount will not appear on the T4 slip, claim the trip in the year that the trip began and include the value of the benefit provided by the employer in income. The maximum claim for each eligible trip is a percentage of the lowest of the following amounts:

- the travel benefits received from the employer for the trip (and included in the taxpayer's income),
- the total travel expenses for the trip, and

- the cost of the lowest return airfare available at the time of the trip between the airport closest to the taxpayer's residence and the nearest designated city. The following cities are designated for this purpose:

  - Calgary, AB
  - Edmonton, AB
  - Halifax, NS
  - Moncton, NB
  - Montréal, QC
  - North Bay, ON
  - Ottawa, ON
  - Québec City, QC
  - Saskatoon, SK
  - St. John's, NL
  - Toronto, ON
  - Vancouver, BC
  - Winnipeg, MB

Travel expenses include any of the following amounts:

- air, train, and bus fares;
- vehicle expenses (actual expenses or a prescribed per kilometer amount);
- meals; hotel and motel accommodations, and camping fees; and
- other incidental expenses, such as taxis and road or ferry tolls.

For taxpayers who lived in a prescribed northern zone, the percentage applied is 100%. For taxpayers who lived in a prescribed intermediate zone, the percentage applied is 50%. For many taxpayers living in a prescribed intermediate zone, it may make more sense to claim the medical travel as a medical expense. Note, however, that no claim may be made for medical travel if the same expenses are claimed by anyone as a medical expense. See Chapter 25.

 The Bottom Line | Use the power of your tax software to help you claim every deduction an employee is entitled to: from sales expenses to auto and home office, to the specialized deductions for those who live in the north, move or have babies. Print each "auxiliary" tax form and attach receipts for use in case of audit.

18

Schedule 1 Tax Credits:
The Costs of Going to Work

Employees will often qualify for non-refundable tax credits that are not specific to their expenditures at work. In this chapter we will discuss three of them: public transit costs, medical expenses and charitable donations.

Amount for Public Transit Passes

Riding the bus or subway these days? Keep your receipts because a non-refundable tax credit is available on Schedule 1, Line 364 for the cost of an eligible public transit pass. If your employer paid for your passes, the amount you can claim is shown in Box 84 of your T4 slip (you can also claim the amount shown on your spouse's T4).

 CHECK IT OUT | **Who can claim it?** Either spouse may make the claim for eligible transit costs of the two parents and the dependent children under 19 years of age at the end of the year, or one person can make the claim for all. If the claim is split between two taxpayers the total amount claimed may not exceed the maximum allowed.

An eligible public transit pass includes:

- a document issued by or on behalf of a qualified Canadian transit organization that identifies the right of an individual to use public commuter transit services of that organization on an unlimited number of occasions and on any day during which the services are offered during an uninterrupted period of at least 28 days,

- an electronic payment card, provided the card provides at least 32 one-way trips in a period not exceeding 31 days, or
- a weekly transit pass covering a period of 5 to 7 days, so long as the taxpayer purchased at least four consecutive weekly passes.

A qualified Canadian transit organization is one that is authorized under a law of Canada or of a province to carry on a business in Canada (through a permanent establishment in Canada) that is the provision of public commuter transit services.

"*Public commuter transit services*" have a specific definition:

- the services must be offered to the general public to and from places in Canada.
- the individual would return daily to the place of their departure.
- the services have to be offered ordinarily for a period of at least 5 days per week by means of a bus, ferry, subway, train, or tram.

A transit pass will qualify if it displays all of the following information:

- an indication of the duration pass;
- the validation date or period;
- the name of the transit authority or organization issuing the pass;
- the amount paid for the pass; and
- the identity of the rider, either by name or unique identifier.

If the above information does not appear on the transit pass, the taxpayer should obtain a dated receipt, or retain cancelled cheques or credit card statements, to support the claim.

Is there a maximum claim? There is no maximum dollar limit for these claims. The cost of the passes must be reduced by any reimbursement received from an employer unless that reimbursement was included in income.

Medical Expenses for Employees

Almost everyone misses claiming medical expenses every year. You want to avoid this because there is a very lengthy list of provisions that can make a difference on your return.

For employees this begins with claiming the group medical expenses you might be paying for every two weeks. This is one of those tax credits where your tax software will rely on you to give it full and complete information. It can then do the calculations in the background properly, and even optimize the claim.

As long as the taxpayer is a resident of Canada, expenses incurred abroad are also claimable, including Blue Cross and other travel or private health insurance premiums. Blue Cross and similar private health insurance premiums are often deducted by the employer; the amount paid by the employer and included in the employee's income will be shown on the T4 slip; amounts paid by the employee will likely be shown on pay stubs.

For more on claiming medical expenses, see Chapter 25.

Charitable Donations on the T4 Slip

A non-refundable tax credit for charitable donations may be claimed to reduce taxes payable. If you are employed, you may have given a donation at work. Look for this on your T4 Slip, box 46. Your software will have automatically entered it on Schedule 9 *Donations and Gifts*, and to the non-refundable credits on Schedule 1 *Federal Tax*, Line 349. Enter other donations you make outside of work, on the Donations data entry sheet. What's important is to consider combining these donations with your spouse's for a higher claim.

For more on claiming charitable donations, see Chapter 27.

 The Bottom Line | The non-refundable tax credits which apply at work: public transit costs, medical and charity expenditures will help you to reduce your federal and provincial taxes payable. You can combine these claims with the costs your family members incurred too.

19

Severance and Unemployment

Losing a job—especially unexpectedly—can be a difficult life event. You should know how to keep the most of a lump sum that might come your way. The taxes on this lifeline can rob you of precious resources while you look for new work or arrange for your retirement income. There are also investment planning decisions to be made.

Begin by answering the common "trigger questions" most people in this situation have:

- Is termination payment acceptable?
- Will you want to contest the termination?
- Do you need to be introduced to a broader professional team that may include lawyers and accountants, recruitment services, or credit counselors?
- How can you develop new networks of potential influencers to assist in seeking the next opportunity?
- Will you be employed or self-employed in your future?

If illness is a reason for job termination, financial relief may be available by applying for the Canada Pension Plan disability benefits, Worker's Compensation or Wage Loss Replacement Plans.

In this chapter we will discuss two important income sources to those who lose a job: severance or retiring allowances and employment insurance.

Retiring Allowances

Employees who are leaving their jobs and who receive job termination payments or retiring allowances should do some tax planning perhaps with RRSP contributions and other income splitting or deferral options.

 CHECK IT OUT | **How can I keep more of my severance package?** An RRSP contribution can help you keep more of your retiring allowance. If adding your retiring allowance to your income brings you into a higher tax bracket, you should consider transferring at least enough of the retiring allowance to your RRSP so that you don't go into that higher tax bracket. The case study in Chapter 12 provided a good planning example.

RRSP Rollovers. You may receive an "eligible" retiring allowance or an "ineligible" allowance, and this will show up on your T4 slip. Here's what this means:

- *Eligible Allowances.* The portion of your retiring allowance that is "eligible" (shown in Box 66) can be transferred into your RRSP, even if you don't have any contribution room. The effect of such a transfer is that you won't have to pay taxes on that portion of the retiring allowance until you take that money out of your RRSP.
- *Ineligible Allowances.* The portion of your retiring allowance that is "ineligible" (shown in Box 67) can also be transferred to your RRSP, but only if you have enough contribution room to cover the contribution.

Avoid Lump Sums. Whenever possible, avoid adding a lump sum to income in one tax year. You might be able to take your severance over two tax years, for example: half in December and half in January. That will often bring a better tax result.

If your only option is to accept a lump sum, check out your RRSP contribution room and contribute as much of your severance to your RRSP as possible. This will offset taxes owing on the severance in the current tax year. You'll get to keep more money, earn investment income on a tax deferred basis and reserve for yourself the opportunity to time RRSP withdrawals in the future to get a better tax result as a family. There may even be an opportunity to split RRSP withdrawals with your spouse.

 Case Study | When Edward left his employer late in 2012, he had already earned $65,000 for the year and received a severance settlement of $100,000.

Had Edward done nothing, the full $100,000 would have been added to his income in 2012 adding more than $42,000 to his tax bill! To minimize the income tax consequences, Edward made an RRSP contribution of $100,000 (having not maximized his RRSP contributions in the past he had sufficient RRSP contribution room). The RRSP deduction eliminated that extra $42,000 in taxes.

If Edward needs to use those funds over the next two years, he could withdraw $50,000 each year and (assuming no other income sources) his tax bill would be about $8,700 per year. This strategy would save Edward $24,600 in taxes simply by parking the money in his RRSP for a year or two. If possible, withdraw money from the RRSP only when other taxable income sources are exhausted to maximize your retirement.

Legal Fees. If you incur legal fees in order to collect money owed to you for severance, pension benefits, or a retiring allowance, you may claim those expenses as Other Deductions on Line 232 so long as those expenses were not reimbursed and the amount collected is included in income. Your legal fees must be reduced by amounts transferred into your RRSP. If unabsorbed by the severance income they can be carried forward for seven years.

Unemployment and Your T4E Slip

For those who become unemployed, EI benefits received in the year are taxable. They are entered from the T4E slip onto your tax return. Be careful to watch for any income tax deductions so you can enter these, too.

The EI benefits received may be subject to repayment, if you have received regular benefits in the previous 10 years, and your income exceeds the annual income threshold for these purposes.

 CHECK IT OUT | **How can I keep more of my EI benefits?** Tax planning with RRSP contributions can help avoid this. Your software will calculate the repayment automatically and add it to the amounts you need to pay for the year. Be sure to check whether you have to repay prior to the RRSP deadline so that you can minimize this clawback by making an RRSP contribution.

Other types of EI benefits which are not considered "regular benefits" and are not subject to repayment include:

• EI-funded financial assistance paid while you are taking part in an approved employment program (Box 17)

- Tax exempt benefits received by status Indians (Box 18)
- Tuition assistance (Box 20 or Box 21)
- Maternity benefits, Parental benefits
- Sickness benefits
- Compassionate care benefits

EI and the Self-Employed. You may find at the end of your employment that you want to earn your living as a self-employed person. Small business owners can now opt in for certain restricted employment benefits available including maternity benefits, parental/adoptive benefits, sickness benefits and compassionate care benefits.

However, there is a trap. Once you opt in, you have 60 days to change your mind. After the 60 days, you are in the program for the calendar year. Assuming you do not collect any EI benefits, you may choose to opt-out at the beginning of any calendar year. If you do receive EI benefits, however, you are no longer eligible to opt-out of the EI program on self-employment earnings, ever. Once you receive a benefit you will continue to remain in the program and have to pay annual premiums on your self-employment income.

 The Bottom Line | If you are leaving your job, reduce any lump sum amounts received with an RRSP contribution if possible. Your legal fees may also be tax deductible.

20

Your T4 Slip Entry Guide

Employer's name – Nom de l'employeur		

Canada Revenue Agency / Agence du revenu du Canada

Year / Année

T4
STATEMENT OF REMUNERATION PAID
ÉTAT DE LA RÉMUNÉRATION PAYÉE

Field	Box		Field	Box
Employment income – line 101 / Revenus d'emploi – ligne 101	14		Income tax deducted – line 437 / Impôt sur le revenu retenu – ligne 437	22
Payroll account number / Numéro de compte de retenues	54			
Province of employment / Province d'emploi	10	Employee's CPP contributions – line 308 / Cotisations de l'employé au RPC – ligne 308	16	EI insurable earnings / Gains assurables d'AE	24
Social insurance number / Numéro d'assurance sociale	12	Exempt – Exemption (CPP/QPP, EI, PPIP / RPC/RRQ, AE, RPAP)	28		
Employment code / Code d'emploi	29	Employee's QPP contributions – line 308 / Cotisations de l'employé au RRQ – ligne 308	17	CPP/QPP pensionable earnings / Gains ouvrant droit à pension – RPC/RRQ	26
		Employee's EI premiums – line 312 / Cotisations de l'employé à l'AE – ligne 312	18	Union dues – line 212 / Cotisations syndicales – ligne 212	44
		RPP contributions – line 207 / Cotisations à un RPA – ligne 207	20	Charitable donations – line 349 / Dons de bienfaisance – ligne 349	46
		Pension adjustment – line 206 / Facteur d'équivalence – ligne 206	52	RPP or DPSP registration number / N° d'agrément d'un RPA ou d'un RPDB	50
		Employee's PPIP premiums – see over / Cotisations de l'employé au RPAP – voir au verso	55	PPIP insurable earnings / Gains assurables du RPAP	56

Employee's name and address – Nom et adresse de l'employé

Last name (in capital letters) – Nom de famille (en lettres moulées)   First name – Prénom   Initial – Initiale

Other information (see over)	Box – Case	Amount – Montant	Box – Case	Amount – Montant	Box – Case	Amount – Montant
Autres renseignements (voir au verso)						

T4 (12)

Box	Claimed on	What is it?	What do you need to know?
14	T1 Line 101	Employment income: salary, wages, bonuses, vacation pay, tips, honoraria, director's fees, and taxable benefits	Includes a cleric's residence allowance in Box 30. Your software will report it on Line 104. You may also be eligible for the Clergy Residence Deduction on Line 231.
			If compensation as a volunteer firefighter is excluded from Box 14, the excluded amount will be shown in Box 87. Your software will add this amount to Line 101 if you claim the Volunteer Firefighter's Tax Credit on Schedule 1.
16/ 17	T1 Line 308/310	Canada Pension Plan/ Quebec Pension Plan contributions	If you are self-employed, your software includes these amounts on Schedule 8 and Line 310. Otherwise, the amounts will be posted to Form T2204. The allowable credit is posted to Line 308.
18	T1 Line 312	Employment Insurance premiums	Your software will post to Form T2204 and calculate any overpayment. The allowable credit is posted to Line 312.
20	T1 Line 207	Registered Pension Plan contributions	Deduction may be limited if the box includes past service contributions.
22	T1 Line 437	Income tax deducted	This will include all source deductions for income taxes from all slips.
24	T2204	EI insurable earnings	Your software will use this number to calculate any overpayment of on Form T2204. If blank, use the amount in Box 14 unless Box 28 indicates you are exempt from EI.
26	T2204	CPP pensionable earnings	Your software will use this number to calculate any overpayment on Form T2204. If blank, use the amount in Box 14 unless Box 28 indicates that you are exempt from CPP.
44	T1 Line 212	Union Dues	
46	Schedule 9	Charitable Donations	Treat as any other donation. May be claimed on the spouse's return if more beneficial or carried forward for up to five years. Usually, your software will optimize this claim for you.
50		Registered Pension Plan or Deferred Profit Sharing Plan number	Do not record on the return.
52	T1 Line 206	Pension Adjustment	Affects your RRSP contribution room for the next tax year. It shows up on your Notice of Assessment/ Reassessment from CRA, which states your RRSP deduction limit and unused contributions. They end up on Schedule 7.

Box	Claimed on	What is it?	What do you need to know?
55		PPIP premiums	The Provincial Parental Insurance Plan is applicable in you live in Quebec.
56		PPIP insurable earnings	as above
66	T1 Line 130	Eligible Retiring Allowances	The amount eligible for transfer to your RRSP or RPP. Any RRSP contributions up to this amount may be made without using RRSP contribution room. Be specific in software.
67	T1 Line 130	Non-eligible Retiring Allowances	This is the amount NOT eligible to be transferred to your RRSP or RPP.
87	T1 Line 101	Volunteer Firefighter Exempt Amount	This amount is excluded from Box 14 but your software will add it to Line 101 if you claim the volunteer firefighter amount on Line 362.

Other Information Section: Entered here are taxable benefits. These are already included in Box 14, so don't enter them again as income. You may be able to claim special deductions to offset the income, which software may do automatically.

Box	What is it?	What else is relevant?
30	Housing, board, and lodging	Amounts may qualify for the Northern Residents Deduction on Form T2222. May represent the clergy residence allowance, which goes to Line 104. Possible Clergy Residence Deduction on Line 231.
31	Board and lodging at a special work site	Not taxable and does not create any deductions.
32	Travel in a prescribed zone	Your software will use this amount to calculate the Northern Residents Deductions on Form T2222.
33	Medical travel	As above.
34	Personal use of employer's auto	Taxable benefit for personal use of an automobile provided by the employer. Reduce this amount if your personal driving is not over 1,667 km per month. Use Form RC18 to calculate.
36	Interest-free and low-interest loan	If the low-interest loan was used for investment purposes, this amount may be used as a carrying charge on Schedule 4. Enter this manually.
37	Employee home-relocation loan deduction	Your software will claim this deduction on Line 248.
38	Security options benefits	Income results when stock option is exercised. If exercised before March 4, 2010, file Form T1212.
39	Security options deduction (public company shares)	Your software will claim this deduction on T1 Line 249.

Box	What is it?	What else is relevant?
40	Other taxable allowances and benefits	This box can include amounts for educational allowances, value of gifts, health benefits (which may qualify as medical expenses). Claim tax credits, as appropriate.
41	Security options deduction (private company shares)	Your software will claim this deduction on Line 249.
42	Employment commissions	Enter on Line 102 (but don't add to total income—already included in Box 14). Other employment expenses claimed at Line 229 may be restricted to this amount.
43	Canadian forces personnel and police allowance	Your software will claim on Line 244.
53	Deferred security options benefits	If the employee deferred stock option benefits using Form T1212, your software will enter this on Line 6520.
68	Status Indian (exempt income)	Eligible retiring allowances. Not included in income.
69	Status Indian (exempt income)	Non-eligible retiring allowances. Not included in income.
70	Municipal officer's expense allowance	The non-taxable portion of the expense allowance received from a municipality.
71	Status Indian employee	This indicates the employee is a status Indian whose employment income is exempt from tax.
72	Section 122.3 income— employment outside Canada	The portion of employment income paid while you were employed outside Canada. Income tax was not withheld. Complete *Form T626—Overseas Employment Tax Credit* to ensure this income is not taxed in 2012.
73	Section 122.3 no. of days outside Canada	The number of days the employee was employed outside Canada to earn amount in Box 72. Use for Form T626.
74	Pre-1990 RPP past service contributions while a Contributor	The amount of past service contributions to an RPP for a period when the employee was a contributor to the plan. Use to calculate RPP deduction on Line 207.
75	Pre-1990 past service contributions while not a Contributor	The past service contributions to an RPP for a period when the employee *was not* a contributor to the plan. Use to calculate RPP deduction on Line 207.
77	Workers' Compensation benefits repaid	Your software will claim a deduction on Line 229 or 232.
78	Fishers—gross earnings	Amount paid or payable to the fisher from the proceeds of a catch. Enter on Form 2121, not Line 101.

Box	What is it?	What else is relevant?
79	Fishers—net partnership amount	This is the product of the gross earnings amount in Box 78, less total amount paid to share-persons reported in Box 80 x the fisher's partnership agreement allocation. Enter on Form 2121, not Line 101.
80	Fishers—shareperson amount	The amount paid to the fisher from proceeds of a catch based on sharing arrangement agreed to prior to start of fishing trip. Use Form 2121, not Line 101.
81	Placement or Employment Agency workers—gross $	These earnings must be reported on T2125.
82	**Taxi drivers** (etc.)—gross $	These earnings must be reported on T2125.
83	Barbers or hairdressers—gross $	These earnings must be reported on T2125.
84	Public Transit Passes	Credit may be claimed on Line 364 on Schedule 1.
85	Employee-paid Premiums to Private Health Services Plans	Premiums may be claimed as a medical expense. Software will post to the medical expense schedule.
86	Security Options Election	The amount of security option cash-outs the employer elected not to claim as an expense and included in the employee's income (as shown in Box 14).

PART 3

Families and Children

Family life is changing significantly in Canada. Consider that in 1961, just over 50 years ago, about 92% of families were headed by a married couple. By 2011 this had dropped to 67%, according to the Canadian Census. Meanwhile significant growth in conjugal relationships includes common-law couples, blended families as well as same sex couples.

Filing a tax return for families is also getting more complex. What hasn't changed, however, is the purpose: getting the best results for each individual, and then "optimizing" all income reporting, deductions and credits to get the best results for the family unit as a whole. That's the subject of this section.

What's New

Most of the changes for families are in the indexed refundable and non-refundable tax credits and the amount of income the family can earn before they lose them. There is also something new for families who take care of someone who is infirm: a "super" non-refundable tax credit called the *Family Caregiver Amount*. This new credit increases several existing credits where the dependant is mentally or physically incapacitated.

Hard Copy

When you gather the hard copy this year, remember to organize all the receipts for the entire family, starting with the lowest income earner and working your way up to the highest. From T4 slips to tuition, subway passes to medical expenses—it's all important.

Software Tips

Your software may automatically link all the family returns together. That's a great option, if you can find it, as it helps you to optimize transferrable deductions and credits which you'll learn about in this section. Also, you will find that many of your personal tax credits will be automatically calculated by your software after you enter details about birthdates and net incomes. To have those figures handy, as you make decisions about income splitting, transfers and carry forward amounts, you may wish to print T1 Summaries for each person in the family.

Tax Sleuthing

Review the summaries of all tax returns and do some "reverse engineering." Do you understand all the numbers? Are they on the right return? What is the net result for the family—have you paid the least taxes possible? Your goal is to maximize refundable and non-refundable tax credits, too. If you have missed a tax deduction, it can affect your income from social benefits throughout the year.

Tax Pro Alert

Do you qualify for income splitting? Can you transfer assets—legitimately—to your spouse or children? Be sure you understand the "Attribution Rules" before you do either. A tax professional can supplement your tax filing knowledge by helping you plan to achieve the most tax efficient results for family income and capital in future years.

21

Conjugal Relationships: Filing With Your Spouse

The number of common-law couples has risen 13.9% in Canada between 2001 and 2006. This compares with a 3.1% increase for married couples in the same period. Lone-parent families increased 8% over the same period. Growth was higher for male lone-parent families (+16.2%) than for female lone-parent families (+6%).

– Statistics Canada Census Data, Sept. 2012

In Canada, we are taxed as individuals. We each qualify for our own Basic Personal Amount (just under $11,000 at the time of writing). We have our own marginal tax rates on our various sources of income. And we individually are subject to a progressive tax system; that is, the more we earn, the more we pay, and the less we receive from income-tested benefits like refundable tax credits or the Old Age Security.

However, most families make financial decisions as one economic unit. Frankly that's how the government redistributes income, too. They look at the size of "net family income" for certain provisions like the refundable tax credits. But that "joint filing" requirement for some provisions but not others can make tax filing and the communications of vital information between family members challenging.

Just when, for example, do families have to declare their relationships and add incomes together? When is income splitting possible? How many tax-exempt residences can a family unit own? These are important questions especially when family life is changing and complicated, as the census data shows. If you are:

• married to someone of the same or opposite sex, with no children just yet,

- living common law with your partner of the same or opposite sex,
- parents of children together,
- adoptive parent of a child, including your spouse's or common-law spouse's child,
- a supporting individual to a sibling, parent, grandchild, aunt, uncle, niece, nephew or any other person whose care you are responsible for, including in-laws, or
- a single parent, or perhaps one who is recently separated or divorced with joint custody or summer visitation rights to your children,

you should discuss joint tax provisions for family, even though each individual might be filing their own tax return. The good news is that your tax software may automatically "optimize" your net family results. But to begin with, you must tell it whether you have a spouse—legally married or otherwise.

 CHECK IT OUT | **What is the definition of a spouse?** A spouse or common-law partner is someone with whom you are living in a *conjugal relationship* (that is, "as married"). You must mark your marital status as "married" or "common-law partner" in the identification area of the tax return, as the following circumstances apply:

- *A spouse*, for tax purposes, is someone of the same or opposite sex to whom you are legally married.
- *A common-law partner*, is someone who is not your spouse but is someone who qualifies under **one** of the following conditions:
  - someone of the same or opposite sex who has been living with you in a conjugal relationship for at least 12 continuous months. (separations of less than 90 days do not affect the 12-month period), or
  - someone you have resumed living with and your current relationship has lasted at least 12 continuous months, or
  - someone who, at the end of the tax year, was the actual or adoptive parent of the taxpayer's child, or
  - someone who has custody and control of your child, or did so immediately before the child turned 19, and who wholly supported that person.

As a general rule, any tax provisions that apply to a spouse apply equally to a common-law partner. Unless specifically noted otherwise, you may assume throughout this book that any time the term "spouse" or "spousal" is used, that the provision applies to both legally married spouses and to common-law partners of the same or opposite sex.

When you indicate you have a spouse whose net income is below the Basic Personal Amount, your software will automatically claim the "Spousal Amount." However, just because your spouse has little or no income, doesn't necessarily mean he or she shouldn't file a tax return. There are several "joint filing" provisions for couples that can bring home tax benefits for your family unit.

 CHECK | **What are the joint filing provisions for couples?** The basic
IT OUT | elements of the tax return that is, the reporting of income, deductions
and various tax credits, should be addressed for the couple, after the information for each individual has been entered on their own return. Quite often your tax software will do this for you in the background. This might confuse you, as you may not understand where the figures have come from.

The tax reporting guide below should help you decipher some of the reporting rules and position you to develop strategies to "average down" the income tax you pay as a family over time, and increase the income redistribution benefits governments may have set aside and waiting for you:

Income Reporting. In some cases, social benefits like the Universal Child Care Benefit must be reported by the spouse. In other cases, it is possible, to elect to split certain income sources, like qualifying pension income or to transfer pools of capital that will result in investment earnings taxed at your spouse's lower tax bracket. However, there are specific rules, especially when it comes to transferring income or capital, as described below:

Line 117 The Universal Child Care Benefit (UCCB). One of the ways the tax system addresses the extra expense of raising children is with a *universal* monthly payment—that is, everyone gets it regardless of income level. The amount is $100 per month for each child under 6. If you're in a conjugal relationship, this must be reported by the spouse with the lower net income.

However, this income will not reduce your family's refundable tax credits, like the *Canada Child Tax Benefit (CTB),* or related provincial credits. If you are a single parent, you may also choose to report this income on the return of a child you are claiming as an "Eligible Dependant" or the return of any other child. Single parents will be discussed in more detail in Chapter 28.

Line 115 Pension Income Splitting: Spouses have a fantastic opportunity to split income from qualifying pensions. They may also assign half of their Canada Pension Plan benefits to their spouse, so that each reports half the benefits the other is entitled to. The result is that the couple will usually pay lower taxes as a unit, than they would if one person reported a high income and the other a lower one. In these cases, a lower level of income between the two may also reduce the clawback of Old Age Security and quarterly tax instalments. We'll discuss this in more depth in Part 5.

Line 120/121/126/127 Investment, Revenue Property and Capital Gains Income Do the same rules hold true when it comes to sharing accumulated savings with family members so the family unit can pay less tax on investment income? Unfortunately, the tax department generally frowns upon higher income earners transferring capital, including investments and revenue properties to lower earners in the family to avoid taxes. For that reason, the "Attribution Rules" disallow most loans and transfers.

CHECK IT OUT | **What are the Attribution Rules?** When income is earned on property that is loaned or transferred to a spouse or minor child, it must generally be reported by the transferor. There are some exceptions, for example, an investment in a TFSA or a Spousal RRSP. These rules will be discussed in more detail in Chapter 28.

Line 135 Self-Employment Income. If your spouse has income from a proprietorship, *Form T2125 Statement of Business Activities* will be completed to self-report income and deductions as well as the ongoing cost of assets used in a business. If the business is a corporation, a separate T2 tax return will be filed and the owner-manager will likely report on the T1 return any salary, wages or dividends drawn out of the corporation.

Businesses must be more than a hobby run out of the basement. There must be a reasonable expectation that a profit will result from a business activity, profession, calling, trade or other activity. While this is a large subject and the focus of my book *Make Sure It's Deductible* (available at www.knowledgebureau.com), an example of the income splitting opportunities appear at the end of this chapter together with a checklist of common write-offs to discuss with your tax professional.

Claiming Deductions. There are numerous deductions leading to net income on Line 236 of the T1, and many of these contain rules that require a look at both spouse's tax returns to make allowable claims. Recall, the refundable tax credits you may be entitled to from the federal or provincial governments are based on your combined "net family income," which is Line 236 of both spouses' returns, or in some cases, Line 234. The lower your family net income is, the more tax credits and social benefits you'll receive.

CHECK IT OUT | **What deductions will reduce your net income?** Pay particular attention to the following deductions, leading to a reduced net income, to determine who should make the claims to get the best family benefit. It's good to address them in the order they appear on the T1, so print it out and follow along:

Common Tax Deductions that Reduce Net Income

Line 208 RRSP Contributions	You may contribute to your own RRSP or to a "Spousal RRSP" based on your own "earned income." You'll get the tax deduction, but it's a good idea to accumulate equal amounts in your RRSP, so you get better tax results with you make retirement income withdrawals. See Part 5, Reporting Pension Income. The deduction is claimed on Schedule 7.
Line 214 Child Care Expenses	Make this claim on Form T778. Usually this must be claimed by the person with the lower net income on Line 234, but in some specific instances the higher earner may make the claim, as described later.
Line 215 Disability Supports Deduction	Receipts are required for supports that enable a disabled person to go to work and earn income at a place of employment or business, or to carry on research or to study at a post-secondary school. This includes the cost of an attendant who assists a severely disabled person. The attendant must be an unrelated person and over 18. Some of the same expenses may qualify as medical expenses but can't be claimed twice. Line 215 deductions will generally get a better result because they can help increase other tax provisions.
Line 219 Moving Expenses	Form T1M is used for this lucrative tax deduction. Either spouse can make the claim, but the move must be at least 40 km closer to new employment or self-employment. There must be income at the new location and in general the person with the higher income will get a better result. A carry forward of the expenses is also possible if there is not enough income earned in the year at the new location.
Line 221 Carrying Charges	Receipts are required for all amounts claimed here including safety deposit boxes and the details of loans taken for investment purposes. Any dual-purpose loans must be prorated (e.g. lines of credit used for both a personal and investment purposes). Either spouse may claim the safety deposit box, one of the most commonly missed deductions for couples.

Refundable Tax Credits. Once you know how much your net income on Line 236 will be for each spouse, your tax software will combine the incomes to calculate many tax credits automatically, including the three federal refundable tax credits below; review their values and income thresholds in *Appendix 3 Refundable Tax Credits Summary*.

- Canada Child Tax Credit (CCTB)
- GST/HST Credit
- Working Income Tax Benefit (WITB)

RRSPs Will Reduce Family Net Income. In Chapter 12, you may recall Rupert, who was single, saved over $4,500 by contributing to an RRSP. The RRSP is equally effective for couples. The following case study illustrates the effect on family net income and credits.

Case Study | **Planning to Increase Tax Credits With an RRSP**

Sarah and Brett live in Vancouver and have two children under age 5; her income is $55,000 and his net income from his consulting business is $25,000.

Without an RRSP contribution, their Child Tax Benefits are $1,474; with a $5,000 contribution based on Sarah's contribution room, they increase to $1,674, plus the couple's tax savings are $1,485. The contribution saves them in total $1,685, a return on their RRSP investment of 34% by way of tax savings.

Non-Refundable Tax Credits. Take a good look at Schedule 1 in your software, where you'll find your federal credits; then visit Appendix 3 for detail about all the non-refundable tax credits claimable on your tax returns. You will note that most of them have been indexed to inflation over the years. You will also notice something new in 2012: some of the non-refundable tax credits are increased if dependants are disabled:

✓ CHECK IT OUT | **What is the new Family Caregiver Tax Credit?** This credit provides a $2,000 "bump" in the value of five tax credits:

- the Spousal Amount (available if you are legally married or living common-law),
- the *Amount for Eligible Dependant* (an "equivalent-to-spouse" amount for families headed by a single parent),
- the *Amount for Children Under 18,*
- the Amount for Infirm Adults, and
- the *Caregiver Amount.*

We will discuss the non-refundable tax credits available to families with children, singles and caregivers in more detail later; now, let's discuss non-refundable credits for spouses.

Line 303 Spousal Amount. For 2012, the maximum claim is $10,822 (the same as the Basic Personal Amount), plus $2,000 if your spouse is infirm and it is reduced by each dollar your spouse makes, as per the example below:

Example: Charles and Jennifer are a common-law couple. Charles earns $46,000 at his job and Jennifer is a student. Jennifer's net income for 2012 was $6,500. Charles may claim the spousal amount of $10,822 – $6,500 = $4,322 for Jennifer. If Jennifer were disabled, his claim would be $12,822 – $6,500 = $6,322.

Your software will calculate this automatically when you add your spouse's income details. For these reasons, it may be wise for your spouse to contribute to an RRSP, as it will reduce net income, thereby potentially increasing or creating a Spousal Amount on your return.

Credits Either Spouse May Claim, Depending on Income. Note that there are three non-refundable tax credits that spouses can potentially claim on either tax return, based on where the best benefit lies:

Line 364 Public Transit Amount. This credit was discussed in detail in Chapter 18. Eligible monthly passes for buses, subways, street cars, commuter trains, and ferries may be claimed by either spouse, or one spouse can make the claim for the whole family. There is no maximum claim.

Line 326 Amounts Transferred from Spouse. Individual taxable income is used to determine whether you can make a Transfer from Spouse on Schedule 2, for five non-refundable credits:

- *Line 303 Age Amount* (available if your spouse is 65)
- *Line 367 Amount for Children Under 18* (available if the child lives with both of you throughout the year)
- periodic benefits from a qualifying pension)
- *Line 316 Disability Amount* (if your spouse is markedly restricted due to a physical or mental infirmity and has a Disability Tax Credit Certificate signed by a doctor
- *Line 323 Tuition, Education and Textbook Amounts* (when your spouse is a student at designated educational institute)

If one spouse's taxable income is too low to benefit from these credits, it's best to transfer these amounts to the higher income earner, which your software will do automatically for you.

Line 330 Medical Expenses. Individual net income is used to determine who should claim the medical expenses for the family. That's because medical expenses are reduced by 3% of net income, and that means the lower income earner generally gets the better result, provided that person is taxable. Your software will figure that out for you. If there is no benefit this year, carry the amounts forward for use next year. You can claim medical expenses for the best 12-month period ending in the tax year, so group larger amounts together over two calendar years.

The detail for what is claimable is discussed in Chapter 24. However, for couples, pay particular attention to the following specific costs, when health issues arise:

- The additional costs for moving into a new primary residence that will accommodate the special needs of a newly disabled spouse. Note that the *RRSP Home Buyers' Plan* can be tapped immediately without waiting for the normal four-year period after owning another home.
- Claim any additional premiums paid for private health care or travel insurance.
- Write off up to 20% of the costs of a van that has to be adopted to accommodate a disabled person to a maximum of $5,000, on acquisition or within six months of

acquisition. This includes conversion kits to allow the disabled person access into and for driving the van.

- *Pension Income Amount* (if your spouse reports Reasonable costs of modifying a driveway for greater access to a bus or Handi Transit services.

Tiered Tax Credits. Depending upon the size of your expenditures; a greater benefit is possible when spouses combine contributions together on one return in the following multi-tiered tax credits:

Line 349 Donations and Gifts. Individual net and taxable income levels are taken into account in determining who should claim the Charitable Donations Amount. Particularly if total gifts are $200 or more, it is usually best to group donations on one return (usually the higher earner's) to maximize the claim, which is calculated as follows:

- 15% of the first $200 gifted and
- 29% of the balance on the federal return;
- provincial governments will add value to this.

Maximum claims for donations are generally limited to 75% of net income, and so the limitation is rarely a factor in claiming the credit. Your tax software will do all the calculations in the background. "Total charitable gifts" include gifts made in the current year or in any of the immediately preceding five years and not previously claimed. That means, you may elect not to claim anything for charitable gifts made in the current year, if it's not to your advantage, and carry the unclaimed gifts forward for five years, especially if you are not taxable this year. The details of these claims will be discussed in Chapter 26.

Line 409 Political Contributions. When you give to your favourite federal political party, you'll need sufficient federal taxes payable to absorb this non-refundable tax credit. Good news is that spouses can claim each other's credits or, better, one spouse can claim for both for a better result. The credit is calculated as follows:

- 75% of the first $400
- 50% of the next $350
- 33⅓% of the balance to a maximum credit of $650, which is reached when a total of $1,275 is given.

Tax Calculations on Spouses' Returns. You will discover, when you review the results of the tax calculations that that one person making a high income, let's say $84,000, will pay a lot more tax than two people making $42,000 each. There are some good opportunities in particular when income is split by families who operate a small business.

Case Study | **Planning to Reduce Taxes With Income Splitting**

Steve currently makes $84,000 in his small business in BC; he wants to pay his new wife Carin half this amount, as they work together in the business. How much will the family save on taxes if they split income?

Currently Steve pays $20,336 in income taxes (including $4,613 in CPP contributions). If he pays Carin a salary of $40,000, his net business income will be reduced to $42,193 (The business will need to pay the employer portion of Carin's CPP contributions.

As a result, Steve's tax bill is reduced to $9,415 (including $3,830 in CPP contributions) and Carin's tax bill will be $5,378 (plus CPP contributions of $1,807). Together they pay $18,407 for income taxes and CPP contributions. That's a savings of *$1,929* each year by splitting the income. As a bonus, Carin will now be eligible for a CPP retirement pension when she is old enough.

Family Business Income and Expense Guide. It is recommended that you visit with a tax professional to properly set up the income and expenses you'll be claiming in a small business and whether or not it will be incorporated. However, the guide below can help families discuss this opportunity and ask better questions.

Expense Type	Criteria for Making the Claim
In General:	Segregate your expenses into two groups:
Operating Expenses	Write off those expenses "used up" in the running of a business. They are 100% deductible if reasonable and incurred to earn income from a business with a reasonable expectation of profit.
Capital Expenses	Only a percentage of costs, known as capital cost allowance, may be deducted, at the taxpayer's option, to write down a notional amount for wear and tear of an income-producing asset.
Mixed Use:	If expenditure contains a mixed business and personal use; isolate personal use (not deductible) and claim business portion
Groceries	Depends on the business but for example the expense of feeding children in a babysitting business is 100%. Always remove personal use components.
Clothing	Clothing is usually not deductible, but may be partially deductible if required and unsuitable for street wear: i.e. a judge's robes; entertainers' costumes.

Expense Type	Criteria for Making the Claim
Footwear	Again usually not deductible, but employed dancers, and certain self-employed taxpayers may make a claim in certain cases if their special footwear is "used up" in the pursuit of business income. For example, those who run a winter resort might write off the cost of snowshoes worn by instructors, or ballerinas may write off the cost of their shoes.
Entertainment	Usually restricted to 50% of costs; except for events that are staff gatherings—but no more than six times a year. If you entertain in your home, keep receipts of food, liquor, etc., specific to the event. Keep entertainment log to record name and address of person being entertained. Claim the most costly affairs first.
Utilities	These may be deductible under employment, business or in some cases, medical expenses. A portion can be claimed if workspace in home claim is otherwise allowed. Keep total bills, but prorate expenses according to square footage of office space.
Repairs and Maintenance	Certain employed musicians, other employees, and the self-employed may make this claim for repairs to musical instruments, home office, revenue properties, certain income-producing equipment and buildings.
Mortgage Payments	Interest costs (not principal) are deductible by the self-employed, according to the space used for business purposes. Certain employees may also make the claim; investors who have leveraged home equity may write off interest costs as carrying charges against investment or business income.
Insurance Payments	Claimable, if home office claims, musician's instrument costs, auto expense claims and insurance for other equipment costs are otherwise allowable.
Car Payments	Never for personal driving; however, costs of running an auto are deductible, if used for business or employment purposes and written off according to information on distance travelled as recorded in an auto log.
Tuition Fees	Usually claimed as a tax credit rather than a deduction if over $100 and paid to a designated educational institute. Sometimes can be claimed as an expense of business as a training cost, in which case either the credit or the deduction must be chosen. For higher income earners, the deduction may result in a higher claim.
Gifts	Personal, no. If made to a client of a self-employed taxpayer, or in some cases, an employed commissioned salesperson, yes. Note gift certificates to restaurants are subject to the 50% restriction on meals. Up to $500 in non-cash gifts given to employees is tax-deductible.
Medical/Pharmacy	Claim as a medical expense credit on the return. Group health plan premiums may be a tax-deductible business expense.

The Bottom Line | The family unit that files together saves tax and prospers together. You'll be able to control the level of net family income to increase refundable and non-refundable tax credits. And, if your goal is to keep more money in the—both income and capital—you'll optimize the tax provisions that allow you to file as one economic unit. When you know net and taxable family income, you are in a better position to make important investment and lifestyle decisions: should we pay down the mortgage or invest in an RRSP? Should we borrow money to invest in the stock market? Should we consider buying life insurance or invest in a TFSA instead?

22

Claiming the Kids:
Yours, Mine and Ours

When you add kids to the family mix, another dimension emerges on the tax return: there are more refundable and non-refundable tax credits to claim, and great opportunities for your family to save money for future generations.

You have learned that the refundable tax credits you file for will be based on your and your spouse's "net family income." However, the amount of non-refundable tax credits you can claim for your child (or other dependant) will depend on two things:

(a) whether or not *the dependant* has *taxable* income; if so they must file their own return to report this and

(b) what your *dependant's net income* is, which could affect the size of some of the non-refundable tax credits you can claim for them.

Blended Families. In the case of blended families, it's possible to make choices about who claims certain credits for the child who lives in different homes. Generally, that will be the parent who claims the Amount for Eligible Dependant (an "equivalent to spouse" amount). See Chapter 28, where we discuss single parents, separations and divorce.

Is Your Dependant's Income Taxable? Your dependant will qualify for a *Basic Personal Amount* and because it's just under $11,000, most children will not make enough money during the year to be subject to tax. Therefore, you will make a claim for various tax credits on your tax return as the supporting individual. (Some credits can be transferred to your spouse as we will discuss below.)

You should now know your child's tax position so you can get better results for the tax returns you file for yourself and your spouse. It's a good idea to print out your child's tax summary to guide you to important figures: net income, tuition, education and textbook amounts, etc. Then, determine whether the child qualifies for any tax deductions that will reduce net income, so you can make claims for deductions and credits for that child on your returns.

Therefore, it makes sense for us to start our discussion with returns that need to be filed for the kids. Because their income is generally lower, we want to know that to maximize claims to be made on the higher income returns of the parents.

Filing Tax Returns for the Kids

We'll discuss this topic in the order of the basic elements of the tax return: income, deductions, refundable credits, non-refundable credits and tax calculations.

Income. It's important for you to file a tax return for children who have any earnings from active employment or self-employment. It really doesn't matter how old they are. If you have a 12 year old, for example, who earns babysitting money, or a 16 year old who works at the local hamburger joint, do file a tax return for that child. There are several reasons:

- *Create RRSP Contribution Room.* This notional account records 18% of earned income, which is the amount eligible for RRSP contribution purposes. Your software will take note and carry the RRSP Contribution Room forward for future use. RRSP contribution room is accumulated by CRA and shown on the Notice of Assessment each year. The records in your software should be compared with this.

- *GST/HST Credits Require Filing by 18 year olds.* When your child turns 18 it's important to file for the purposes of making Canada Pension Plan contributions on qualifying earnings (there is a $3,500 exemption, so that means earnings above this are subject to CPP contributions the month after the child turns 18.) In addition, 18 year olds should file so they can start receiving their quarterly GST/HST refundable tax credit the month after they turn 19. Check out the case study in Chapter 7.

  Example: Justin was born February 15, 1994 so he turned 18 in 2012. His parents will receive any GST/HST credit payable for him until he turns 19. However payments after February 15, 2013 will not be made to his parents. Instead, the credit payment on April 5, 2013 will be paid to Justin but only if he files a 2012 return to apply for the credit.

- *Report Investment Earnings.* Your child will not qualify to invest in a *Tax Free Savings Account (TFSA)* until he or she turns 18; at which time this should be strongly encouraged. However, in the meantime, your child may have enough savings based on their own earnings to open a non-registered savings account. Resulting investment earnings are reported by the child. Be aware that a T-slip may not have been issued if the earnings are under $50; they must be self-reported in that case.

You can also run afoul of the *Attribution Rules* previously introduced, when adults loan or transfer capital they have earned to the child. Resulting investment income is attributed back to that adult, so keep the birthday money in a separate account. You'll learn in Chapter 27 about an exception here: capital gains (but not dividends and interest) earned on capital that has been loaned or transferred to a child will circumvent these rules.

Deductions Your Working Child Can Claim. Some of the common ones that apply to a working child include the following:

RRSP Contributions. If your child's taxable income exceeds the Basic Personal Amount, and the child has the required RRSP Contribution Room, you may wish to make a contribution to take an RRSP deduction. Note that children under 18, however, are not allowed to make an RRSP overcontribution, which is permissible (up to $2,000) in the case of adults.

Depending on income level, the deduction may help the child avoid taxation, but in addition, if the child is attending post-secondary school and qualifies for a tax credit under the tuition, education and textbook amount, a lower net income may open up a transfer of up to $5,000 of that credit to your return. See Chapter 23.

If the child's income is too low to be taxable, carry forward the undeducted contributions to the future when income is higher. In the meantime, your child benefits from the power of tax-deferred compounding of investment earnings in the RRSP. That means the investment will grow faster.

In addition, if you are claiming child care expenses for a child you are supporting, as described in Chapter 15, making an RRSP contribution may reduce net income below the Basic Personal Amount, so you can claim child care for that child, if under 16 or if over 16, disabled.

Moving Expenses. Your child may take a deduction for moving expenses on Line 219 if they have moved at least 40 kilometers closer to a new work location or to begin self-employment. Look for Form T1M on which to make the claim and see Chapter 16 for details.

In addition, students who move to attend a post-secondary school in Canada or abroad full time, may claim moving expenses to offset income at the new location, including taxable awards such as research grants, as long as one of the residences was in Canada (before or after the move). Registration for regular full-time attendance in an academic year is required, even if, for post-graduate studies, required attendance is minimal. In the case of "co-op" courses that have a work component attached to them, only those months of attendance at the school qualify as "full-time" attendance.

A good guide for deciding whether attendance is full or part time is that at least 60% of a normal course load is required to meet the full time rules. Students will be addressed in more detail in Chapter 23.

Business Income and Losses. It's not unusual to fill in a business statement for children who are making money babysitting, doing lawn care or other activities of self-employment. In fact, do file Form T2125 reporting this income for that entrepreneurial child because it will help to create unused RRSP contribution room.

In the unlikely event that your child has incurred losses from a business (the lemonade stand may not cut it—unless it had a reasonable expectation of profit), or the sale of a capital property, a tax write off is possible.

In the case of the unincorporated business, a non-capital loss will offset other income of the year, or if unabsorbed by income, the loss may be carried over (three years back and 20 years into the future to offset income in those years).

In the case of capital losses from the disposition of investment assets, other capital gains of the year would first be offset with the loss; then, the net capital loss remaining would be applied to the carry over years (against capital gains in the prior three years, or an indefinite carry forward may be scheduled using form *T1A Request for Loss Carry Over*).

Refundable Tax Credits. Minor children don't normally qualify for refundable tax credits, as it is assumed their parents will be claiming federal and provincial tax credits for them: the Canada Child Tax Benefit, GST/HST and Working Income Tax Benefit all have provisions for children. This is true of most provinces who distribute refundable tax credits as well. However, in some instances, for example, if the minor has a child of his or her own, filing for refundable tax credits is possible. Single parents are discussed in Chapter 28.

Non-Refundable Tax Credits for Children. Your minor child will commonly qualify for these credits:

- **Line 300** Basic Personal Amount
- **Line 312** Employment Insurance Premiums Paid (no premiums are payable if employment income is $2,000 or less)
- **Line 363** Canada Employment Amount on T4 earnings

The amounts below are transferrable to supporting individuals or in some cases may be carried forward if the child is not taxable.

- **Line 318** Disability Amount (if a Disability Tax Credit Certificate is available— transferrable to supporting individuals)
- **Line 319** Interest Paid on Student Loans (can be carried forward five years if the child not taxable)
- **Line 323** Tuition, Education and Textbook Amounts (up to $5,000 can be transferred to a supporting individual if the student is not taxable)
- **Line 330** Medical expenses, although this is usually claimed by the supporting individual

- **Line 349** Donations and gifts made personally or through employment (these can be carried forward five years if the child not taxable)

Note that students and children with infirmity will be cover in later chapters.

Tax Calculations. Your child's tax refund will generally relate to any withholding taxes at part time jobs or a return of Canada Pension Plan premiums deducted in error for those under 18. However, there may be one other provision that causes a balance due and that's the "*Kiddie Tax*" or *Tax on Split Income*.

 CHECK IT OUT | **What's the Kiddie Tax?** The "kiddie tax" is a punitive tax on dividends paid to children from corporations owned by their parents. The tax is payable at the highest marginal rate to discourage income splitting with minor children using a corporation. Use *Form T1206 Federal Tax on Split Income* to compute this. Be sure to consult a professional before paying dividends to children from your corporation.

Claiming the Kids on Your Return

Let's turn now to a discussion of family-filing provisions on your and your spouse's returns, beginning with deductions and then moving to tax credits.

Child Care Expenses. You may have enrolled your little ones in activity day camps while you work over the summer, with a babysitter in your home, or you may take your little ones out for daycare. If so, you'll want to claim child care expenses on Form T778 and Line 214. But there is a host of things to know, to make a proper claim. See Chapter 15 for a complete discussion of claiming Child Care Expenses.

Disability Supports Deduction. This will be discussed in more detail in Chapter 25. However, the deduction is used to account for supports required by a disabled person to go to work or to school. Many of these items also qualify for the medical expenses credit. Only the disabled person can make this claim, so if your child doesn't need the deduction, it may be best to claim the supports as medical expenses which can be claimed on your return.

Non-Refundable Tax Credits. There are numerous non-refundable tax credits that could be claimed for your family members.

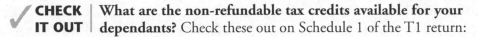

CHECK IT OUT | **What are the non-refundable tax credits available for your dependants?** Check these out on Schedule 1 of the T1 return:

- Amount for Eligible Dependant (claimed by single parents for one child)
- Amount for Dependent Children under 18
- Amount for Infirm Dependant Age 18 or Older
- Adoption Expenses
- Amount for Children's Fitness
- Amount for Children's Arts
- Disability Amount Transferred from Dependant
- Tuition, Education and Textbook Amounts Transferred from a Child
- Medical Expenses

For the purposes of the discussion in this chapter, we will assume your child lives with you in a home you share with your spouse, and that you do not share custody of this child with anyone else. In some cases your software will automatically claim the amounts; in others you'll need to tell it to do so, as noted below:

Line 367 Amount for Minor Child. This amount, for children under 18, shows up on Schedule 1 of the T1 General as the *"Amount for children born in 1995 or later"* (the year changes annually to reflect the right age). Available since 2006, this credit may be claimed by either parent. The amount has been indexed each year to a formula linked to the Consumer Price Index, and it's not income-tested.

If there are multiple children under 18 in the family, one spouse must claim all of them. If that parent is not taxable, any unused amounts are then transferred to the other spouse using Schedule 2. When your returns are linked, your software will generally do all of this in the background for you, but it's best for you to check to be sure you get the intended results.

CHECK IT OUT | **What is the maximum claim for a minor child?** The amount of the credit is $2,191 for 2012. This amount is increased by $2,000 to $4,191 if the child is infirm. A child is considered infirm only if he or she is likely to be, for a long and continuous period of indefinite duration, dependent on others for significantly more assistance in attending to their personal needs and care when compared generally to persons of the same age.

Line 306 Amount for Infirm Dependants Age 18 or Older. When you support a dependant age 18 or over, it is assumed the person will file their own return, and receive their own refundable and non-refundable tax credits to offset any taxes payable. However, if that person is dependent on you by reason of mental or physical infirmity, it is possible to claim this non-refundable tax credit. You'll do so on the details of dependants form in your software or your software may allow you to enter details right on Schedule 5 and the numbers will end up on Schedule 1 to offset taxes payable. Some things to watch for in making this claim:

- *Qualifying Dependants.* If anyone else claims any tax credits for this infirm adult, you cannot do so. Otherwise, claim it for an adult you are supporting who is at least 18 and dependent because of their infirmity. This can include:
  - your child or grandchild, or that of your spouse
  - your parent, grandparent, brother, sister, uncle, aunt, niece or nephew or that of your spouse but in these cases, the dependent must have been resident in Canada at any time in the year.
- *Infirmity Definition.* The adult dependant does not need to be "markedly restricted" by their infirmity for the purpose of claiming this credit. That definition is used to qualify for the Disability Amount, described later. Rather, CRA's Interpretation Bulletin 519 describes the term as "lacking muscle or mental strength or vitality."

CHECK IT OUT | **What is the maximum claim for an infirm dependant for 2012?** The claim is $6,402 per dependant but it is reduced by the dependant's net income in excess of $6,420 so if the dependant has net income in excess of $12,822, the claim is reduced to zero. If your qualifying dependant is a senior, for example, your parent, it's possible that person may be receiving income from the CPP and OAS, which could knock out the claim. However, you may get relief from the Caregiver Amount on Line 315, if the dependant resides with you.

Example: Beth and Tom take care of Tom's mother, Sophia, who lives with them. Sophia's only income for 2012 was a taxable foreign pension of $15,000 CDN. While Sophia's income is too high to claim the amount for infirm dependants, they can claim the caregiver amount of $4,402.

Line 364 Public Transportation. Described earlier, don't forget to save those transportation travel passes for a federal non-refundable tax credit of 15% of your monthly expenditures. All the travel pass costs for every member of the family can be claimed by one parent. There is no maximum claim.

Line 365 Children's Fitness Amount. Claimable since 2007, this credit recognizes eligible expenses for sports and fitness activities taken by each child under age 16, up to a maximum of $500. (Parents of a disabled child under 18 get to claim $500 more if they spend at least $100.) Some interesting activities qualify—sailing, bowling and golf lessons, for example, in addition to the more typical hockey and soccer.

CHECK IT OUT | **How much can you claim for the Children's Fitness Amount?** You'll save 15% of every dollar you fork out, up to the maximum limits above. That's a maximum of $75 for each healthy child. Because this is a non-refundable tax credit, it offsets federal taxes you otherwise pay. No benefit, in short, for those who pay no federal tax.

Line 370 Children's Arts Amount. A federal tax credit for costs of participation in artistic, cultural, recreational or developmental activities should be claimed for the costs of enrolling children in literary, visual and performing arts, or music or language lessons, too. Costs of instruction, equipment, uniforms, facility rental and administration costs included in the registration or membership fees will qualify.

 CHECK IT OUT | **How much can you claim for the Children's Arts Amount?** It is structured much like the Children's Fitness Credit, so expect your refund to grow by up to another $75 as described above. Again, that's a maximum of 15 per cent of $500 (up to $1,000 if your child is disabled), used to offset other federal taxes payable. If your children participate in fitness and arts activities, you can make two claims: one for each credit. Not allowed: fees paid for programs that are part of a regular school curriculum. Nor are costs for travel, meals and accommodation.

Be careful to choose programs of the right length, too. For both the Children's Fitness and Children's Arts Amount, the program must last at least eight consecutive weeks if it is a weekly program or in the case of children's camps it must last at least five consecutive days.

Line 313 Adoption Expenses. Either parent may claim the costs of adopting a child or they may split the costs as long as no more than the actual amount spent is claimed.

 CHECK IT OUT | **What is the maximum claim for Adoption Expenses?** Allowable expenses include

- fees paid to a provincially or territorially licensed adoption agency
- court, legal and administrative expenses
- reasonable travel and living expenses for the child and adopting parents
- document translation fees
- mandatory fees paid to a foreign institution
- any other reasonable expenses required by a provincial or territorial government of a licensed adoption agency.

The adoption period is the period that begins at the earlier of the time the adoption file is opened with an authorized adoption agency or the time a file is applied with a Canadian court, and ends at the later of the time the file is acknowledged by the Canadian government or the moment the child begins to reside with the adopted parents. The maximum claim for 2012 is $11,440 and must be made in the year that the adoption period ends.

An eligible child for whom the credit is to be claimed is an individual who has yet to turn 18 years old at the time the adoption file was acknowledged by the Canadian government. You'll need to enter the amounts paid into your software, which will then calculate the credit against taxes payable. There are no provisions for carrying over expense claims where the parent is not taxable.

Line 316 Disability Amount for Children. It is possible your child will qualify for the Disability Amount if there is a severe and marked restriction in daily living activities due to a physical or mental infirmity, as confirmed by a qualified medical practitioner on a signed Disability Tax Credit Certificate.

 CHECK IT OUT | **How much can you claim for a disabled child under the Disability Amount?** Children qualify for the normal disability amount of $7,546 (for 2012). Also, for children under 18, the disability amount will be increased by a *Disability Amount Supplement*. This adds $4,402 to the value of the Disability Amount. However, Child Care Expenses (Line 214) and the Disability Supports Amount (claimed at Line 215 or as medical expenses on Line 330) claimed in excess of $2,578 by anyone for the child will reduce the Disability Amount Supplement.

Your medical practitioner must assess how the impairment of the child affects the ability to perform one or more basic activities of daily living where the child is three years of age or older. From birth to three the assessment is different: the development progress of the child as it relates to a normal range of development is observed. If the child's impairment is obvious and medically proven, the credit may be allowed.

Note that children who require therapies administered to them 14 hours a week or more, including kidney dialysis and insulin injections and other care for diabetics, will qualify for this claim. *See Chapter 25 for more details on this credit.*

Line 327 Tuition, Education and Textbook Amounts. Because this claim is made for post-secondary education at a designated educational institution leading to a diploma or degree, there are few claims available for those with younger children under this provision. However, it is possible in some cases. See Chapter 23 for more details.

Line 330 Medical Expenses. A parent or other supporting individual will generally claim medical expenses incurred for the child. An extensive list will be shared in Chapter 24, but specifically, allowable medical expenses can include the following for children:

- Medical devices and equipment such as braces, glasses, artificial limbs, wheelchairs
- Costs of medical practitioners such as speech therapists, language pathologists, audiologists, sign language interpreters
- Costs of caring for a physically or mentally disabled person, including children suffering from behavioural problems and attendance problems and dyslexia in an institution.
- Costs of care for those addicted to drugs or alcohol for outpatient or car in detoxification centres.
- Premiums paid for tutoring and textbooks for a person with learning disabilities if certified by a medical practitioner.

Note that the cost of maternity clothes, diapers or diaper services is not deductible.

Allowable expenditures must be supported by hard copy and will be entered on the return with the lower net income. That's because total medical expenses must be reduced by 3% of net income, and claiming them on the lower earner's return will generally result in a better family benefit. However, if that person is not taxable, and the spouse's returns are linked, many software packages will provide the opportunity to transfer the amounts to the higher income earner or optimize the credit, by carrying forward the amounts for use next year.

Tax Calculations. Your tax software will calculate your federal and provincial taxes for each family member in the background, automatically claiming any of the federal and provincial tax credits that result from all the net income thresholds. You'll find this quite remarkable, especially if provisions like tuition fees and medical expenses magically appear on the right returns in the right amounts. Your software is "smart" but you'll need to explain it all to a tax auditor, so be sure you get the intended results on the right returns and have the documentation in your files to back the numbers up.

The Bottom Line | An RRSP for each family member with RRSP contribution room can work wonders to increase refunds and tax credits. Try some "what if solutions" and look at the difference. Also, remember to save all your receipts for discretionary claims like the RRSP, child care and moving expenses, as well as Tuition, Education and Textbook Amounts, medical expenses and charitable donations as these are often subject to review after tax season.

23

Students in the Family

Filing a tax return for a student can involve several provisions and they are all quite important because they generate transferred credits to supporting individuals in some cases, or they can be carried forward for the student's use to reduce taxes payable in the future.

Tax software does an impressive job of both optimizing these claims between family members and keeping track of the carry forwards. Especially if students study abroad, the amounts can be large. In addition, several provinces provide rebates to graduates of their tuition fees paid to attract them to stay in the province. Therefore, this is an important tax filer profile.

Because of the joint filing requirements between family members, we will discuss the rules for students according to the basic elements of the tax return: income, deductions, tax credits and tax calculations specific to students and then the parents or supporting individuals.

Filing for the Student

Income. Students report employment or self-employment income in the normal manner, but you should be aware of the following income sources commonly earned by students working their way through a post-secondary educational experience and some special rules:

Line 104 Other Employment Income. There are two income sources common to students you'll want to report here:

- *Tips and Gratuities.* Waiters and waitresses often turn into doctors, lawyers and teachers. Along the way they can make lots of money in the service industry to pay their way through school. That can become a problem if the income is not reported as required, especially when the employer is audited and credit card chits are reviewed for average tips left. You will want to avoid this.

Be sure to report those tips on the tax return and build RRSP contribution room, which can be very valuable to you along the way, as you'll see in this chapter. If you can afford to do so you can also voluntarily contribute to the Canada Pension Plan, using form *CPT 20 Election to Pay Canada Pension Plan Contributions*. Because youth brings with it a long period of compounding, these opportunities will serve you particularly well over the years as your money compounds on a tax deferred basis. In addition, saving within an RRSP allows you tax-free access to the money later, under the *Lifelong Learning Plan*, described under deductions below.

Finally, be sure to open a Tax Free Savings Account (TFSA) when you turn 18. It's a great place to "park" money and earn tax-free income too, possibly to fund next year's tuition.

- *Line 104 Net Research Grants.* If you receive a research grant, you'll be taxable on the net amount—that is, you can deduct any costs of completing the research. There is no special form for deducting your costs, simply report the net amount on Line 104. The net amount is considered earned income for both RRSP and child care purposes. If the grant is received in relation to a post-secondary program leading to a degree then the net research grant may qualify as exempt scholarship income (see Line 130 below).

Line 119 Employment Insurance (EI). Sometimes, people who lose their jobs can apply for EI to help them go back to school. Know that those amounts may be taxable and that the regular benefits received may be subject to a clawback if net income is above $57,375 in 2012. An RRSP contribution can help you avoid this.

Line 126 Rental Income. Parents will sometimes buy a property for the university-bound child as a principal residence. That's a good way to avoid the Attribution Rules, as some or all of the future capital gains will be tax exempt. If the child rents out some of that residence to help pay for its upkeep, the rental income is reported by the child. In general, there is no attribution of income reporting back to the parent as the child is now an adult and there is likely no profit motive—the income will cover the expenses in most cases. See Chapter 33.

Line 130 Scholarships, Bursaries and Fellowships. Great news! Students who win awards to go to school now qualify for full tax exemptions in most cases. But you should review the list of rules below, because there have been lots of rule changes recently, and you might want to adjust prior filed returns if you made any errors or omissions:

- Prior to tax year 2006, up to $3,000 of income from scholarships, fellowships and bursaries was exempt from taxable income. Since then, the amounts are excluded from income if you qualified for the full-time education tax credit. This credit is discussed in more detail under the Tuition, Education and Textbook Amount below.

- If the student does not qualify for the education amount, a $500 exemption applies; you'll report the rest as income on Line 130 Other Income. Your software may simply call this "Other Income" on your selection screens.
- For 2007 and later years, scholarships and bursaries that relate to attending elementary or secondary school programs will also be exempt from tax if the student qualifies for the full-time education amount.
- Beginning in 2010, students in part-time programs will limit their scholarship exemption to tuition paid plus costs of program-related materials. An exception is where they also qualify for the Disability Tax Credit, in which case the full scholarship is exempt.
- Where the scholarship is received in respect of a program that consists mainly of research, the education amount (and therefore the scholarship exemption) is allowed only if the program leads to a degree.

Line 130 RESP Income. Many families save for years within a Registered Education Savings Plan (RESP) for their child's education. When it comes time to take money out of the plan, here's what will happen:

- The student will report the Educational Assistance Payments (EAPs), which include investment earnings on the principal contributed by the benefactors, as well as the Canada Education Grants and Bonds on Line 130.
- The capital contributed may be withdrawn tax-free.

The maximum amount of EAPs is $5,000 until the student has completed 13 consecutive weeks in a qualifying education program at a post-secondary educational institution (3 weeks if the student is studying abroad). Once the 13 weeks have been completed, there is no limit to the amount that may be withdrawn from the plan.

However, if, for a period of 12 months, the student does not enrol in a qualifying education program, the 13-week period and the $5,000 limitation will be imposed again. There are no restrictions on how the EAPs are actually spent so long as the student is enrolled in a qualifying educational program.

Line 135 Self-Employment. The student may have a variety of self-employment income sources; for example, tutoring others, marking exams or providing consulting services. Be sure to report these amounts on Form T2125 *Statement of Income and Expenses.* Auto and home office expenses may be claimable and certain equipment, like computers depreciable on Capital Cost Allowance schedules. Business ownership is discussed in detail in my book *Make Sure It's Deductible.* Any business losses can be used to offset other income sources of the year; if there is a net profit, it will build RRSP contribution room. In addition, CPP premium may be payable.

Deductions. Students may qualify for a number of deductions on the tax return, which may reduce net income on Line 236 or taxable income on Line 260. Of note is the RRSP contribution, based on the student's unused RRSP contribution room built up over the teenage years by smart parents who have filed tax returns for their children. This deduction will reduce net income, which in turn will make it possible for the parent or supporting individual to claim a transfer of the Tuition, Education and Textbook amounts the student may qualify for.

Refundable Tax Credits. All students should file a tax return to claim their *GST/HST Tax Credit*. In addition, some students may qualify for the *Working Income Tax Benefit (WITB)*, which is provided to those who earn at least $3,000. Your software will calculate this automatically, but to illustrate, please see the case study below.

Case Study | Planning to Maximize Student Credits

Jonathan is a 19-year-old part-time commerce student living in Ontario. He works part time as a waiter and reports T4 income of $5,000 and tips of $6,000 on his tax return. His wife Amanda is not a student and has no net income because she stays at home to look after their son Joshua. He receives both a GST/HST Credit and a WITB.

GST/HST Credit. Jonathan can claim the GST/HST credit for himself, his wife, and his son. The total credit for July 2013 to June 2014 is approximately $670.

WITB. Because Jonathan has an eligible dependant he qualifies for the Working Income Tax Benefit. With a combined family net income of only $11,000, Jonathan qualifies for a WITB of $1,762.

Non-Refundable Tax Credits. Students will qualify for two specific tax credits: The *Amount for Interest Paid on Student Loans* and *the Tuition, Education and Textbook Amount*, described below.

Line 319 Interest Paid on Student Loans. Taxpayers who pay interest on student loans under the *Canada Student Loans Act*, the Canada Student Financial Assistance Act or a provincial statute that governs the granting of financial assistance to students at a post-secondary level, may claim a non-refundable credit against taxes payable for the interest paid. You should have official receipts for the amount paid. Keep these in case CRA asks for them.

Although not transferable to another person such as a spouse or common-law partner, any credit not claimed in one year may be carried forward for up to five years. Keep back-up documentation on file.

Line 323 Tuition, Education and Textbook Amounts. This is a combo of three great tax credits in one! Post-secondary students may claim the Tuition amount, the Education amount and the amount for Textbooks.

The student must make the claim on his or her tax return first, but if not taxable, or if the full amount is not needed, this credit may be transferred from a student to the supporting individual. Alternatively, the student can decide not to transfer the amount and instead carry any unused amount forward to be used in future years to offset income tax payable.

The claim for these credits originates on the student's Schedule 11 *Tuition, Education, and Textbook Amounts.* But then, depending on who claims the amount, you may have to check out three different lines:

 CHECK IT OUT | **Where is the Tuition, Education and Textbook Amount claimed?**
- Claim the credit for the student on Line 323 of Schedule 1 Federal Tax.
- Claim the amounts transferred from a child on Line 324.
- If the transfer is to the student's spouse, complete Schedule 2 *Federal Amounts Transferred From Your Spouse or Common-law Partner.*

Qualifying Programs. The educational institution will issue an official receipt or Form T2202 *Education and Textbook Amounts Certificate* or Form T2202A *Tuition, Education, and Textbook Amounts Certificate* showing the amount of tuition paid. Qualifying institutions in Canada post-secondary institutions like universities or colleges or private designated educational institutions.

Universities outside Canada. These may qualify too. They will send the student Form TL11A *Tuition, Education, and Textbook Amounts Certificate—University Outside Canada,* TL11C *Tuition, Education, and Textbook Amounts Certificate—Commuter to the United States* or TL11D *Tuition Fees Certificate—Educational Institutions Outside Canada for a Deemed Resident of Canada.* Flying schools may send Form TL11B *Tuition Fees Certificate—Flying School or Club.*

Qualifying Course Duration. The required study period for claiming the Tuition and Education amounts as well as qualifying to withdraw Education Assistance Payments from an RESP is 13 weeks. However, if the student is studying abroad, that duration has been shortened to three consecutive weeks effective the 2011 tax year.

Transferring Amounts to Supporting Individual. Look to the back of the forms above and have the student "sign over" the credit to the supporting individual, which can be a supporting parent, grandparent of spouse. Note that if there is a spouse who claims the student as a dependant, that person must make the transfer, even if the young couple lives at home.

Then indicate the transfer on your tax return, Schedule 11 *Tuition, Education, and Textbook Amounts* as described below. Here's what you'll be able to enter for your claim.

- Tuition fees paid in excess of $100 to each individual qualifying post-secondary institution can be claimed. This includes admission fees, charges for the use of library or laboratory facilities, examination fees and ancillary fees that exceed $100 including the cost of identification cards and certain prerequisite study materials.
- Education amounts of $400 per month for full-time students and $120 for part-time students are possible.
- Textbook amounts claimable are $65 a month more for full time students and $20 a month more for part time students.

Tax Calculations. Students will want to file their no income returns to transfer their tuition, education and textbook amount to supporting individuals and from a provincial perspective, to take advantage of tuition rebates or provincial tax credits. The following tuition rebate programs are refundable (i.e. do not require tax provincial taxes be payable):

- Saskatchewan Graduate Retention Program Tuition Rebate
- Manitoba tuition fee income tax rebate
- The NB Tuition Rebate is claimed on a separate application form (NBTR_01 for 2009) and is not integrated into the NB provincial tax forms.

On the Parent's Return

The question you must answer when filing returns for children in the family is whether they will be claimed by you and how their income affects that decision.

✓ **CHECK IT OUT** | **What provisions on my return are affected by my child's income?** A simple chart illustrates them well:

Child's Income Has No Effect on These	Child's Income Will Affect These
Line 117 Universal Child Care Benefit	Line 214 Child Care Expenses*
Line 367 Amount for Children under 18	Line 305 Amount for Eligible Dependant
Line 364 Public Transit Amount	Line 324 Tuition, Education, Textbook Amounts
Line 365 Children's Fitness Amount	
Line 370 Children's Art Amount	
Line 313 Adoption Expenses	
Line 318 Disability Amount Transferred	
Line 330 Medical Expenses	
Canada Child Tax Benefit	
GST/HST Tax Credit	
Working Income Tax Benefit	

* For a dependent child from a relationship other than your and your spouse's.

The Bottom Line | Filing a tax return for a student can be complicated, but if completed properly, tax credits can spill over and reduce taxes for supporting individuals, or reduce the graduate's taxes in the future if carry forward provisions are properly managed. Remember too that many provinces offer rebates of tuitions paid against provincial taxes payable if graduates stay in the province to work and raise families. The benefits will keep coming back if you are tax savvy.

24

Medical Expenses

I love this topic! That's because just about everyone I know has an "aha moment" when the topic of tax-deductible medical expenses comes up. We may have skirted around the edges as we have discussed various tax filing profiles so far, but now it's time to get down to business and tell you about the lucrative claims you qualify for when someone becomes sick in the family.

 CHECK IT OUT | **Where are medical expenses claimed?** Medical expenses qualify for a non-refundable credit on Schedule 1. Often your software will have a worksheet for you to enter data on. It may also optimize the claim between family members.

Your total expenses for the immediate family (spouses and dependent children) for *any 12-month period* ending in the year are itemized and claimed on Line 330. This means, that if your biggest medical expenses occurred between June 2011 and May 2012, this is the period you'll claim on your 2012 return. You'll save the rest of your receipts for 2012 until next year.

Unfortunately, many higher earners can't actually claim medical expenses. That's because we must reduce the total by 3% of net income on Line 236. Generally that means the spouse with the lower income will get the biggest claim, but it is worth nothing if that spouse is not taxable.

Whose expenses can be claimed? Medical expenses paid may be claimed for any of the following people:

- the taxpayer,
- the taxpayer's spouse or common-law partner;
- a child or grandchild of the taxpayer or the taxpayer's spouse who depended on the taxpayer for support, and
- a parent, grandparent, brother, sister, uncle, aunt, niece, or nephew of the taxpayer or the taxpayer's spouse who lived in Canada at any time in the year and depended on the taxpayer for support

Software Tips. Claims for dependants other than the immediate family should be made on whichever return provides the most benefit. They are claimed on Line 331 and are reduced by 3% of that dependant's net income, which can provide an additional benefit to the higher earner in the family. Your tax software can be used to quickly optimize those results.

Allowable medical expenses. The following is a list of common medical expenses you may have forgotten to claim. Be sure to adjust prior filed returns if this is to your advantage. Remember, you can go back up to 10 years to recover missed deductions and credits.

Medical Expenses

Medical Practitioners
- a dentist
- a medical doctor
- a medical practitioner
- an optometrist
- a pharmacist
- a psychologist
- a speech-language pathologist
- an osteopath
- a chiropractor
- a naturopath
- a therapeutist or therapist
- a physiotherapist
- a chiropodist (or podiatrist)
- a Christian science practitioner
- certain psychoanalysts
- a psychologist
- a qualified speech-language pathologist or audiologist
- certain occupational therapists
- an acupuncturist
- a dietician
- a dental hygienist
- a nurse including a practical nurse whose full-time occupation is nursing
- a Christian science nurse
- an audiologist

Medical Treatments

- medical and dental services
- attendant or nursing home care
- ambulance fees
- transportation
- travel expenses (see below)
- eyeglasses
- guide dogs
- transplant costs
- alterations to the home for disabled persons (prescribed)
- lip reading or sign language training
- sign language services
- cost of training a person to provide care for an infirm dependant
- cost of deaf-blind intervening services
- reading services provided under a medical practitioner's prescription
- cost of drugs obtained under the Special Access Program
- for medical marihuana or marihuana seeds purchased from Health Canada, or a licensed person under Marihuana Medical Access Regulations (MMAR)
- therapy provided by a medical doctor, psychologist or occupational therapist for a patient who qualifies for the disability amount
- tutoring services for a patient with a learning disability or mental impairment
- drugs prescribed by a medical practitioner (see list above) and recorded by a pharmacist
- lab tests
- private health plan premiums, including group insurance premiums
- Blue Cross premiums including travel costs

Medical Devices

- an artificial limb
- an iron lung
- a rocking bed
- a wheelchair crutches
- a spinal brace
- a brace for a limb
- an ileostomy or a colostomy pad
- a truss for a hernia
- an artificial eye
- a laryngeal speaking aid
- hearing aid
- an artificial kidney machine

Home Modifications as Medical Expenses. Also watch for these eligible expenses that relate to home or auto modifications:

- Incremental costs of building or modifying a new home for a patient who is physically impaired or lacks normal physical development where those costs are incurred to enable the patient to gain access to or be functional within the home. However, the expenditure must not be of a type intended to increase the value of the home or would not typically be incurred by someone who was not impaired
- costs of alterations to the driveway of a residence of a person with a mobility impairment to facilitate access to a bus
- moving expenses for a disabled person to move to a more suitable dwelling to a maximum of $2,000

- lesser of $5,000 and 20% of the cost of a van that has to be adapted for the transportation of an individual who requires a wheelchair

Special needs persons. The following costs are claimable, provided they are not claimed elsewhere on the tax return:

- incremental cost of gluten-free food products for persons with celiac disease
- cost of purchasing, operating and maintaining phototherapy equipment for treating psoriasis and other skin disorders
- cost of real-time captioning, note-taking services, for a person with speech or hearing impairment
- cost of voice recognition software for persons with a physical impairment
- beginning in 2004, the cost of talking textbooks used by individuals with a perceptual disability if the expenditure is not claimed as a medical supports deduction
- cost of operating and maintaining an oxygen concentrator
- a device that is a Bliss symbol board for use by an individual who has a speech impairment need for which is certified in writing by a medical practitioner
- a device that is a Braille note-taker for use by a blind individual to allow that individual to take notes, need being certified in writing by a medical practitioner
- a device that is a page turner or other devices used by an individual with a severe and prolonged impairment to turn pages of a book or to read print as certified in writing by a medical practitioner

Medical Travel Costs. The taxpayer may claim travel expenses for the patient and one attendant who must travel 40 km or more to receive medical services not available in their community. If the taxpayer is required to travel more than 80 km from their place of residence, then travel expenses may include hotel and meal costs. Actual receipts can be used for costs of travel including gas, hotel and meals.

Alternatively, or you can claim vehicle expenses using a *simplified method* based on a rate per kilometre. This method does not require receipts to be kept for vehicle expenses, only a record of the number of kilometres driven. If more than one province is involved, the rate is calculated based on the province in which the trip began. An updated list of rates is available early in the New Year from CRA.

 The Bottom Line | It pays to hunt down your medical expenses and claim them over the best 12-month period **ending in the tax year**. (Note: please confirm this makes technical sense.) Baby boomers in particular are at risk of under-reporting medical costs when they care for their aged parents or if their own spouses or siblings become ill. Visit with a tax professional when life events involving the health of a family member occur.

25

Caring for the Sick and Disabled

Did you know that one in 5 Canadians aged 45+ provides care to seniors living with long-term health problems[2]? Because of the cost of hiring help, the range of services that fall into the gap that family members must fill are extensive. From meal preparation and household chores to time off for appointments with doctors and to deal with financial matters, the time commitment is great and cuts into economic activities for the caregiver, such as employment and self-employment.

In addition, the caregiver may require supports at home as a result: child care for the nuclear family, personal and respite care and resources for specialized nursing care if publicly-provided home care is unavailable or inadequate.

The physical and psychological toll on family caregivers is also huge: up to 75% will develop psychological illnesses; 15 to 32% suffer from depression. These are significant numbers. As our population ages, disability-related caregiving for family members will increase.

In this chapter, we'll discuss the tax supports available when you give care in the family to someone who is disabled from two points of view: the return of the disabled person and that of the supporting individual who gives care.

The Disabled Person's Return

The objective in preparing a tax return for the disabled is first to properly report all the income sources that may come your way, and to keep an eye on tax efficiency.

---

[2] Canadian Study of Health and Aging (CSHA), 1991, 1996, 2001.

Similar to retirement income planning, the opportunity is to layer voluntary income withdrawals from private plans to meet spending needs into the unpredictable and often frustrating receipt of income from government sources like EI, CPP and Workers' Compensation.

Because the adjudication periods can be long and prone to appeals, these sources can come in lump sums, which bump up marginal tax rates and affect how much is received for various refundable and non-refundable tax credits. In addition, some of the amounts may need to be repaid as a result of any overlaps. Finally, the amounts that can be claimed by supporting individuals will change, too, as net income levels fluctuate.

For all of these reasons, it's necessary to look at the income for a disabled person over several tax years in the year of change to average down the taxes payable. You may wish to seek professional help.

Income. The disabled person may need to leave work, temporarily or permanently. Various insurance plans may be available for income replacement, but if they do not produce enough, other investments must be tapped. Following are some of the common income replacement sources that may be available, and how to report them on the tax return.

CPP Disability Pension. After a three-month waiting period, benefits under this plan may be payable up to age 65 if the applicant is permanently disabled. CPP disability pension benefits are taxable and will be reported to you in Box 16 of a T4A(P) slip. Your software will post this amount to Line 114 and Line 152 of your tax return. This is because the benefits are also considered to be earned income for RRSP purposes and this notation will take them into account to enable you to make additional RRSP contributions in future years, which can offset the taxes that may be generated by the benefits.

The payments are made for conditions that are "severe and prolonged."

 CHECK IT OUT | **What is the definition of severe and prolonged?** For CPP Disability Benefit purposes, this refers to a mental or physical disability that regularly restricts the purpose from doing any type of substantially gainful work. Prolonged means the disability is likely to be long-term and last indefinitely or will likely result in death.

In the year you begin receiving CPP disability benefits, your required CPP premiums will be prorated. Be sure to enter the number of months shown in Box 21 of the T4A(P) slip so your software can complete Form T2204 and determine if you've overpaid CPP. You can apply for the benefits retroactively, but only for 11 months.

When you qualify for CPP Disability Pension, a Children's Benefit is also available, if the child is your natural or adopted child, or a child in your care and custody, and either under the age of 18 or between 18 and 25 and attending a recognized school or university full time. The child will report that income.

Special averaging will occur on your tax returns if you receive a lump sum that is over $300. CRA will do this automatically for you. When that happens, see a tax pro to ensure other tax deductions or credits—like medical expenses or spousal amounts—require optimization between spouses with the new results.

EI Benefits. You may be entitled to receive benefits from Employment Insurance as a result of your inability to work for up to 15 weeks. These benefits are taxable. They can amount to up to 55% of your average insurable earnings to a dollar maximum. Lower income families can receive up to 80% of the average insurable earnings. However, applying for them involves a qualification process with Service Canada, including health information with a doctor's certificate, as well as detailed employment records. If you are eligible the payments will start in 28 days, after a two-week waiting period.

Complications arise when EI is received in conjunction with other income. For example, any money you receive during the two-week waiting period will be deducted from the benefits you are entitled to receive for the first three weeks, dollar for dollar.

Likewise if you work while receiving EI sickness benefits, or receive commissions, compensation under a work accident plan, group health or group wage loss replacement plan, payments under an accident insurance plan, or retirement income under a public or private plan, the amount you earn will be deducted dollar for dollar.

The good news is that the following types of income noted on the EI benefits website have no impact on EI:

- retroactive salary increases.
- disability benefits;
- survivor or dependent benefits;
- workers' compensation benefits paid under specific regulations;
- additional insurance benefits paid under a private plan that is approved by Service Canada (for example, payments for pain and suffering or medical expenses that you receive from an insurance company after you have been injured in a car accident);
- additional sickness benefits paid by your employer from a supplemental unemployment benefit plan (as long as the income, benefits, and additional amounts combined do not exceed 100% of your weekly earnings);
- sickness or disability payments received under a private wage loss replacement plan.

Repayments of EI and CPP. Because there is often a multi-year process to sort out repayments of those various income sources that overlap in the onerous qualification process and waiting periods. If a repayment is necessary, it is claimed as a deduction on Line 232 Other Deductions, in the year the repayment took place.

Legal fees. Paid to object to or appeal a decision under the *Income Tax Act*, the *Unemployment Insurance Act*, the *Employment Insurance Act*, the *Canada Pension Plan Act* or the *Quebec Pension Plan Act* are deducted here, too.

Workers' Compensation. If you receive Workers' Compensation benefits, you will receive a T5007 slip showing the amount received. When you enter the slip, your software will include the amount on Line 144 of your return. The good news is it will also claim a deduction at Line 250. The result of including this amount in income and then deducting it at Line 250 is that the payments are included in your net income but not your taxable income. These payments may then reduce your refundable tax credits and may also reduce any non-refundable tax credits that may be claimed for you.

Wage Loss Replacement Benefits. If you paid all of the premiums for your wage loss replacement plan, then benefits you receive from the plan are not taxable. However, if your employer paid some or all of the premiums, the benefits you will receive will be taxable. You can deduct the premiums you paid from that income before you report the net amount on Line 104.

Example: Connor was injured at work and received benefits from a wage loss replacement plan that was jointly funded by employee and employer premiums. Because Connor's employer paid a portion of the premiums, the benefits are taxable, but Connor can claim a deduction for all of the premiums he paid into the plan that he has not deducted previously.

Severance. If you're leaving your employment due to a disability, you may receive a severance package or job termination payment. See Chapter 19 for details.

RDSP Income. If you have a Registered Disability Saving Plan and are receiving disability assistance payments from the plan, a portion of these payments will be shown in Box 131 of a T4A slip. That amount must be reported and is taxable. When you enter these benefits in your tax software, they will be posted to Line 125 of your return. The portion of your disability assistance payments that represents contributions to the RDSP will not be taxable.

Critical Illness and Long Term Care Insurance. Premiums paid for private disability or critical illness insurance are not tax deductible, but benefits received are not taxable, they are often paid within a month after the critical illness diagnosis and the money can generally be used for any purpose.

If your life insurance provides for it, a lump sum payment may be available as an advance on the death benefit if you are diagnosed with less than one (or sometimes two) years to live. This is also a good way to receive a tax-free benefit to help pay for the costs of end-of-life care.

Deductions. If you are disabled and incur expenses of an attendant or other disability supports purchased to enable you to earn employment or self-employment income or to pursue education, then you can claim the costs of Disability Supports on Line 215 so long as the expenses were not reimbursed.

If you are employed or self-employed, your claim is limited to your earned income (employment, net self-employment, taxable scholarships and net research grants).

If you are a student, your claim is limited to the least of:

- $375 for each week you attended school
- Your net income less your earned income
- $15,000

Your combined claim is limited to the amount of your expenses. Unclaimed amounts due to the restrictions above can be claimed as a medical expense on Line 332 may also claim the Medical Expense Supplement on Line 452, discussed below. Your software will make the claim automatically for you.

Non-Refundable Tax Credits. The disabled individual must first claim certain credits on the tax return; then if not taxable, the amounts can be transferred to a supporting individual.

Disability Amount. If you become disabled, you can claim the disability amount on Line 316 of your return. You'll need to get a medical professional to certify that you're disabled and send the completed Form T2201 *Disability Tax Credit Certificate* to CRA to qualify for this credit. Unless you have a T2201 Form already on record with CRA, you'll not be able to use NETFILE to file your return.

If you do not require the full disability amount to reduce your federal taxes to zero, you may transfer the unused portion of the credit to a supporting person. In the case of spouses, that transfer is made on Schedule 2 and on Line 326.

 CHECK IT OUT | **What is the maximum claim for the disability amount?** The maximum claim is $7,546 per adult dependant. Taxpayers with "a severe and prolonged impairment in mental or physical functions" may claim it. Here is what that means:

- A **prolonged impairment** is one that has lasted or is expected to last for a continuous period of at least 12 months.
- A **severe impairment** in physical or mental functions must restrict the patient all or substantially all of the time, which is another way of saying 90% of the time or more.

Home and Attendant Care. There are some special rules in making this claim if home or attendant care is involved:

- You may not claim both the costs of nursing home care or full-time attendant care as a medical expense, together with the Disability Amount. One or the other can be claimed but not both.
- Those who pay someone to come into the home to provide care for the sick may claim expenditures up to $10,000 ($20,000 in the year of death) as medical expenses and still claim the Disability Amount.
- Individuals who qualify for the disability amount will also be considered to be infirm for the purposes of the Amount for Eligible Dependants, the Amount for Infirm Dependants, and the Caregiver Amount.

If possible, you should send in the completed T2201 form before filing your return to minimize the delays in sending refunds caused by review of the form. Once the form is accepted by CRA, you may file using NETFILE.

Note: Fees for the completion of the T2201 form are considered to be medical expenses.

Medical Expenses. Disabled individuals often incur medical expenses that cannot be reimbursed. Note the following medical expenses that are often missed. If the disabled person does not have enough income to claim these, a supporting person may use them:

- incremental costs of building or modifying a new home for a patient who is physically impaired or lacks normal physical development where those costs are incurred to enable the patient to gain access to or be functional within the home. However, the expenditure must not be of a type intended to increase the value of the home or would not typically be incurred by someone who was not impaired
- costs of alterations to the driveway of a residence of a person with a mobility impairment to facilitate access to a bus
- moving expenses for a disabled person to move to a more suitable dwelling to a maximum of $2,000
- lesser of $5,000 and 20% of the cost of a van that has to be adapted for the transportation of an individual who requires a wheelchair

Also note the limitation noted above: you cannot claim the disability amount if you claim more than $10,000 for attendant care costs as a medical expense. See Chapter 24 for a more complete discussion of claiming medical expenses.

Refundable Medical Expense Supplement. Individuals who have at least $3,268 in earned income and medical expenses may be able to recover some of those medical expenses by claiming the refundable medical expense supplement. This supplement equals 25% of the medical expenses claimed to a maximum of $1,119 but is reduced by 5% of net income in excess of $24,783 for 2012.

The Caregiver's Return

The biggest concern for caregivers is the maintenance of income sources while they give care to their sick loved ones. This can cause stress and burnout and financial pressure. Your tax return may also be more complicated, but that can be a good thing because you will likely get a bigger tax refund as a result of the circumstances.

Income. Many employers are accommodating when their employees have to take time off to give care. Speaking to the HR department at work can uncover a host of assistance. However, if you must take a leave without pay, consider the following:

EI Compassionate Care Coverage. Employment Insurance will provide benefits for a maximum of six weeks of compassionate care benefits if your relative is at risk of dying in next 26 weeks. This can be used for psychological or emotional support; arranging for care by a third party or directly providing or participating in the actual care.

To qualify, there must be a 40% or more decrease in income, you must have accumulated 600 insured hours in the last 52 weeks and there is a two-week waiting period. At the time of writing the maximum assistance was $485 per week.

Investment Accounts. You may have to withdraw money to fund the non-working gap period. Taking a tax-free return of capital from one of your non-registered accounts can make sense. The same is true of a TFSA. A less attractive option from a tax viewpoint is to withdraw from a registered account as the amounts will be taxable in the year withdrawn. Use your tax software to do some "what if" scenarios to judge your tax liabilities.

Self-Employment. You may have to hire extra staff to cover your workload in your small business. If that results in a loss, you will be able to offset other personal income of the year if your business is unincorporated. Speak to a tax professional to project your income and losses.

Tax Deductions and Credits. Imagine a situation where a single daughter brings her mother into her home to care for her after she has suffered a stroke. The daughter will find that several tax preferences will open up for her:

Child Care Expenses. You may be able to claim child care expenses in an amount up to $10,000 if you must hire care to look after your disabled adult while you work. Complete Form T778 and record the amount on Line 214.

Amount for Eligible Dependant. As a single person caring for an infirm dependant in her home, a daughter becomes eligible for this "equivalent to spouse" credit if her mother's income is under $12,822. The amount claimable on Line 305 is $12,822 less the amount of the net income.

Amount for Infirm Adult Over 18. This credit is generally not as lucrative as the Caregiver Amount, because the net income threshold for the dependant is lower. However in this case, the dependant does not have to live with you. You could claim it if you are the supporting individual and the infirm person is living in their own home, hospital or nursing home. Also, another person, perhaps a sibling could also make this claim so long as those making the claim split it between them.

Caregiver Amount. If you provide care for an infirm dependant in your home, you may be eligible to claim the Caregiver Amount if your dependant's net income is less than $21,435.

For 2012, the maximum claim for the Caregiver Amount is $4,402 if the dependant is not infirm. This definition refers to situations where children look after their parents, age 65 or older, who are not infirm. If the dependant is infirm, the claim is $6,402.

In either case, the claim is reduced by the dependant's net income in excess of $15,033. Your tax software will do this in the background.

Disability Amount. Claim this first on the return of the disabled adult; it can then be transferred to a supporting individual, including the spouse.

For those supporting a disabled minor, this amount is enhanced by an indexed supplement of $4,402 (for 2012). This amount is reduced by amounts claimed under child care expenses on Line 214 and the disability supports deduction on Line 215 in excess of $2,578 (for 2012). Your software will usually calculate this in the background but be sure that all of the information is available. For example, if child care is being claimed by someone else, your software will not know this automatically.

Some provinces also provide tax relief for the care of disabled persons.

Medical Expenses. Caregivers can claim the medical expenses of the people they are supporting, if the dependants do not need the amounts to reduce their taxes payable. The medical expenses in this case are not based on family net income, or the net income of the individual who is claiming the expenses. Rather it is based on the net income of the disabled person and that generally means a tax reduction will result.

Example: Pierre and Yvette care for and support Pierre's mother, Sophia who lives with them. Sophia's net income is only $5,000 for 2012. Her unreimbursed medical expenses total $9,000. Pierre can claim these medical expenses, reduced by 3% of Sophia's net income ($9,000 – $5,000 x 3% = $8,850 claim).

 The Bottom Line | Illness is a life event that has multiple tax consequences in the family, both for the disabled person and their caregivers. It may require an inter-advisory team of financial professionals. Be sure to involve a legal advisor for the completion of the will, the Power of Attorney and a health care directive. A financial advisor can assist with the planning of investments, withdrawals and insurance and a tax advisor with complex and often-missed tax provisions, especially in a year of change.

26

Charitable Donations

Canadians are charitable people… almost all Canadians (94%) aged 15 and over gave food, goods or a financial contribution to a charitable or non-profit organization. The average annual financial contribution per donor was $446 and the median amount (half the donors gave more and half gave less) was $123. Interestingly, women give slightly more so than men[3].

When you make a financial contribution, and sometimes, a gift in kind, to a charitable cause, the government rewards you too, with a non-refundable tax credit that reduces taxes payable.

 CHECK IT OUT | **How much is the credit for charitable donations?** It can be close to 50 cents on the dollar, depending on how much you give. The amount is calculated on Schedule 9 and then posted to Line 349 of Schedule 1. Your software will have a screen to list your donations and calculate the credit, as follows:

1. The first $200 of total gifts is eligible for a credit at the rate equal to the lowest federal tax bracket (15%).
2. The remainder of the gifts is eligible for a credit at the federal tax rate for the highest tax bracket for the year (29%).
3. When provincial taxes are factored in charitable donations over $200 often return close to 50% of amounts donated.

---

[3] Canada Survey of Giving, Volunteering and Participating (CSGVP), 15,482 respondents in 2010 and 21,827 respondents in 2007.

Donations may be claimed either by the person who made the gift or by the spouse or common-law partner. Because of the increased tax credit above the $200 threshold, it is often best to group the donations made by the family on one return for a better claim.

What can you give? The allowable claim is calculated as follows, based on your qualified gifts which can include cash, publicly traded securities and mutual funds, life insurance policies, personal use property, capital property, depreciable assets, cultural and ecological gifts. Also, be aware that your software will calculate the allowable donations automatically based on your proper data entry:

- First, your donations credit is the least of
  - your total charitable gifts for the year
  - 75% of your net income for the year **plus** 25% of
  - capital gains on gifts
  - reserves from the prior year on gifts of non-qualifying securities
  - recapture on gifts of depreciable property
  - the lesser of net proceeds from gifted depreciable property and the capital cost of that property
  - **minus** any capital gains deduction claimed on gifted property
- Then add 100% of your total cultural gifts and total ecological gifts.

Cultural gifts are gifts of objects that the Canadian Cultural Property Export Review Board has determined meet the criteria set out in the *Cultural Property Export and Import Act.*

Ecological gifts are gifts of land which is certified by the Minister to be ecologically sensitive land, the preservation of which is important to the preservation of Canada's ecological heritage. Such gifts must be made to Canada, a province, a municipality, or a registered charity whose main purpose is the preservation of Canada's environmental heritage. The taxation of the capital gains on such gifts is completely eliminated.

✓ **CHECK IT OUT** | **When can I avoid capital gains on transfers of securities to charity?** You can use a 0% capital gains inclusion rate, rather than the normal 50% rate when transfer qualified securities to your favorite charity, including a private foundation. This can include the following:

- a share, debt obligation or right such as a stock option, listed on a designated stock exchange
- unlisted securities, partnership interests or shares of a private corporation that are donated within 30 days of an exchange for publicly traded securities
- a share of the capital stock of a mutual fund corporation or mutual fund trust
- an interest in a related segregated fund trust

- a prescribed debt obligation
- ecologically sensitive land (including a covenant, an easement, or in the case of land in Quebec, a real servitude) donated to a qualified donee other than a private foundation

What this means is that you can transfer these assets, upon which you have an accrued taxable gain, directly to your favorite charity, avoid paying the tax on the gain and then also receive a charitable donation receipt. If you decide to do so, complete *Form T1170, Capital Gains on Gifts of Certain Capital Property.*

There are more complicated rules for more sophisticated investors who want to donate flow-through shares or shares in a private corporation:

Donations of Flow-through Shares. These are shares in an oil and gas exploration company that renounces its eligible exploration, development and project start-up expenses and flows them through to its investors. These flow-through shares are deemed to have a cost base of zero and that results in a capital gain or loss on disposition. For flow-through shares acquired after March 22, 2011, if such an investment is donated to charity, the portion of the capital gain that is exempt from capital gains is calculated as the actual increase in value of the shares over the cost of the shares to the investor. The donor will pay capital gains tax on the lesser of the value of the shares at the time of donation and their original cost.

Donation of Non-Qualifying Securities. A donor will not receive a donation receipt for a donation of a NQS (non-qualifying security, i.e. share in a private corporation) until, within five years of the donation, the shares have been sold for consideration that is not another NQS. In other words, there will be no receipt until the real value of the donation has been realized. This rule will apply to securities disposed of by donees on or after March 22, 2011.

Qualifying Donees. Charitable gifts may be made to the following organizations:

- registered Canadian charities,
- registered Canadian amateur sports associations,
- a Canadian municipality or province, or Canada,
- charities outside Canada to which the Government of Canada has made a donation in the prior 12 months, although beginning in 2013 that government donation is no longer a requirement of the "qualified donee" works to provide disaster relief or urgent humanitarian aid or provides services in the national interest of Canada.
- the United Nations and its agencies,
- donations to U.S. charities. Under the Canada-U.S. Tax Convention, Canada is required to give equivalent tax treatment for U.S. charities to the extent that the taxpayer has U.S. source income that is taxed in Canada. Thus, the donations claim limit is *75% of U.S. source income* for U.S. charities that do not otherwise qualify.

The amounts donated to registered Canadian charities must be supported by receipts that have official registration numbers. This means if you have a donation receipt that does not have the charity's registration number, you don't have valid documentation to back up your donation. Charities may issue interim receipts without their registration number and issue one receipt for all your donations in the year with the registration number on that receipt.

However, gifts made through employment are supported by an entry on the taxpayer's T4 *Statement of Remuneration Paid (slip)* rather than an official receipt. Cultural gifts must be certified by the Cultural Review Board as to their Fair Market Value and gifts of ecologically sensitive land must be certified by the Minister of the Environment.

Donation of Options. The donation of an option to acquire a property is allowed and, in the past, a receipt has been issued immediately when you make the donation. New rules will delay the receipt until the option has been exercised. As well, the donation receipt will be issued for the difference between any amount paid for the property and/or option by the donee (the advantage) and the Fair Market Value of the property at the time the option is granted. As is the case with all donations, if the advantage exceeds 80% of the FMV then it is not considered a gift and there will be no receipt. These rules have applied to options granted on or after March 22, 2011.

Timelines for Claiming Charitable Donations. Gifts made by you or your spouse in the current year or in any of the immediately preceding five years can be claimed on this year's return so long as those donations have not already been claimed. If it's not to your advantage to claim the donation credit this year, you can even elect not to claim your donations and carry the unclaimed gifts forward for *five years*. This would be advantageous if you are not taxable or where claiming the total gifts would create a non-refundable credit in excess of your taxable income.

 The Bottom Line | Recent charitable donation schemes and scams have added hardship for well-meaning donors. There are specific rules regarding the valuation of various gifts and in addition, if someone offers to sell you a big charitable donation receipt for a fraction of its value, beware: this is fraud and it is against the law to purchase a receipt for these purposes. Stay on the right side of tax law when it comes to making charitable donations for a well-rewarded community experience.

27

Attribution Rules

A discussion about family tax filing cannot be complete without addressing what the Attribution Rules are. These rules deny you the opportunity to split income in the family when you transfer assets to your spouse or minor children. If you do this, any earnings from the transferred property are "attributed" back to you, which means, you report the income.

Case Study | **Planning for the Attribution Rules**

John transfers $75,000 to his wife Sue to invest in the stock market. John has a very high income and wants Sue to be able to report future capital gains. Unfortunately, John will have to report those gains because of the Attribution Rules.

Now, let's say John transfers $75,000 to his 15-year-old son. This money earns interest, dividends and on disposition a capital gain. In this case, John must report the interest and dividends until his son turns 18. However, his son may at any time sell the shares and the resulting gain is taxed to his son.

May is 79, very ill and has an adult daughter. May wants to put her daughter's name on her bank accounts so she can look after her affairs if she becomes incapacitated. May, however, will continue to report the income from those accounts, even though her daughter's name appears on the account and the T5 slip.

Confused? Many people are. Here are the rules:

Property transferred between spouses is subject to attribution: If the higher earner transfers property to the lower earner for investment purposes, resulting income from the investment is taxed in the hands of the transferor. Exceptions include:

- *Tax Free Savings Account contributions*—Although the attribution rules apply to contributions to a TFSA, the earnings within the TFSA are not taxable so no earnings are attributed back to the transferor. Thus the higher-income spouse may provide funds to the lower-income spouse for contributions to their TFSA with no income tax consequences. Parents may also provide funds to their children for contributions to their TFSAs (children must be 18 or over to contribute to a TFSA).

  Example: Terri earned $45,000 in 2012 while her husband Uri was a full-time student with no taxable income. Terri gave Uri $5,000 to contribute to his TFSA. So long as the funds remain in the TFSA, no taxes are payable on the earnings either by Uri or by Terri.

- *Registered Disability Savings Plan (RDSP) contributions*—earnings on contributions to an RDSP are not taxed while the funds remain in the plan. Once they are withdrawn, the earnings are taxable to the plan beneficiary and are not attributed back to the contributor.

- *Spousal RRSP contributions*—contributions to a spousal RRSP, including the earnings on those contributions become income of the spouse three years after the last contribution is made to a spousal RRSP. If the funds are withdrawn from the spousal RRSP in the same year as the last contribution or in either of the following two calendar years, then a portion of the withdrawals will taxable to the contributor. The calculation of the allocation is done using Form T2205 *Amounts from a Spouse or Common-law Partner RRSP or RRIF to Include in Income*.

  Example: Quentin contributed $5,000 to a spousal RRSP for Rosie in 2009 and 2010. In 2012, Rosie took $6,000 out of the plan. Because of the 2010 contribution, $5,000 of the amount withdrawn must be added to Quentin's income in 2012. The remaining $1,000 is Rosie's income.

- *Non-Registered Investment Accounts*. Income resulting from transactions in which bona fide "inter-spousal" loans are drawn up to transfer the capital and, where interest is charged at the prescribed rate or more and is actually paid to the lender at least once a year during the year or within 30 days after the year end.

  Example: William earns $150,000 annually while his common-law partner Jackie is an aspiring writer with annual earnings of $15,000. Because William is in the highest tax bracket and Jackie is in the lowest, William would like to have the earnings on his $500,000 investment portfolio taxed in Jackie's hands. To do this, they drew up a loan agreement for $500,000 with interest payable at 1% (the current prescribed rate). Jackie then used the loan proceeds to purchase William's investment portfolio. So long as Jackie pays the interest each year by 30 days after the end of the year, the earnings on the investment portfolio are not attributed back to William. Note that the $5,000 interest on the loan is income to William and Jackie can claim the expense as a carrying charge.

- *Profits resulting from investments in a business*—only income from property is subject to the attribution rules; business income is not subject to these rules. Thus one spouse may give the other funds to start a business and, so long as they are not a partner in the business, the business income is taxed only to the business owner.

  Example: Anne gave her husband, Bruno, $25,000 to start a business in 2010. In 2012, the business made a profit of $20,000. The $20,000 income is Bruno's income and is not attributed back to Anne even though she provided the funds to start the business.

- *Transfers resulting from marriage breakdown*—the Attribution Rules do not apply to assets transferred as a result of a marriage breakdown (e.g. assets transferred as part of the separation or divorce agreement). Also the attribution rules no longer apply to assets transferred between spouses once they are no longer spouses.

  Example: While they were married, Carl gave Dianne money to invest. In 2012, Carl and Dianne were divorced. Any income earned on those investments prior to the divorce is attributed back to Carl. However, any income earned after the divorce is taxable to Dianne.

- *Income on property after it is inherited*—income earned on assets transferred at death is income of the beneficiary. Attribution does not apply to the deceased taxpayer.

Property transferred to minor children. Income in the form of dividends and interest will be attributed back to the transferor, however capital gains will be taxed in the hands of the minor.

Example: Each year Evan gave 100 shares in The Walt Disney Company to his grandson David. While David is under age 18, all of the dividends earned on those shares are attributed back to Evan. However, when David turned 16, he sold the shares to buy a car. The capital gain on the sale is David's income and not attributed back to Evan.

Kiddie Tax. A "tax on split income," will be applied if minors receive dividends from private corporations owned by their parents. This "kiddie tax" also applies to income paid to minors from a trust or partnership, and cancels the advantage of income splitting.

Example: When Frank set up his corporation, he issues shares to himself, his wife and his three children. Originally he thought that he could pay $8,500 in dividends to each of his children on a tax-free basis each year. His advisor explained to him that if he paid dividends to his minor children from his corporation then these dividends would be taxed at the highest marginal rate (43.3% in his province) so he decided not to pay dividends to the children until they turn 18.

Other exceptions to the Attribution Rules on transfers of capital to minors include:

- **Contributions to RRSPs and RESPs.** When parents make contributions to an RESP, the earnings are not taxed while in the plan and it becomes income of the children if they become students. Likewise, when parents give their children money to make RRSP contributions based on that child's earned income, the earnings are not taxable while the funds remain in the RRSP and are taxable to the child when they are removed from the plan.

  Example: Greg gave his daughter Amanda (who is a full-time student) $6,000 to contribute to her RRSP. Amanda had sufficient earned income based on her summer jobs. By taking the RRSP deduction, Amanda did not need to deduct so much of her Tuition, Education and Textbook amount and was able to transfer it back to Greg. The earnings within the RRSP remain untaxed until Amanda removes them from her RRSP. At that time, they are taxed to her.

- *CCTB and UCCB*. Any income earned on the investment of Child Tax Benefits or Universal Child Care Benefits in an account held in trust for the child.

  Example: Each month Irene takes her Child Tax Benefit and Universal Child Care Benefit cheques and deposits them into an account for her only son Jacob. So long as the only amounts deposited to that account are from the CTB and UCCB payments, the income earned in the account is Jacob's income (and consequently is not taxed).

- Employment income actually earned by a child working in a parent's business—so long as amounts paid to a child are reasonable and the work is actually done by the child, those earnings are income of the child and deductible as a business expense to the business.

  Example: Ken operates a small business. He pays his daughter Kim $100 per week to clean the office on Sundays. Kim's earnings are taxable to her (and deductible as a business expense to Ken's business).

Property transferred to adult children. There are no restrictions on the type of property that can be transferred to adult children, and all resulting income will be taxed in their hands except if the tax department believes the main reason for the loan was to reduce or avoid taxes by including the income on the adult child's return.

Case Study | Example of Tax Avoidance

Lisa is in a high tax bracket but her son Jeffrey is in the lowest tax bracket. Jeffrey dropped out of college and currently lives at home in his parent's basement. With no income, Lisa and her husband provide Jeffrey with spending money while he figures out what he wants to do with his life.

Lisa decided it would be a good idea to temporarily transfer to Jeffrey the portion of her stock portfolio that is paying dividends. Jeffrey could then use the dividends for spending money and Lisa would not have to provide it. The net result of this transfer is that the taxable dividends that were once reported on Lisa's return would now be reported on Jeffrey's return, one could expect that the CRA would see this as a tax avoidance maneuver and attribute the dividend income back to Lisa.

The Attribution Rules will not apply if:

- Amounts transferred are used for non-taxable investments: in a TFSA for example, principal residence, in the costs of education, car purchases, and so on.
- Contributions are made to the child's RRSP, RESP, or RDSP[4].
- A bona fide investment loan is drawn up, with interest actually paid at least once a year within 30 days after year-end, similar to inter-spousal loans.
- Transferred funds are used to start the child's business.

Q & A | Understanding the Attribution Rules

The following are other common questions families may have about the economic activities they have with one another. See if you can answer the questions:

Q. How are amounts in joint accounts reported?

A. Income earned in joint accounts must be reported by the person who earned the capital in the account. Where more than one person contributed capital earned in their own right, then the income in the account must be allocated based on the capital provided by each contributor.

Q. How do I report income from a rental property we jointly own as spouses?

A. Income from a rental is income from property so the Attribution Rules apply and require that the rental income be reported by the person (or persons) that provided the capital to acquire the rental property—this would be the down payment if the rental income is used to make the mortgage payments. Where

---

[4] Registered Retirement Savings Plan, Registered Education Savings Plan or Registered Disability Savings Plan.

both spouses contributed capital, the rental income should be allocated to them according to the capital provided by each.

Q. I lent my spouse money for a business she runs out of our home. Who reports the income?

A. Business income is not income from property so the Attribution Rules do not apply. Any income earned by the business is income of the owner of the business. So, unless you drew up a partnership agreement with your spouse, then the income earned in the business is her income.

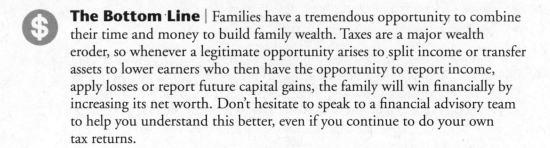

The Bottom Line | Families have a tremendous opportunity to combine their time and money to build family wealth. Taxes are a major wealth eroder, so whenever a legitimate opportunity arises to split income or transfer assets to lower earners who then have the opportunity to report income, apply losses or report future capital gains, the family will win financially by increasing its net worth. Don't hesitate to speak to a financial advisory team to help you understand this better, even if you continue to do your own tax returns.

28

Relationship Breakdown

According to Statistics Canada, there are approximately 71,000 divorces in Canada each year. Over 40% of marriages will end up in divorce, which is less than the U.S. divorce rate at 46% and the Swedes, which have the highest rate at 55%. There are all kinds of reasons for divorce: communications breakdowns, infidelity, a midlife crisis, abuse and financial issues.

Those financial problems can be exasperated when there is trouble with the taxman, and there often is, unfortunately, because people who separate don't understand the rules for reporting income, assets and expenses. This is worse if the couple isn't communicating.

A couple need not be legally or formally separated for their tax status to change. A couple is considered separated if they cease co-habitation for a period of at least 90 days.

Software Tips. When a couple separates, each person will be taxed as an individual and income and assets will be separated. Your software should ask you the date that your marital status changed if it changed in the year. If you are separated or divorced at the end of the year, enter that as your marital status and your software should take care of making claims on that basis. However keep in mind what you learned in the last chapter when deciding what income to report on your return. Remember, attribution ends with the relationship.

Support and Alimony. One of the most expensive failures, from a tax preparation point of view, is the recipient of taxable child support or alimony payments must report those amounts as income and pay the tax.

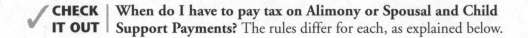

✓ CHECK | **When do I have to pay tax on Alimony or Spousal and Child**
IT OUT | **Support Payments?** The rules differ for each, as explained below.

Support for Spouses. Alimony or support payments made to a spouse or common-law partner are taxable to the recipient and deductible by the payor. In the year of separation or divorce, however, the payer may claim either the deduction for support or the spousal amount, but not both. The only way for the recipient to avoid this tax status is to receive a lump sum, in which case the payment is neither deductible nor taxable.

Making Instalment Remittances. The spouse who receives the taxable amount will often be unprepared for the tax consequences when a large balance due is due on April 30. In addition he or she may need to pay quarterly instalment payments on this income in the year after it is first paid and reported. This should be discussed before the separation or divorce papers are finalized to ensure the net tax result intended is actually paid and received.

Support for Children. For all agreements or court orders after May 1997, child support payments are not taxable to the recipient or deductible by the payor. For income tax purposes, any support stipulated in an agreement or court order is deemed to be child support if it is not identified as spousal support.

Complications can arise when support payments are in arrears. All arrears payments are deemed to be child support payments until child support is up to date. Subsequent payments are considered to be spousal support payments that are taxable to the recipient and deductible to the payor.

Example: Martin lost his job in 2012 and was not able to keep up with his required support payments. He was required to pay $500 per month in spousal support and $1,000 per month in child support. For the year, he paid $15,000. For income tax purposes, this is deemed to be $12,000 child support (the required amount) and $3,000 spousal support. Martin may deduct only $3,000 of the $15,000 paid and his ex-wife is only required to report $3,000 as income from spousal support.

Separating Assets. Income attribution ends when there is a separation providing that the couple continues to live apart. Therefore the new owner of the property after a relationship breakdown is responsible for all tax consequences on the earnings and capital appreciation (depreciation) of the property. The cost at which the assets are transferred is also important, because it determines what numbers you will use to calculate future gains and losses from taxable investments or income from registered investments, as described below:

Spousal RRSPs. Spousal RRSP contributions will no longer be allowed. Withdrawals from spousal or common-law partner RRSPs made by the annuitant are generally reportable by the contributing spouse if any RRSP contribution has been made in the current year or the previous two years. However, this rule is waived for separated/divorced couples.

Example: In 2011 Hans made a $10,000 spousal RRSP contribution. In June 2012, his wife Heidi left him and did not return. Had Heidi removed funds from the RRSP prior to the separation, the income would have been reportable by Hans. However, if she withdrew funds from the RRSP after the separation, those funds are considered to be her funds and Hans does not have to include them in his income.

RRSP Accumulations. Funds that have accumulated in RRSPs may be rolled over on a tax-free basis to the ex-spouse when the parties are living apart and if the payments follow a written separation agreement, court order, decree or judgment. The transfer must be made directly between the RRSP plans of the two spouses and one spouse cannot be disqualified because of age (over age 71). The same rules for tax-free transfer of funds apply to RRIF accumulations. Form T2220 is used to authorize the transfers between the plans.

TFSA Accumulations. These can also be split on a tax-free basis. The funds from one party's TFSA may be transferred tax free to the other party's TFSA. This will have no effect on the contribution room of either of the parties.

Principal Residence. After separation, CRA recognizes two family units, and therefore it is possible for each to own one tax-exempt principal residence.

Other Property. The transfer of depreciable property (those upon which Capital Cost Allowance can be claimed) takes place at the Undepreciated Capital Cost of the property. As a result, no recapture, terminal loss, or capital gain takes place on the transfer.

For other capital property, the transfer takes place at the Adjusted Cost Base of the assets, so again, there is a tax-free rollover.

Case Study | Planning For the Transfer of Property on Divorce

Rachael owned two rental properties but in her divorce settlement, one of the properties was transferred to her ex-husband Daniel. The rental property consists of two assets: the building (which is a depreciable capital asset) and the land that is not depreciable.

Per the assessment at the time of purchase, the land was worth $100,000 and the building $120,000. At the time of transfer, the land was worth $130,000 and building was worth $140,000. Rachael had claimed CCA on the building so its UCC was reduced to $110,000.

The land is transferred to Daniel at is original cost ($100,000) so Rachael has no capital gains tax to pay on the transfer. Daniel's cost base is $100,000 so he already has an accrued capital gain of $30,000.

The building is transferred to Daniel at $110,000 so Rachael has no recapture or capital gain to report as a result of the transfer. Daniel is deemed to have acquired the building for $120,000 and to have already claimed $10,000 in CCA.

By special election, assets may be transferred at their Fair Market Value. This could result in significant tax savings if, for example, the transferor had unused capital losses to apply to gains on the transferred property. See Part 4.

Deductions. Three deductions need to be addressed regarding separation or divorce:

Line 214 Child Care Expenses. Child care expenses must normally be claimed by the lower-income spouse but may be claimed by the higher-income spouse during a period where the taxpayer was separated from the other supporting person due to a breakdown in their relationship for a period of at least 90 days as long as they were reconciled within the first 60 days after the taxation year.

If the taxpayers were not reconciled within 60 days after the taxation year, then each spouse may claim any child care expenses they paid during the year with no adjustment for child care expenses claimed by the other taxpayer.

Example: Susan and Ron separated in September 2012. They both work and so had child care expenses for the full year. If they reconcile before March 1, 2013, then the spouse with the lower net income (Susan in this case) must claim the child care expenses less the $175 per week that Ron may claim for the period of separation. If they do not reconcile by March 1, 2013, Ron may claim whatever child care expenses he incurred and Susan may claim the expenses she incurred.

Line 220 Support Payments. These will be deductible in the following cases, and qualify for RRSP earned income purposes.

The payments must be periodic spousal support payments made pursuant to a written agreement or court order are deductible and only if the spouses remain living apart and payments are made directly to the spouse or to a third party for maintenance of the spouse. Note the following:

- Lump sum payments in lieu of periodic spousal support payments are not deductible (or taxable) as mentioned above. However, a lump sum payment to pay deductible periodic payments that are in arrears is deductible.

- Child support payments are not deductible (or taxable) unless they are made pursuant to a written agreement or court order dated prior to May 1997 which has not been altered since that date

Line 232 Legal fees on separation or divorce. Legal fees to obtain a divorce or separation agreement are normally not deductible. However, CRA considers legal costs incurred to obtain support relating specifically to the care of children (not the spouse) under the *Divorce Act* or under provincial legislation, as well as the costs incurred to obtain an increase in support or make child support non-taxable, to be deductible.

Tax Credits on Separation or Divorce. Refundable and non-refundable tax credits will be allocated based on individual net income levels, and certain social benefits can be split as described below.

Universal Child Care Benefit. In the case of joint custody, each parent can apply to receive equal shares of this income the month following the month of marital status change by filing Form RC65.

Child May Report UCCB. A single parent may choose to claim any UCCB received as the income for the child rather than as his or her own income. This is generally beneficial if the parent's income level is above the lowest tax bracket.

Example: Megan is a single mom with two children under age six. She received $2,400 UCCB income in 2012. Her taxable income is $45,000 so she is in the second tax bracket. If she includes the UCCB in her income, she'll pay $528 federal tax on the income (plus provincial tax). She is claiming Kyle as an eligible dependant. Her claim for him is $10,822, which results in a federal credit of $1,623.30.

If she elects to include the UCCB in Kyle's income, her federal taxes are reduced by the $528 she would have paid and her claim for Kyle is reduced by $2,400, which results in a reduction of $360 in her federal credit for him. The net result is a federal tax saving of $168. She also saves on her provincial taxes by making this election.

Federal Refundable Tax Credits. The Child Tax Benefit (CTB) and Goods and Services/ Harmonized Sales Tax Credit (GSTC) are calculated based on net family income from the prior tax year.

When a family breakdown occurs, CRA should be immediately notified so that the calculation of the credits for the next CTB or GSTC payment may be made without including the estranged spouse or common-law partner's net income. Notify CRA no later than the month following your change in marital status if you become divorced. If you become separated, the separation is not recognized if you reconcile within 90 days so do not notify CRA until the 90 days have elapsed. In the case of joint custody, each parent has the right to receive half these amounts.

Otherwise, the *Income Tax Act* assumes that the eligible CTB recipient is the female parent. However, "prescribed factors" will be considered in determining what constitutes care and upbringing and who is fulfilling that responsibility.

For example, if after the breakdown of a conjugal relationship, the single parent and child returns to live with his or her parents (the child's grandparents), the single parent will still be presumed to be the supporting individual unless he or she is under 18 years old. In that case, the grandparents may claim the Child Tax Benefit for both their child and grandchild.

Provincial Tax Credits. Many provinces have tax reductions or refundable credits that are based on family net income. In most cases, in the year of separation, it is not necessary to include the estranged spouse or common-law partner's income in the family income calculation and normally no credits or reductions on behalf of the estranged spouse or common-law partner will be allowed. Each partner will claim the credits or reductions to which he or she is entitled.

Non-Refundable Tax Credits. Here are the general rules on who claims in sole or joint custody cases:

- *Spousal Amount*—The spousal amount may not be claimed when a couple is separated or divorced except in the year of separation where no claim is made for spousal support.
- *Age Amount and Transfers*—No transfers are allowed between spouses if they are separated or divorced at the end of the year.
- *Amount for an Eligible Dependant*—A single parent may claim an amount for an eligible dependant if they support that child in their own home at some time during the year. No claim may be made for a child by a taxpayer who is required to make support payments for that child. In the case of joint custody, if both parents qualify to claim the amount for an eligible dependant, they must agree who will make the claim—it cannot be split between them.
- *Amount for Children Under Age 18*—In the case of sole custody, the parent who has custody may claim the amount for children for the child. In the case of joint custody, only the parent who qualifies to claim the amount for an eligible dependant for the child may make this claim. The claim may not be split. No claim may be made by a taxpayer who is required to make support payments for the child unless both parents are required to make support payments, then only the one who claims the amount for an eligible dependant may make this claim.
- *Public Transit, Fitness and Arts Amounts*—These amounts may be claimed by either spouse so long as the same expense is not claimed twice and the total claim is not more than the maximum allowed for the child.
- *Caregiver Amount*—The Caregiver Amount may be claimed by more than one individual so long as the combined claim does not exceed the maximum allowable claim

for the dependant. However, if anyone claimed an amount for an eligible dependant for that dependant, no one else may claim the caregiver amount for the same dependant.

- *Disability Amount Transferred from a Dependant*—The transferred disability amount may be claimed by more than one taxpayer so long as they agree on how much will be claimed by each and the total claim does not exceed the maximum allowed.
- *Medical Expenses*—Medical expenses for a child may be split between parents so long as the same expense is not claimed twice. Medical expenses may not be claimed for your spouse or common-law partner after separation or divorce.

 The Bottom Line | Separation and divorce is expensive and complicated. Filing a tax return to the best benefit if the family unit is harder, too. Make sure you get the right results to minimize the financial impact. Consider consulting with a tax pro if you are unsure.

PART 4

Reporting Investment Income

According to CRA, approximately four million investors in Canada reported dividend and interest income of $44 billion. Recent statistics tell us that the number of investors who receive dividends has declined 15.3% but those whose income came from interest declined 24.2%. Despite the financial crisis, the equity markets still got better results.

What's New

Over the past several years, corporate income tax rates have decreased which has affected reporting by individual investors on their personal returns for dividend income. The current gross-up for "eligible dividends" is 38%, meaning you'll have to report $138 for each $100 dividend income you receive. You'll get a federal dividend tax credit for $20.73 for each $100 dividend income you receive, as well as a provincial credit. There are also changes under the "kiddie tax" rules this year.

Hard Copy

Gathering up documentation for investors can involve not just the various T-slips, but a thorough search for the cost base information on assets you have disposed of this year and may have purchased years ago. You may need appraisals of Fair Market Value on others. Wise investors will start their document retrieval tasks early in the tax year.

Software Tips

Your tax software will do an excellent job of posting most information found on T3 or T5 slips to their proper destinations. However, beware of tricky entries. For example, for foreign income, you'll need to ensure that the foreign tax credits are claimed.

If you have capital dispositions, the dispositions must be entered in the appropriate section of Schedule 3 so the software can apply the correct rules for that type of disposition, especially when applying losses. If you have capital gains reserves, a capital gains deduction, principal residence designation or rental property, be sure you understand where to find the required forms and how they work, as the software can do little more than add up the numbers that you enter. We'll help you with this part.

Tax Sleuthing

The most common deductions and credits relating to investment income are listed below; they are also often missed:

- carrying charges, including your safety deposit box, investment counsel fees and interest paid on money borrowed to invest and the foreign tax credit; and
- all reasonable expenses of earning rental income including mortgage interest, property taxes, advertising, routine maintenance costs. Improvements like the cost of a new roof are often misclassified and can cause audit problems.

Tax Pro Alert

Consider consulting a tax pro if you have any of the following transactions this year:

- purchase of sale of a rental property, debt forgiveness, mortgage fore-closure (rental or business) or repossession of business assets
- capital gains election or capital gains deduction
- conversion of rental or business property to personal use or vice versa

29

Reporting Dividends, Interest and Other Investment Income

It's been difficult to find a safe place to invest money during the recent financial crisis, while protecting it against market volatility, taxes and inflation. At a time that interest rates on consumer credit cards have been 20% or more, the $50,000 you have on deposit with the same institution earns less than the rate of inflation. So, getting the best after-tax return is very important. This chapter will help you through the nuances.

While we are going to focus on helping you understand how to report the investment earnings you had this year, I hope you'll also learn there is no better time to understand the investing options you have for your money. First, some important terms and parameters:

Income from property, for example, is any income earned from investments which produce interest, dividends, rent or royalties. This is passive income, which differs from active income that is earned "actively," through employment or self-employment.

Income from property also differs from the capital gain or loss which may occur on the disposition of an asset. That's important because it affects where and how to report the earnings and also expenses like interest costs. Income from property is also treated differently than capital gains and losses, under the Attribution Rules.

Schedule 4 Statement of Investment Income is used to report amounts from taxable dividends, interest and other investment income, net partnership income, and the carrying charges that have been incurred to earn that income. Schedule 3 is used to report *Capital Gains or Losses*. This will be discussed in the next chapter.

For most people, reporting investments in non-registered accounts is as simple as entering the data from various T-slips. The tax software does most of the rest of the calculations, with little human intervention required.

CHECK IT OUT | **How are investment earnings reported on Schedule 4?** The slips you receive can include a T3 slip from investments held in a trust, a T5 slip when the source is a corporation, a T5013 slip from an investment in a limited partnership, a T600 slip for Canada Savings Bonds investments, a T5008 slip for securities transactions. In some cases this income will be self-reported.

No T-Slips. An issue facing investors in recent times is the very low rates of return these investments have garnered. A $10,000 deposit earning half of one per cent, for example, will only have earned $50 for the year. Financial institutions must only issue a slip if the earnings are $50 or more. So, investors must self-report interest on deposits under this. Be sure to dig out your bankbooks or statements, as well as your *Notice of Assessment* or Reassessment to find any interest paid to you from CRA, too. The amounts should be entered into Schedule 4 and from there they will be posted by your software to Line 121.

Joint Accounts. Report the interest earned in the same ratio as the principal was deposited into the accounts, based on who earned that capital in his or her own right.

Example: Debra, who normally stays home and raises the children, deposited all of the money in a joint account with her husband, as a result of an inheritance. In this case, 100% of the earnings are reported by Debra. If her husband, Jason, who earns all the other income for the family, deposited 100% of savings in another joint account, he reports 100% of the earnings from that account. A third account holds their gain on the sale of their principal residence last year; to which they each contributed one half of the cash gifts they received from their wedding. In this case, each spouse reports 50% of the interest earnings.

T-Slip Entry Guide. When entering amounts from your T-slips, it's important for you to compare all the data on your hard copy with the results on your return, which will be added together when there are multiple slips. It's easy to forget a slip or miss a box so double-checking is important. See the *T-Slip Entry Guide* at the end of this Part to help. The following are line links to possible deductions and credits. Carrying charges will be discussed later, but you will find out more about the dividend tax credit, which is used to reduce taxes payable, in this chapter.

Income Lines	Possible Deductions	Possible Credits
120 Taxable amount of dividends	**221** Carrying charges like interest or investment counsel fees	**425** Federal dividend tax credit on Schedule 1
121 Interest and other investment income	**221** Carrying charges like safety deposit box fees	

Income Lines	Possible Deductions	Possible Credits
122 Net partnership income	**251** Limited partnership losses of other years	
127 Taxable capital gains	**253** Net capital losses of other years **254** Capital gains deduction	

Registered vs. Non-Registered. The income, dividends or capital gains earned within a registered account, like an RRSP of RRIF, lose their tax attributes or unique tax identity. When the money is withdrawn, it is all taxed as "ordinary income;" that is, both principal and earnings are included as part of your total income when withdrawn.

However, the investments in non-registered accounts and the different sources of income—interest, and dividends, for example—all have unique tax attributes, which means that they are subject to differing tax treatment. Interest, for instance, is taxed in full as "ordinary income" while dividends are taxed more advantageously.

Layer and Average Down. Astute investors will try to arrange the realization of income for tax purposes in "layers" of different sources so as to average down the overall rate of tax they pay. Let's look at reporting dividends, interest and net partnership income in more detail, as required on Schedule 4.

Line 120 Taxable Amount of Dividends

Dividends are earned as a result of an investment by an individual in a Canadian corporation, that is incorporated and resident in Canada throughout a period that began at any time after June 18, 1971. Dividends are the after-tax distribution of earnings in a company.

When dividend amounts are reported on the income tax return of the individual shareholder, the actual dividends received are "grossed up" so the taxpayer reports an amount higher than that received. Offsetting this *grossed-up amount* is a "*dividend tax credit*" (DTC), which is computed on *Schedule 1 Detailed Tax Calculation* as a reduction of federal taxes payable. A provincial credit is also calculated on the tax calculation schedule for your province of residence. The objective with these calculations is to integrate the corporate and personal tax systems to avoid double taxation.

The amount of the gross-up and DTC will depend on whether the corporation is a public or private company and, as a result, there are two specific terms for the dividends earned:

- *Other Than Eligible or "Ineligible" Dividends.* These are dividends by *Canadian Controlled Private Corporations (CCPCs)*, whose income was within the Small Business Deduction (SBD) and therefore subject to a lower rate of corporate tax. The SBD is $500,000 federally and in most provinces. For ineligible dividends, the taxable amount is 125% of the actual dividends with an offsetting dividend tax credit of 13.33% of that taxable amount.

- *Eligible Dividends*: Eligible dividends are those paid after 2005 by Canadian resident public corporations and also *CCPCs*, where the income from which the dividend is paid has been subject to tax at the "general" corporate rate because it exceeded the small business deduction. After 2011, the taxable amount for eligible dividends is 138% of the actual dividends with an offsetting dividend tax credit of 15.02% of that taxable amount.

Good news: the tax software will calculate this for you. You'll also see that the provinces have adjusted their dividend tax credit rates in response to the increased federal gross-up. When you earn dividends, there are several planning issues:

Grossed-up Dividends and Net Income. The increased gross-up may be problematic for taxpayers who are in a clawback zone for non-refundable tax credits, refundable tax credits, or the OAS or EI Benefits. It may reduce or eliminate these provisions, and so you'll want to plan your investment income sources with this in mind. An RRSP contribution will also reduce net income to protect your benefits.

Example: Tyler earns $40,000 employment income as well as $5,000 eligible dividend income. Because of the dividend tax credit, his net income is $46,900. Also because of the dividend tax credit, Tyler's payable taxes on his investment income are $886 less than had he earned the $5,000 as interest income. Tyler has three children, and because of the $1,900 dividend gross-up increases his net income, his family's Child Tax Benefit is reduced by $76 and their GST Credit is reduced by $95.

A $1,900 RRSP contribution would restore these refundable credits while retaining the tax benefits of the dividend income.

Dividends are otherwise tax efficient. Canadian dividends can produce very tax efficient results because they are subject to lower marginal tax rates than ordinary income sources like interest or pensions. Where income is in the lowest tax bracket, the dividend tax credit may in fact, exceed the tax levied on the grossed-up dividends.

This may result in a "negative marginal tax rate" on dividend income. What this means is that the dividend tax credit will help to offset taxes owing on other types of income earned in the year, and that makes dividends very tax efficient. To illustrate, the marginal tax rates for 2012 for the province of BC, appears below:

Marginal Tax Rates on Investment Income Sources

	Taxable Income Range in 2012	Ordinary Income	Capital Gains	Ineligible Dividends (SBC)	Eligible Dividends
BC	Up to $10,822	0%	0%	0%	0%
	$10,823 to $11,354	15.00%	7.50%	2.08%	-2.03%
	$11,355 to $37,013	20.06%	10.03%	4.16%	-6.84%
	$37,014 to $42,707	22.70%	11.35%	7.46%	-3.20%
	$42,708 to $74,028	29.70%	14.85%	16.21%	6.46%
	$74,029 to $84,993	32.50%	16.25%	19.71%	10.32%
	$84,994 to $85.414	34.29%	17.15%	21.95%	12.79%
	$85,415 to $103,205	38.29%	19.15%	26.95%	18.31%
	$103,206 to $132,406	40.70%	20.35%	29.96%	21.64%
	Over $132,406	43.70%	21.85%	33.71%	25.78%

Spousal Income Transfer is Possible. The Attribution Rules generally require the spouse who earned and invested the capital that generated the dividends be the one to report the dividend income. However, if the lower-income spouse has dividends but cannot benefit from the dividend tax credit because his or her income is too low, the higher-income spouse may report the dividends. Technically the rule is that higher-income spouse can report the dividends if the claim for the spousal amount is created or increased by removing the dividends from the lower-income spouse's income. You may wish to check your tax software to ensure it made the transfer.

Example: Ryan earns $55,000 from employment. His wife Ashley's only income is $3,000 from eligible dividends on shares she inherited from her grandfather. If Ashley reports the dividends, her net income will be $4,140 reducing Ryan's claim for her to $6,682. Ashley is not taxable so she cannot benefit from the dividend tax credit. If Ryan elects to include the dividend income on his return, he will have to pay $403 taxes on the income, but the additional claim for Ashley will reduce Ryan's taxes by $788. The net result of the election is a tax savings of $385.

Minimum Tax Possible. Taxpayers who receive a large part of their income by way of eligible dividend may find themselves subject to *Alternative Minimum Tax,* if the dividend tax credit entirely eliminates tax payable. This calculation is made automatically by your tax software on Form T691 and it's a long complicated form. However, if you had to pay minimum tax, the carry-over functions in your software will record this for you and that's important, because any minimum tax paid this year, will be used to offset regular taxes payable in the following seven years until used up. But if you continue to earn a large part of your income from dividends, you may continue to be subject to minimum tax which you may never be able to recover.

Example: In 2011, Clyde's only income was $100,000 from eligible dividends. Normally, after the dividend tax credit, his federal taxes would have been $6,041 but, because Clyde is subject to minimum tax, his federal taxes for 2011 were $7,421. The extra $1,380 Clyde had to pay may be used to reduce his federal taxes in 2012 so long as he is not subject to minimum tax again in 2012.

Other Dividends. Other types of dividends may confuse you and if so, do speak to a professional about the source documents you may have received from your investment firm. Here is a short list of some unique circumstances:

Capital Dividends. These are dividends paid out of the Capital Dividend Account (CDA) of a private corporation and they reflect the 50% tax exempt portion of capital gains earned by the corporation on the disposition of capital property, capital dividends received from other corporations or life insurance policy proceeds, for example. These distributions are therefore not taxable. The corporation must file Form T2054 on the day the dividend becomes payable or on the first day any part of such a dividend is paid, whichever is earlier. As the recipient of a capital dividend, you will not receive any documentation because the income is not taxable to you.

Capital Gains Dividends. These dividends are received from mutual fund companies and reported on a T5 slip and on *Schedule 3 Capital Gains and Losses,* because they reflect capital gains realized in the fund rather than dividends. These dividends are eligible for a 50% income inclusion rather than the gross-up and dividend tax credit. These dividends will be reported in box 18 of your T5 slip.

Example: Amber's T5 slip shows $550 as a capital gains dividend (Box 18). When she keys this into her tax software, it gets posted to Line 174 of Schedule 3 and $275 is then posted to Line 127 of her return as a capital gain.

Deemed Dividend. When a corporation reorganizes, shareholders may be deemed to have received a dividend, and a T5 will be issued. This can occur, for example, where a share is redeemed or cancelled. Where the dividend is deemed to have been paid by a Canadian corporation, it is subject to the normal gross-up and dividend tax credit rules.

Dividend Reinvestment Programs. When a corporation reinvests the dividends in shares of the corporation rather than paying a cash dividend, the amount of the dividend is included in income in the tax year the cash dividend would have been paid. The cost base of the asset is then increased by the amount of the reinvestment. This is a popular method used by mutual funds and segregated funds.

Example: Brandon held 1,000 CIBC Series 32 preferred shares that were redeemed in 2012. He received $26 per share that was allocated by CIBC as $25 per share proceeds and $1 per share deemed dividend. Brandon received a T5 slip showing the $1,000 actual dividend ($1,380 taxable) that is eligible for the dividend tax credit. The remaining

$25,000 is considered proceeds of disposition of the redeemed shares and is used to calculate his capital gain for the year.

His wife Lauren owned 1,000 common shares of CIBC that were in a dividend reinvestment plan. The cost of the shares was $75,000. During 2012, the stocks paid $376 in eligible dividends that were reported to Lauren on a T5 slip. She did not receive the money but instead received five additional shares. She must report the $376 ($518.88 taxable) dividends on her 2012 return. By the end of the year, she owned 1,005 shares with a cost base of $75,376).

*Income Bonds and De*bentures. These instruments may be issued with terms up to five years by corporations in financial difficulty and under the control of a receiver or trustee in bankruptcy. A return on such an income bond is paid only if there is a profit on the operations, in which case the amount paid or received is considered to be a dividend. In the year that the income is paid, a T5 slip will be issued with the deemed dividend shown in Boxes 24, 25, and 26.

Foreign Dividends. The tax treatment of dividends in the foreign country is not relevant for Canadian tax purposes. Here, foreign dividends do not qualify for the gross up and dividend tax credit that Canadian dividends do. Rather, the actual amounts are reported in Canadian funds when received. The value of the dividends depends on the paid up capital

If the dividends were subject to withholding taxes in the foreign country, the Canadian resident will qualify to claim a *foreign tax credit*, which offsets taxes on Schedule 1 *Detailed Tax Calculation*. This will be calculated automatically by your tax software if you record the amounts in the right boxes on the data entry screen. However, there are three possible provisions that will be involved in making sure as much of that foreign withholding tax as possible is offset to avoid double taxation: the *federal foreign tax credit* (form T2209), the *provincial foreign tax credit* (Form T2036 for all provinces but Quebec, which has its own calculations and forms) and, if an unabsorbed balance of tax still remains, a deduction is claimed on *Line 230 Other Deductions*. That's because your foreign tax credit cannot be more than 15% of your net income from the investment. Where your effective tax rate is less than the foreign tax rate, you may claim the taxes that are not credited as a deduction instead.

After this, the taxpayer may carry forward unabsorbed foreign taxes paid on business income for a period of 10 years; but unfortunately there is no carry forward provision on non-business income.

Non-Residents Receiving Canadian Dividends. Non-residents must pay tax on the income earned in Canada either through *withholding taxes* on passive income sources such as investments, pensions and management fees (Part XIII Tax—you may elect to file a Canadian return in this case) or by filing a Canadian tax return on actively earned sources or the disposition of certain taxable capital property. (Part I tax).

When a Canadian corporation issues dividends to a non-resident, it is necessary to withhold taxes and issue an NR4 Slip. A remittance number must be obtained from CRA for these purposes by filing form NR75, *Non-Resident Account Information* Form. This is all the tax the non-resident will need to pay and there is no need to file a tax return, unless there are other sources specifically subject to tax, listed above.

Tax Treaties. The amount of withholding tax is determined by the tax treaty in force between Canada and the foreign country. At the time of writing there were 90 tax treaties in force, 10 signed but not yet in force and another nine under negotiation. You can look this up by going to the Finance Canada website.

In general the withholding tax rate is 15% for non-residents of countries with whom we have a tax treaty, and 25% for those resident in non-treaty countries. CRA is now requiring a certificate of residency from each shareholder in order to apply withholding taxes properly, with re-certification required every third year, as well as Form *NR301—Declaration of Eligibility for Benefits Under a Tax Treaty For A Non-Resident Taxpayer*.

These rules will impact tax planning for family businesses where family members travel or work abroad as non-residents. A more tax-efficient method of distribution of family wealth may be required in planning for those people. Failure to remit can attract penalties of up to 10%, 20% for repeat omissions.

Patronage Dividends (Allocations). Patronage dividends or allocations are received from cooperative corporations and reported on a T4A slip in Box 30. If you are operating a business, such as a farm, add the portion of the amount to income that represents a rebate on expenditures for business purposes. If you are a consumer, the amounts represent a discount off your purchases and are not taxable. You'll be asked to show the breakdown of taxable and non-taxable patronage allocations on your tax software screen.

Example: Farmer Ben buys groceries and fuel at the local co-operative. At the end of the year he received a T4A representing his patronage dividend in the amount of $950. He notes that $100 tax was also withheld, which would show up as a credit on Line 437 of his tax return. His farm books show that 50% of expenditures at the Co-op related to groceries (personal use), with the balance to fuel (farm use). The portion of the patronage dividend that relates to fuel purchases is taxable ($450) because it represents a reduction in the amount paid (and already deducted) for fuel costs.

Stock Dividends. These dividends are paid by the corporation by issuing of additional stock of that corporation, rather than cash. They can also be known as "dividends in kind." For tax purposes they are treated the same way as an ordinary dividend. You will report the grossed-up amount (as shown on your T5 slip) on your tax return and claim the dividend tax credit if the amounts are issued by either a public Canadian corporation or a Canadian Controlled Private Corporation. The actual amount of the dividend is deemed to be the cost of the new shares.

Stock Splits. There are no immediate tax consequences on a stock split. This occurs when there is an increase in the number of outstanding shares of a company's stock but the percentage of ownership remains the same. No T-slip will be received. Most commonly investors would experience a 2-for-1 split, in which case one share owned becomes two, which will affect the cost base of the shares. The tax consequences are later recorded on the sale or loss of the securities. Please see the next chapter.

U.S. investment accounts. Financial transactions between Canada and the U.S., with whom we have a tax treaty, can be complicated and expensive. Canadian residents holding investments in U.S. securities may have tax consequences in both countries; dividends earned on U.S. securities, for example, are taxed in the U.S. first through withholding taxes and then in Canada. Portfolio gains on US securities held by Canadians will be taxed in Canada. You can get relief from double taxation through a foreign tax credit in Canada to offset federal and provincial taxes. Unabsorbed foreign taxes from non-business investments cannot be carried forward although they can be deducted if you have Canadian taxes to pay.

U.S. Citizens Residing in Canada. U.S. citizens living in Canada must pay tax in the US on world income no matter where they live, so filing a 1040 tax return no later than June 15 is required. Investors face a minimum penalty of $10,000 for failing to report details of their foreign financial accounts, including those in Canada. Starting in 2014, Canadian financial institutions will be required to disclose financial information to the IRS about funds held for U.S. citizens. You will be asked if you are a U.S. citizen, where you were born, and whether either of your parents are U.S. citizens for these purposes.

Reporting Interest and Other Investment Income

Interest income results from an investment in a "debt obligation." That is, you loan capital to a financial institution, company or another person, and in return for the use of your money, you are paid interest at a certain percentage. That interest can be paid to you periodically—once a month, once or twice a year, and so on—depending on the terms in your contract. Or the interest may be automatically reinvested and left to compound.

Examples of interest-bearing investments are Guaranteed Investment Certificates (GICs), Canada Savings Bonds (CSBs), Treasury Bills or T-Bills, strip bonds or income bonds or debentures, which link interest paid to a corporation's profits or cash flow. Indexed debt obligations can be linked to inflation, too. Government of Canada Real Return Bonds are an example of this.

Interest Reporting Methods. Most tax filers will receive a T3 or T5 slip on which interest is reported. That data is then entered on the appropriate screen in your tax software.

Behind the scenes, however, know that some investments will report interest on a calendar-year basis (January to December); alternatively, on a bond year basis as in the case of

Canada Savings Bonds, October 31 to November 1. Therefore, the anniversary date of an interest-bearing investment is important: it will either be one year from its date of issue less a day, the anniversary of that date in each subsequent year or the day of disposition.

Compounding vs. Simple Interest. An investment compounds when earnings are reinvested so that you can earn on those earnings as well as the principal. For compounding investments acquired after 1989, annual reporting is required. All interest that accrues in the year ending on the anniversary date must be reported, even though you may not have received the money.

Simple Interest Received. Interest is considered earned for tax purposes when it is received or receivable by the taxpayer. This can be cash or by cheque, as a credit to your bank account, in kind in lieu of cash or when a new term deposit certificate is issued for interest earned on a matured certificate. Matured bond interest is considered to have been received when the bond is cashed, sold, given in payment of a debt or another form of negotiated payments.

Interest Accrued. As indicated above, interest must be reported on your tax return each year even if it continues to accrue and is not paid or payable. For example, if you have a five-year investment that pays interest only when it matures at the end of the five-year period, you'll still receive a T-slip and you'll have to report the interest that accrues each year. In the final year when you actually receive the interest, you'll only have to report the difference between the amount received and the amount already reported.

Other Interest-Bearing Investments. Interest earned on corporate or government bonds is reported according to the rules above. If your bond is purchased at a discount to maturity, the interest amount reported will increase your adjusted cost base when you sell the bond on the open market. This is discussed in the next chapter.

Other interest. Sometimes parents will lend money to kids to buy their first home or corporations will lend money to employees to buy stocks in the company. Here is how to handle the interest paid:

- *Mortgages.* You must report the interest on the mortgage you hold for another, including your child, as "other investment income" on your tax return. Don't report the principal in the blended payment—just the interest.
- *Employer-provided loans.* In this case a taxable benefit will be reported in employment income in Box 14 of the T4 slip to account for the difference in interest rates between the low rate and the prescribed rate of interest. The current prescribed rate is 1% and has been for several years. If your employer provides you with an interest-free loan, then your taxable benefit will be the interest that you would have paid had the loan been at the 1% prescribed rate and the amount of interest you actually paid. For an interest-free loan that would be zero so your taxable benefit will be 1% of the

loan balance. This amount is included in income (as shown in Box 14) and this is important, because that amount can be used as a carrying charge as interest paid to earn investment income.

Limited Partnership Income

Some investors like the opportunity to participate in tax shelters known as limited partnerships. Because the partnership does not pay taxes itself but passes on a portion of its income, losses and credits to its partners, partnerships offer an attractive opportunity for immediate tax savings based on losses that are shared amongst the partners.

A limited partner is an inactive member of a partnership whose liability in respect of the partnership interest is, as the name implies, limited by law. In general terms, investors in a limited partnership will be responsible for reporting a portion of the taxable activities. For example, a partnership must calculate its net income for the fiscal year as it were a separate "person." All partners must then include in their income a portion of the partnership's net income for the year.

Limited partnership income is generally reported to the investor on Form *T5013 Statement of Partnership Income* and transferred to the tax return on Line 122 or as Rent or other investment income depending on the nature of the business operated by the partnership. The T-slip guide at the end of this part will help you enter the data.

Limited Partnership Losses. Unfortunately, this is where things get tricky. Losses that exceed the partner's "*at-risk amount*" cannot be used to reduce income from other sources.

That means that unless you have income from the limited partnership, your losses will not be deductible beyond the amount that you invested in the partnership. Limited partnership losses may not be carried back, either, but may be carried forward indefinitely to be applied against future income from the limited partnership that gave rise to the loss. Limited partnership losses of other years are deducted on Line 251. The partner's at-risk amount is shown in Box 22-1 or 22-2 of the T5013 *Statement of Partnership Income* slip.

Investors often do not understand the tax reporting and are angered that they can't write off all the losses immediately. For that reason, ask your investment advisor to run you through all the tax consequences before you invest.

 The Bottom Line | Many investors are fleeing to the safety of guaranteed, interest-bearing investments at a time when the yield is not great. Should interest rates go up in the future, they may be locked into a term at low rates or worse, lose on the sale of a bond in the open market because no one wants a low return investment. That's why you need to do some careful tax planning.

30

Reporting Gains and Losses

I would now like to introduce you to a topic that I have to admit boggles the minds of many taxpayers. But, if you can get past the tax jargon—and we'll help you here—you'll find that managing your capital assets and their gains and losses can make you very wealthy over time. So isn't that good motivation to dive right in?

 CHECK IT OUT | **What is a capital property?** A capital property is usually acquired for investment purposes (securities such as stocks, bonds or mutual fund units) or for business purposes to earn income (land, building, equipment).

Capital property does not include inventory or insurance policies, with the exception of segregated fund trusts. It is also arranged in certain classifications, because tax treatment on the assets will differ.

Classification of Property. There are special rules for the classification of certain capital properties relating in particular to the claiming of losses and a very special tax break, the Capital Gains Deduction. We'll discuss those in more detail later. But first, what is a capital gain or loss?

A **capital gain** or loss can occur if you have disposed of, or are "deemed" to have disposed of a capital property. For many taxpayers, however, the capital gains on their investments in mutual fund corporations and trusts will be reported on a T5 or T3 slip respectively, so reporting is simple. In other cases, it will be necessary to gather documentation from your investment advisor to properly compute the gain or loss.

How is a Capital Gain Calculated? A capital gain will occur, and you will need to report this on your tax return, when a capital property is sold or "deemed" to be sold for more than its adjusted cost base and the outlays and expenses you have incurred to dispose of the property. If you dispose of the asset for less than its cost base, there is a capital loss. We'll define those terms in more depth later. A capital gain is basically the following:

Proceeds of Disposition – Adjusted Cost Base – Outlays and Expenses = Capital Gain (or Loss)

Capital Gains Inclusion Rate. One half of this capital gain is included in your taxable income. The income inclusion rate, in other words, is 50%. (That income inclusion rate has changed over the years. A short history appears at the end of this chapter, in case you need to go back to the information for assets held over time.)

Example: An investor buys a share for $50 and sells it for $75 (with no outlays or expenses). The capital gain in this case is $25. ($75 – $50 = $25). The amount added to income and subject to tax is 50% of this or $12.50.

Proceeds of Disposition. This part of the equation can simply mean the selling price. However, in some cases, there is a "*deemed disposition.*" A *Fair Market Value (FMV)* must be determined because there is no actual sale.

✓ **CHECK IT OUT** | **When do you have a "deemed disposition" for tax purposes?** A deemed disposition occurs when:

- One asset is exchanged for another.
- Assets are given as gifts.
- The property is stolen, destroyed, expropriated or damaged.
- Shares held by the taxpayer are converted, redeemed or cancelled.
- An option to acquire or dispose of property expires.
- A debt owed to the taxpayer is settled or cancelled.
- Property is transferred to a trust.
- The owner of the property emigrates from Canada, becoming non-resident
- The owner changes the use of the asset from business to personal (and vice versa).
- The owner dies (the disposition is considered to have taken place immediately prior to death).

Fair market valuation. In the dispositions above the FMV is determined as the price a stranger (unrelated to the taxpayer) would pay for an asset on the open market. To get that value, it's important to see appraisals or listings of similar assets sold recently on the open market.

Valuation days. Due to the history of the taxation of capital gains in Canada, numerous valuation days for various assets may also be used as proceeds of disposition. For example, capital gains were not taxable at all prior to 1972, so valuation was required at that time. At the end of this chapter is a history to be used in your calculations as various assets are disposed of.

 CHECK IT OUT | **What is adjusted cost base (ACB)?** Simply put, this is the value of your property that is not subject to tax on disposition. It's what you paid for it or its value at the time you acquired it, if you received it as a result of a deemed disposition. The cost to the taxpayer acquiring the asset is equal to the proceeds of disposition of the party who disposed of it. Some exceptions apply to this rule. More on that later.

Outlays and Expenses. The costs of disposing of a capital property may be used to reduce a capital gain or increase a loss, as the case may be. Examples are:

- advertising costs
- brokerage fees
- commissions
- costs incurred to improve the property
- finder's fees
- professional fees: legal, surveyor's, appraisals
- transfer taxes

Example: Marissa acquired a rental property she wanted to fix up and sell. The real estate cost $250,000. She replaced the roof and upgraded the carpets for $10,000. The roof and carpets were improvements, which she added to her cost base, bringing it up to $260,000. She sold the property within two months for $325,000 and incurred expenses of $25,000 on the sale. Her capital gain was $40,000 ($325,000 – $260,000 – $25,000).

Capital Losses. Capital losses are important. They can offset capital gains of the year, the prior three years or any future capital gains.

Example: Marissa funded her real estate improvements by selling one of her investments. She had purchased the shares for $12,000 and at the time of sale, they were worth $11,500. She paid brokerage fees of $125 on the trade. Her loss was calculated as follows:

Proceeds of Disposition	$11,500
Adjusted Cost Base	($12,000)
Outlays and Expenses	($ 125)
Capital Loss	($ 625)

This loss will be used to offset the capital gains of the year, $40,000 in this case. Marissa's net capital gain, therefore is $40,000 less $625 = $39,375 and the taxable gain is 50% of this or $19,687.50.

Many investors think that because they have no capital gains this year to absorb losses, as Marissa did, that the capital loss they incurred is worthless. This is not so.

Capital Loss Carry Back. Marissa's brother, Mark, was not so lucky this year. He lost $30,000 in the stock market. He had no other capital gains this year, but last year he had a great year; he made $40,000 in the stock market. He can now reach back and recover some of the taxes he paid last year with a loss carry back. He would use Form *T1A Request for Loss Carry Back* to do so.

Capital losses can be carried back to offset capital gains in the previous three years or, at Mark's option, he could have carried those losses forward, for use against future capital gains. The carry over options (back or forward) do not need to be made in any particular order.

In Mark's case, his other income of the year was $65,000 from employment. He paid $13,365 in taxes on his total income. The loss carry back created a refund of $4,672 and so was very worthwhile. Mark contributed that extra money to his TFSA.

There are some special classifications of property where the loss application rules are restricted or varied. These are discussed next. But in the meantime, if you have missed claiming a capital loss anytime in the past 10 years, consider making an adjustment to those prior-filed returns.

 CHECK IT OUT | **What are the classifications of capital property?** You won't get a convenient T-slip for some of the capital dispositions you may make for the assets you own. Let's discuss those in three profiles: dispositions by individuals, investors, and business owners.

Individuals

What are the tax consequences when you sell your home, a personal use property, for a loss or make a bundle on grandma's antique silver goblets, a listed personal use property? Here are the rules.

Personal Use Properties. The gains and losses on the sale of a personal use property, which includes all items used for personal use, such as homes, cars, boats and furniture, must be reported as they are subject to the "$1,000 Rule." That is, the Proceeds of Disposition and Adjusted Cost Base of personal use property are deemed to be no less than $1,000 for the purposes of computing any gain or loss. This eliminates reporting small transactions. Losses on personal use properties are not deductible, however.

Example: Peter put a lot of money into his cabin at the lake. He bought it for $50,000 and then put in a deck and an addition for another $50,000. He did not use it as a rental property and after a year, he had to sell it for only $80,000 as he took a job in another city. His $20,000 loss, unfortunately is not deductible.

Listed Personal Use Properties. These possessions usually don't depreciate in value. They can include artwork, jewelry, rare books or stamp and coin collections. Again the $1,000 Rule applies, however, in this case, losses can be deducted but only against other listed personal property gains of the year. If there are none, you can apply unabsorbed losses by carrying them back three years or forward seven years.

Investors

Investors may need to record capital dispositions for three types of assets:

- Publicly traded shares, mutual fund units, other shares
- Bonds, debentures and promissory notes
- Real estate, such as vacant land or a revenue property

Publicly Traded Shares, Mutual Funds and Other Shares. For many tax filers, the reporting capital transactions for mutual or segregated funds is easy: simply enter the amounts from the T-slips into your software data sheet and they will all appear on Lines 174 and 176 of Schedule 3. The software will keep track of any unabsorbed capital losses as well. These transactions reflect trading within managed accounts and the resulting capital gains and other income that has flowed through to the investor.

However, when you sell or otherwise dispose of the securities or mutual fund units themselves, you'll need to report that disposition separately. That involves finding your statements for the cost of acquisition and any additions (reinvested amounts in the case of mutual or segregated funds) as well as outlays and expenses (brokerage fees) to properly compute the Adjusted Cost Base (ACB). This can be tricky in some cases, as described below:

Identical Property. Shares in the same class of the same corporation or units in a specific mutual fund are known as "identical properties." Each share or unit is the same as the others and you can't tell one from another. When a taxpayer trades a portion of a group of identical properties, the taxpayer must calculate an *average cost* of all properties in the group to determine the adjusted cost base (ACB) of the property sold and report the capital gain or loss. Simply stated, each time there is a purchase, add the adjusted cost base of all the shares or mutual units in the group and divide by the total number of shares or units held.

Example: On January 1, Sarah purchased 1,000 shares of QRS Corp. for $12,000. On March 15, she purchased another 1,000 shares in the same corporation for $8,000. Then she disposes of 1,000 shares on July 15, for $11,000. There are no other transactions in the year and for these purposes, no outlays or expenses. The capital gain to be reported is calculated as follows:

- The average cost of the share is: $20,000 / 2,000 = $10 per share.
- The Adjusted Cost Base of the shares she sold is $10 x 1,000 or $10,000.
- The capital gain is $11,000 – $10,000 or $1,000.
- This is reported on Schedule 3.
- Half of this is added to total income.

Mutual Fund Exchanges and Switches. In the year you acquire a mutual fund, you will usually receive a full annual distribution, even if you invested late in the year. These amounts will generally be reinvested for you and you'll need to keep track of this to increase your cost base. If you exchange an investment in one fund for another (e.g. You switch from an equity fund into a balanced fund), a taxable disposition is considered to have occurred. However, there are no tax consequences when you switch from one class or series of funds to another, provided the investment is in corporate class funds.

Example: In 2011, Justin purchased 1,000 units of ABC Equity Fund for $8,547. He received a T5 slip in 2011 showing allocated earnings of $174.50 which was not paid to Justin but was used to acquire 21.86 more units in the fund. In July 2012, Justin decided he would transfer his investment to ABC Balanced Fund. The ABC Equity Fund units were selling at $8.05 per unit at the time of the sale and the ABC Balanced Fund units were selling at $7.45 per unit so Justin's 1021.86 Equity units were exchanged for 1104.16 units in the Balanced Fund. There were no transaction fees associated with this transfer.

As a result of this transaction, Justin has a capital loss, calculated as follows:

Capital Gain or Loss = Proceeds of Disposition – Adjusted Cost Base – Outlays
Proceeds = 1021.86 units @ $8.05 per unit = $8,225.97
ACB = $8,547.00 + $174.50 = $8,721.50
Outlays = $0.00
Gain or Loss = $8,225.97 – $8,721.50 – $0.00 = $495.53 Loss

Justin can use this loss to decrease any other capital gains in 2012. If his losses exceed his gains in the year, he can carry the loss back to reduce capital gains reported in 2011, 2010, or 2009. If the losses are not applied to gains in those years, he can carry the loss forward and apply it against gains in future years.

Segregated Funds. These are mutual funds wrapped up with a life insurance policy to provide a death benefit as well as a guarantee of principal. The money is held in trust and income is distributed to the beneficiaries and then generally immediately reinvested, much like mutual fund distributions. Income allocations do not affect the value of the segregated fund, unlike mutual funds. In addition, losses can be flowed through to the segregated fund holder to offset other capital gains.

Insurance segregated funds differ from mutual funds primarily in that they offer maturity and death guarantees on the capital invested and specifically, reset guarantees—the ability to lock in market gains. This is usually 75% to 100% of the amount invested, which will be returned to the taxpayer on death or maturity. Depending on the insurer, a reset can be initiated by the investor two to four times per year. The guaranteed period on maturity is usually 10 years after the policy is purchased, or after the reset. There are no tax consequences at the time the accrued gains in the investment are locked in by way of reset.

Guarantee at Maturity. If the value of the fund has increased over the reset amount, the disposition is reported as a normal capital gain.

Example: Ariel purchased 500 units in a segregated fund for $5,450. In 2012, she sold her 624 units (the number had increased over the years due to reinvestment of income allocations) for $9,048. The ACB of her units was $8,161. Her last reset was at $14 per unit. Since her proceeds amount to $14.50 per unit, the guarantee was not invoked. She has a capital gain on disposition of $9,048 – $8,161 = $887 assuming no expenses of disposition.

If at maturity the value of the fund has dropped, the insurer must top up the fund by contributing additional assets to bring the value up to the guaranteed amount. When it is sold at maturity, the difference between the adjusted cost base (which will include all allocations of income over time) and the proceeds received to the guaranteed amount will be accounted for. This is how to report this on Schedule 3:

Example: If the value of Ariel's investment (previous example) was only $13 per unit, the guarantee would have been revoked and Ariel's proceeds would be $14 per unit x 624 units = $8,736 and she would still have a capital gain but for $8,736 – $8,161 = $575 in spite of the fact that the actual value of the units was less than her ACB.

Guarantee at Death. The policyholder is deemed to have disposed of the contract at its FMV at death. If the value of the assets in the fund increases, the gain will be a capital gain to the policyholder when the policy matures or to his estate if the policy owner dies. The example below demonstrates how to report this on Schedule 3:

Example: Mark had purchased 1,000 units in ABC segregated fund for $8,450 which, through income allocations had increased to 1,247 units at the time of his death in 2012. The ACB of the units was $10,600 at the time of his death. At that time the value of the fund units was $9.05 per unit. On Mark's final return, a capital gain of $685.35 must be reported in Part 3 of Schedule 3:

> Proceeds of disposition: $9.05/unit x 1,247 units = $11,285.35
> Adjusted cost base: $10,600.00
> Outlays and expenses: $0.00
> Capital gain: $11,285.35 – $10,600.00 – $0.00 = $685.35.

If the value of the assets in the fund decreases, the taxpayer is deemed to have acquired additional notional units in the fund, so no gain is incurred even though the taxpayer receives more than the value of the notional units. A capital loss may occur if the guaranteed value is less than 100% of the investment. Report as follows:

Example: When Ester died, she owned 1,500 units in DEF segregated fund. The ACB of her units was $7.49 per unit. She had a guarantee at death of $10 per unit but the unit value at that time was $9.00 per unit.

Ester's estate will receive $15,000 (1,500 units x $10.00 per unit guaranteed value). Technically this is accomplished by allocating more units to Ester at $9 per unit to ensure the $15,000 guarantee is met. However, on Schedule 3 of Ester's final return the gain is calculated in the normal manner:

Proceeds of disposition: $15,000
Adjusted cost base: 1,500 units x $7.49/unit = $11,235.00
Capital gain: $15,000 – $11,235 = $3,765.

Income Trusts. If you have investments in income trusts, these investments now pay income to investors in the form of dividends. In some cases, these investments pay a *Return of Capital*, which must be tracked in order to properly reflect a declining adjusted cost base, as described below.

- *Return of Capital.* In some cases, most commonly with mutual funds, distributions are made to investors that represent a portion of the original investment rather than earnings. Because the return of capital does not represent earnings, these distributions are not taxable when received. You'll find them reported Box 52 of a T3 slip or in a footnote on a T5 slip. Since these are not taxable distributions, you will not find an entry field for them in your tax software.

  However, since some of your investment was returned to you, the adjusted cost base of the units is decreased by the amount returned. You'll need to take that into account when reporting any capital gain or loss when the units are disposed of.

- *Gifts.* Where property is acquired by gift or bequest, the cost to the recipient of the property is deemed to be its FMV at the time of the gift. An exception is a gift to a spouse where a tax-free rollover can take place. FMV may be elected, however if FMV consideration is paid in cash or through a spousal loan.

Example: Henry and Elizabeth purchased their cottage many years ago and, because of health issues are no longer able to use it. The cottage was worth $200,000 in 2012 when they decided to pass it on to their son Michael. The ACB of the cottage was $120,000. The fees associated with the transfer were $5,000.

Although Henry and Elizabeth received no proceeds from the transfer, they must report a capital gain on the disposition to Michael.

Gain = Proceeds (FMV deemed proceeds) – ACB – Outlays
Gain = $200,000 – $120,000 – $5,000 = $75,000.

This gain will be reported on each owner's tax return on the basis of his/her ownership interest in the property.

Non-Arm's Length Consideration. Where a taxpayer acquires a property in a non-arm's length transaction (a related party like a spouse for example), for more or less than the fair market value (FMV) special rules apply. Where the proceeds are more than the fair market value, the transferor will show the actual proceeds as FMV but the cost to the transferee is FMV. Where the proceeds of disposition were less than FMV, the transferor is deemed to receive FMV but the cost to the transferee is the actual proceeds. These rules are meant to discourage transfers at amounts other than the fair market value.

Example: Peter has an antique automobile that is currently worth $50,000. He agrees to sell it to his brother Andrew for $40,000. Peter's ACB is $25,000. He was expecting to report a capital gain of $15,000 since he sold the car for $40,000. However, because this is a non-arm's length transaction at less than fair market value, Peter is deemed to have received $50,000 (FMV) for the car and has to report a capital gain of $25,000 ($50,000 FMV – $25,000 ACB). Andrew's ACB of the car is the amount he paid ($40,000) so if he were to sell it again for $50,000, he would have to report a $10,000 capital gain.

Capital Gains Election. With the exception of flow-through entities, when a taxpayer elected to trigger the $100,000 capital gains deduction on accrued gains in 1994, the taxpayer was deemed to have disposed of the property and re-acquired it at a cost equal to the elected amount. This is particularly important for executors. There still may be securities or cottages in the family to which this election is connected. Get professional help and make sure you inquire about whether an election was made if a loved one in your family passed away.

Example: Cecil purchased his cottage for $40,000 in 1985. In 1994, he took advantage of the capital gains election to report the $20,000 accrued gain on the property (which was exempt because of the election). The ACB of the cottage as a result of the election then became $60,000. Between 1994 and 2012, he made improvements to the property that totaled an additional $25,000. Cecil passed away in 2012 and the value of his cottage was $175,000. On Cecil's final return, the executor must report a capital gain of $90,000 ($175,000 (FMV) – [$60,000 + $25,000] (ACB)).

Immigration. When a taxpayer immigrates to Canada, the taxpayer is deemed by to have acquired the capital properties owned at that time at a cost equal to the fair market value of the property at the time of immigration. This becomes the cost base of those assets for the purposes of reporting future capital gains.

Example: When Myron immigrated to Canada in 2010, he brought with him a piece of artwork that was valued at $10,000 CDN. Myron had purchased the artwork some years earlier for the equivalent of $3,000 CDN. When he sold the artwork in 2012 for $12,000, he had to report a capital gain of $2,000 ($12,000 – $10,000) on his Canadian return. The gain that accrued prior to Myron immigrating is not taxed in Canada.

Securities Traders. It is possible for a taxpayer to make an election that all disposed securities in this and future tax years will be treated as qualifying for capital gains treatment (i.e. only 50% of the gain is taxable). The election is made on Form T123 *Election on Disposition of Canadian Securities.* Once the election is made, it is permanent, and cannot be revoked.

The reason you might make this election is to avoid situations where you might be considered to be running a business trading securities. If that were the case, then any gains would be fully taxable, instead of only 50% taxable. The downside of the election is that losses are also considered to be capital losses and can only be deducted against capital gains rather than being 100% deductible against all other income sources.

This election cannot be made by taxpayers who are traders or dealers in securities or non-residents. If a taxpayer who has made this election becomes a trader or dealer, the election will not apply during the period in which the taxpayer is a trader or dealer. If the taxpayer ceases to be a trader or dealer, then the election will again apply to transactions after that time.

CRA will consider factors such as the frequency of transactions, the period of ownership of the securities, the taxpayer's knowledge of the securities market, the amount of time spent on the market, and any level of advertising to purchase shares in deciding whether to allow the permanent status for all future dispositions.

 CHECK IT OUT | **Retirees may benefit from the election.** A taxpayer who closely follows the stock market and buys and sells securities is not likely to be considered to be a trader. However, if a taxpayer has quit their job, or retired and "day trades" as their main source of income, they likely would.

Bonds, Debentures and Promissory Notes. In this category we include gains on the sale of foreign currencies in excess of $200 and repayments of amounts that were previously used to reduce the adjusted cost base of an asset, such as government assistance, inducements, reimbursements, etc. You would also include the sale of bonds, debentures (a type of bond) or T-Bills.

Treasury Bills or T-Bills. These are short-term government debt obligations generally available in three-, six- or 12-month terms. If the terms exceed one year, the normal interest accrual rules apply. These instruments are acquired at a discount to their maturity value and have no stated rate of interest. On maturity you receive the face value which includes the accrued interest. This will generally be reported to you on a T5008 Slip. When entering the T5008 information in your tax program be sure to enter the proper Type Code (Box 15) as this will determine whether the income is reported as interest on Schedule 4 or a capital gain on Schedule 3.

When you sell the T-Bill prior to maturity, a capital gain or loss could result, depending on its value in the marketplace. That portion of the transaction would be reported on Schedule 3.

Report the interest on Schedule 4 as the difference between the cost and face value of the T-Bill times the number of days you held the investment.

Example: A T-Bill has a face value of $10,000 and Sam acquired it for $9800, maturing in 365 days after acquisition. Brokerage fees were $50. He held it for 100 days and then sold it for $9,500 and paid another brokerage fee of $50.

1. Report as interest income: $10,000 – $9,800 = $200 x 100/365 = $54.79
2. Claim the brokerage fee as a carrying charge on Line 221 (Schedule 4)
3. Calculate the Adjusted Cost Base: $9,800 + $54.79 = $9,854.79.
4. Calculate Capital Loss: $9,500 – ($9,800 + $54.79) – $50 = $404.79

Debentures are debt instruments that carry a fixed interest rate, and are secured by the general credit of the issuing corporation. The sale of debentures prior to maturity may give rise to a capital gain or capital loss. The Adjusted Cost Base (ACB) will be the price originally paid for that debenture. The proceeds of disposition are the actual amount that a debenture is sold for and the gain is, of course, reduced by disposition costs (e.g. commissions).

Where a debenture is held to maturity, a capital gain or capital loss may arise if the purchase price (ACB) is different from the maturity value. The proceeds of disposition will be the maturity value actually received. The capital gain or capital loss will be the maturity proceeds less that ACB of the debenture. Where the debenture was purchased directly from the issuing corporation, the ACB would be equal to the maturity value, therefore, no capital gain or capital loss would arise if held to maturity.

When a debenture is exchanged for shares of a corporation, or another bond or debenture, the exchange is not considered to be a disposition and therefore it should not be reported on the tax return.

Promissory Notes. A promissory note is an agreement to pay a certain sum of money at some point in the future to another party which loans the money. Depending on the nature of the agreement, there may or may not be a requirement to pay interest as well. If someone defaults on a promissory note, the investor receives nil proceeds for his investment and therefore has a capital gain equal to the ACB of the note (the amount loaned).

Example: John lent his son, Tom, $50,000 at 1% interest to start a bicycle repair shop. Tom defaulted on the loan, closed the business and went to China. On John's tax return he will report a capital loss of $50,000.

Real Estate. Lots of people like to dabble in real estate when markets are hot. The issue for tax filing purposes is whether you held the property for personal use, as a passive investment or whether you are in fact in the business of buying and selling real estate.

We have previously discussed the tax consequences of selling personal use properties (losses are not deductible) and in the next chapter will have a closer look at tax-exempt personal residences and rental properties.

When real estate is held for investment purposes, any income it earns will be *"income from property,"* generally in the form of *rent*. Upon disposition of the property, any increase in value will usually be taxed as a capital gain. However, if you are continuously flipping your properties, it's possible you're in business.

 CHECK IT OUT | **When are you considered to be in the business of buying and selling real estate?** The *Income Tax Act* does not prescribe when gains from the sale of real estate will be considered income rather than capital. In making such determinations, the courts have considered factors such as:

- the taxpayer's intention with respect to the real estate at the time of its purchase;
- feasibility of the taxpayer's intention;
- geographical location and zoned use of the real estate acquired;
- extent to which the intention was carried out by the taxpayer;
- evidence that the taxpayer's intention changed after purchase of the real estate;
- the nature of the business, profession, calling or trade of the taxpayer and associates;
- the extent to which borrowed money was used to finance the real estate acquisition and the terms of the financing, if any, arranged;
- the length of time throughout which the real estate was held by the taxpayer,
- the existence of persons other than the taxpayer who share interests in the real estate;
- the nature of the occupation of the other persons who share interest as well as their stated intentions and courses of conduct;
- factors which motivated the sale of the real estate; and
- evidence that the taxpayer and/or associates had dealt extensively in real estate.

The more closely a taxpayer's business or occupation is related to real estate transactions, the more likely it is that any gain realized by the taxpayer from such a transaction will be considered to be business income (100% income inclusion on a business statement) rather than a capital gain (report on Schedule 3 as a capital gain—50% income inclusion).

In addition, it's not necessary for you to buy and sell properties. If CRA considers the transaction to be an *Adventure or Concern in the Nature of Trade*, even a one-time transaction can be considered to be a business transaction. The result? Again, you must report business profits (100% taxable) as opposed to a capital gain (50% taxable.)

Generally, when the intention of the taxpayer is to earn income from the sale of real estate, based on these factors, the income is included in income from business. When the asset is held for investment purposes (i.e. to earn income from property—interest or rent is earned—the gain on sale is capital in nature).

Vacant Land. Special rules apply to vacant land. If it's held for speculation; that is there is no potential for income from the property, a capital gain or loss will eventually occur. Further interest, land transfer taxes and property taxes cannot be deducted along the way, either. You must be able to show the potential for rental income to deduct interest and property taxes, but if there is no potential for rental income the expenses cannot be deducted. However, so long as the land is not held for personal use, interest and property taxes may be added to the adjusted cost base of the land reducing the capital gain on disposition.

Vacant land that is capital property used by its owner for the purpose of gaining or producing income from the sale of lots, will be considered to have been converted to *inventory* at the earlier of:

- the time when the owner starts making improvements with a view to selling it; and
- the time of making application for approval of a plan to subdivide the land into lots for sale, in order to develop a subdivision.

The subdivision of farmland or inherited land in order to sell it will not, of itself, constitute a conversion to inventory and so capital gains treatment should be preserved in these cases.

Options on Real Estate. Where an arm's length lease-option agreement exists, reasonable rental paid prior to the exercise of the purchase option by the lessee is considered to be rental expense to the lessee and income to the lessor. This is true even where a rebate or discount on the purchase price for a portion of the previous rentals paid is given at the time the option to purchase is exercised.

Upon exercise of the purchase option, the option price for the property, less adjustments for previous rentals paid, if any, will be considered the cost of property to the lessee purchaser.

Example: Susan operates a proprietorship. She wanted to purchase a storefront for her business but was unable to provide the required down payment for financing so she entered into a lease option agreement to purchase a property. Under the agreement, she paid

$1,000 per month for five years and at the end of the lease could purchase the building for $150,000. As the $1,000 per month was reasonable rent on the building, she was able to deduct the payments as rent. If she purchases the property for $150,000 at the end of the lease, her ACB will be the $150,000 paid (plus any additional expenses of acquisition).

Selling Land and Building. When land and building are held to earn income (either business income or rental income) then the building is a depreciable property (see below). Because special rules apply to depreciable property, the land and building are considered to be separate assets and the ACB must be established for each at the time of purchase. Likewise, proceeds of disposition must be allocated to the land and building according to their value.

In the simplest case, where no CCA has been claimed and the value of the property increases, the result of the allocation is simply to split the capital gain into two parts. However, where CCA has been claimed, the value of the property decreases, or the value of the land increases and the value of the building decreases, then the rules become more complicated. You may want to seek professional assistance if you sold real estate that was held for investment or business use.

Case Study | Planning to Sell a Rental Property

Dexter purchased a rental property in 2009 for $250,000. Per the appraisal, the building was worth $150,000 and the land worth $100,000. In order to reduce his rental income to zero each year, Dexter claimed a total of $5,000 CCA as a deduction. In 2012, Dexter sold the property for $275,000. Per an appraisal done at the time of the sale, the $170,000 of the proceeds were allocated to the land and $105,000 to the building. Outlays and expenses totalled $18,000 which were allocated on the same basis as the proceeds ($11,127 to the land and $6,873 to the building).

The capital gain on the land (as shown on Dexter's Schedule 3) is $170,000 − $150,000 − $11,127 = $8,873.

Because the net proceeds for the building ($105,000 − $6,873) are more than the depreciated value ($100,000 − $5,000 CCA), Dexter has over-claimed depreciation and he must add back the excess (recapture) of $3,127 into income.

Business Owners

Small business owners may dispose of three types of properties on their personal tax returns: depreciable property and eligible capital property in the case of unincorporated businesses as well as qualifying shares of a small business corporation.

Depreciable Property. Whether incorporated or not, when you sell a depreciable property, that is assets upon which you claimed or were entitled to claim *Capital Cost Allowance (CCA),* a tax consequence can occur. A capital gain will occur only if you sold the property for more than its original cost plus improvements. There can be no capital loss on the disposition of a depreciable property. Rather, any amounts received below the *Undepreciated Capital Cost (UCC)* of all the assets in the Class is shown on the business statement as a Terminal Loss, which reduces other income of the year.

Recapture is another possible consequence. That is, if one or more assets in the Class is disposed of for proceeds that exceed the UCC, the excess is added to business income of the year.

In the case of *Class 10.1 Passenger Vehicle* or luxury vehicles, neither recapture nor terminal loss can be claimed on disposition. Instead, there is a "half year rule" on disposition. (Only one half the normal depreciation rate is claimable.)

Eligible Capital Property. This is tax talk for purchased goodwill, customer lists, trademarks or patents, licenses or quotas that don't have a pre-defined life. Generally these types of assets go into a special account call the *Cumulative Eligible Capital (CEC) Account.* An allowance for depreciation is then claimed. When a disposition occurs, there may be recapture, terminal loss or a capital gain.

Qualified SBC Shares. The disposition of the shares of a Canadian-controlled small business corporation is often a happy occasion. When a business owner sells or otherwise disposes of the business, it's possible to claim a ***Capital Gains Exemption (CGE)*** of up to $750,000 on Line 254 for each shareholder in the family business. But not all shares qualify. Here are the rules for qualification:

- Mostly all (90% or more) of the assets of the business must be used in an active business carried on primarily in Canada.
- The shares must be held throughout a 24-month period before disposition, and in that period.
- 50% of the fair market value of the corporation's assets must have been used in an active business.

The 24-month holding period, by the way, cannot be circumvented by the issuing of shares from treasury. Do not report other publicly traded shares here, either.

Capital Gains Deduction (CGD). As discussed above, after March 18, 2007 the CGE increased to $750,000 from the prior $500,000. (50% of those amounts are claimed as the CGD on Line 254). To do so, go to *Form T657 Calculation of Capital Gains Deduction.* Also see the history of CGE changes at the back of this chapter, which you might find helpful to do this form properly. Your software will do the calculations automatically if it has this history of prior capital gains deductions you may have claimed, prior *Business Investment Losses (BIN)* claimed and your *Cumulative Net Investment Losses (CNIL)*.

- *Business Investment Losses (BIL).* Did you have a loss on the sale of the shares in a family business? If so, there is a consolation. The net loss on those qualifying SBC shares can be claimed on Line 217 of your return, which means it will reduce other income this year and reduce your net income on Line 236 as well, so you may be able to claim more refundable tax credits. This makes the BIL very valuable. If unabsorbed, it can be carried back as a "non-capital loss" using form *T1A Request for Loss Carry Back*, to offset other income in the previous three years and for up to 10 years in the future. If there is still an unabsorbed BIL after this, it becomes a regular "capital loss," which can offset gains indefinitely in the future. However, a claim for a business investment loss will reduce your CGD.
- *Calculation of Net Business Investment Loss (CNIL)*: As you report investment income and expenses (interest costs, for example) over the years, your tax software will have kept track of your CNIL balance, the excess of expenses over income, on Form T936 *CNIL*. At the time of disposition of a qualifying SBC, a positive CNIL balance will reduce your CGD.
- *Reserves.* Where a taxpayer has disposed of a capital property and a portion of the proceeds is receivable after the end of the taxation year, the taxpayer may claim a reasonable capital gain reserve for the funds not yet received. The amount of the reserve claimed in one year is included in income in the following year, against which an additional reserve may be claimed for amounts receivable. Use form T2017 *Summary of Reserves on the Disposition of Capital Property* to do this. Note that there is a limitation on how large a reserve may be claimed:
  - *80% or less in the year of disposition*
  - *60% or less in the next year*
  - *40% or less in the third year*
  - *20% in the fourth year*
  - *0% in subsequent years*

  If you claim a reserve on the disposition of qualified small business shares, then your capital gains deduction for that disposition will be reduced.
- *Replacement Properties.* It is possible to defer paying tax on a capital gain if you acquire a replacement property for a "former business property" or a property that was stolen, expropriated or destroyed. This is generally real property used in earning business income as opposed to a rental property. Certain time limits must be met in replacing the property to qualify, depending on whether the disposition was voluntary or involuntary. Another rule allows for a "capital gains rollover" for small business owners who sell one business and then reinvest in another. Speak to your tax advisor about this. These occurrences will affect your CGD if the gain reported in the year is reduced to less than your available deduction.

Qualified Farming and Qualified Fishing Properties. The disposition of certain property owned for a full 24 months prior to disposition by an individual or their spouse, child, grandchildren or parents, certain trusts or interests in a family farm or partnership or corporation will qualify for the CGD if the property was actively used in the course of carrying on a farm business. Similar rules exist for qualified fishing enterprises after May 1, 2006.

Qualifying properties can include real property, such as land and buildings, as well as eligible capital property such as egg and milk quotas for farmers or fishing licenses for fishers, and depreciable property such as fishing vessels.

In the case of farm businesses that have been held in the family for several generations, those acquired *after June 17, 1987*, will be considered qualified property for CGD purposes if all or substantially all (90% of more) of the Fair Market Value (FMV) of the property was used throughout the 24 months immediately before disposition by the qualified family members named above. As well, for at least two years during ownership, the gross revenue of the individual who used the property in an active business must have exceeded income from all other sources.

If acquired *before June 18, 1987*, the farm must have been used by the individuals, partnerships or corporations defined above, in the year of disposition, or at least five years in the ownership period in an active farming business to qualify. Otherwise the property is considered to be "non-qualified" and is claimed under "Real estate, depreciable property and other properties" on Schedule 3.

Farm Property Succession Planning. If properties are transferred to the taxpayer's child during the farmer's lifetime, the child or the child's representative may elect that the deemed proceeds of disposition on the transfer be *any amount between the transferor's cost amount and the fair market value of the transferred property*. In addition, a reserve of up to 10 years may be claimed when taxable capital gains arise upon disposition.

When a farm property is transferred on death to the spouse or child of a taxpayer, it is deemed that non-depreciable assets be acquired by the survivor at a cost equal to the cost to the deceased. In other words, there is a "tax-free rollover." However, an election may be made to have the transfer take place at an amount greater than the cost to the deceased, but not greater than the fair market value of the asset. This would be helpful to use up the deceased's losses or capital gains deduction, and to bump up the cost base for the survivor.

Mortgage Foreclosures & Conditional Sales Repossessions. Sometimes the creditor repossesses an asset, which has been financed, because the purchaser fails to make payments. When this situation arises, there are tax consequences for two sides—the debtor and the creditor.

The creditor is deemed to have purchased the property for the amount of principal owing on the asset, plus any expenses required to protect the creditor's interest in the asset. This forms the cost of the asset for purposes of computing its ACB, and may result in a capital gain or capital loss in the future when the asset is actually disposed of. The creditor will also be able to deduct any accrued interest reported in a prior year that will have already been reported but not received. The debt is deemed to have been disposed of at its cost amount. If the debt is not extinguished by the foreclosure, then the debt is deemed to have been re-acquired with an ACB of nil. A future sale will result in a capital gain in this case.

When a debtor has a property repossessed, the property is deemed to have been disposed of for the principal amount owing at the time of repossession plus interest. This may result in a gain or loss.

Example: Judy purchased a rental property for $300,000, with a mortgage of $285,000. Several years later, the property was repossessed. The amount owing at the time of the repossession was $305,000, made up of principal of $280,000, unpaid interest owing was $10,000 and fees were $15,000. How is this reported?

Capital gain = $305,000 (Proceeds of Disposition) – $300,000 (ACB) = $5,000

Those taxpayers who suffer a mortgage or conditional sales repossession may exclude any capital gain realized as a result of this transaction from net income for the purposes of the calculation of the Age Amount, GST/HST Tax Credit, Child Tax Benefits (CTB) and any Social Benefits Repayment.

Bad Debts: What are the tax consequences when you assume someone else's debt? A bad debt is written off at its adjusted cost base unless you make an election for it to be considered a capital loss, providing the money was loaned for business purposes or on the sale of a capital property to an arm's length party. In this case, you can claim the capital loss in the year the debt went bad, but only up to the capital gain you previously reported on the sale.

If you later recover the bad debt which you claimed as a capital loss, claim a capital gain in the year of recovery.

Debt Forgiveness. If you have a commercial debt obligation—a debt on which interest would have been deductible in computing income from a business or property—and that loan is forgiven, you'll have a tax consequence. This may affect other provisions on the tax return. Professional help is recommended because the consequences can affect your tax filings for many years to come. What's important is you have enough knowledge to ask good questions should this happen to you.

 CHECK IT OUT | **What is the consequence of debt forgiveness?** Where the forgiven amount cannot be allocated to a specific asset (which is often the case for a commercial loan) the forgiven amount is used to reduce the debtor's other "tax preferences" in the following order:

- Non-capital loss balances (except for allowable business investment losses)
- Farm losses
- Restricted farm losses
- Net capital losses
- Depreciable property's capital cost and Undepreciated Capital Cost (UCC) balances
- Cumulative eligible capital
- Resource expenditure balances
- Adjusted Cost Base (ACB) of certain capital properties
- Current year capital losses

In the case of *Business Investment Losses* from small business corporations, reductions due to debt forgiveness are applied to the earliest such loss first. It is also possible to transfer unused balances of forgiven debt to another taxpayer.

Assumption of Debt. Where another party assumes a debt, the debt is not considered to be forgiven. Therefore, in this situation, the debt forgiveness rules above do not come into effect.

Significant Dates in Capital Gains Taxation and Valuation Days

- Prior to 1972: Capital gains were not taxable in Canada
- December 22, 1971: Valuation day for Canadian publicly traded securities
- December 31, 1971: Valuation day for all other capital property
- January 1, 1972: Capital gains inclusion rate is **50%**; two tax-exempt principal residences allowed per household comprised of a legally married couple.
- December 31, 1981: Valuation day for family homes—one tax exempt principal residence allowed per household comprised of a legally married couple.
- January 1, 1985: Capital gains deduction is introduced
- January 1, 1987: Capital gains deduction is capped at $100,000, but the Super Exemption of $500,000 is introduced for qualifying farms and small business corporations.
- January 1, 1988: Capital gains inclusion rate increases to **66⅔%**
- January 1, 1990: Capital gain inclusion rate increases to **75%**
- January 1, 1993: One tax-exempt principal residence per common law couple of the opposite sex
- February 22, 1994: Capital gains election date, which occurred on the elimination of the $100,000 Capital Gains Deduction
- January 1, 1998: Same sex couples could *elect* conjugal status with the result that only one tax exempt residence is allowed per couple.
- February 27, 2000: Capital gains inclusion rate drops to **66⅔%**

- October 18, 2000: Capital gains inclusion rate drops to **50%**
- January 1, 2001: Same sex couples are now limited to one tax exempt residence per conjugal relationship (no election)
- May 1, 2006: Qualified fishing property allowed for CGD purposes
- March 18, 2007: Capital gains exemption increases to **$750,000**

 The Bottom Line | The buying and selling of assets can help you build your family's wealth. You'll want to control the timing of those transactions for the best tax consequences. Make sure you keep a current list of valuations handy. Also, a personal net worth statement filed in your safety deposit box every year will make life much easier for your executors, who must compute gains or losses on your final return due to a deemed disposition.

31

Personal Residences

Did you just buy your first home? Inherit a second home when your grandmother passed away? Are you wondering about the taxes on the big increase in value on your family cottage? What about the rental income you get for that spare room downstairs?

These are common questions about one of the most significant assets Canadians have—their principal residence.

 CHECK IT OUT | **What's a principal residence?** It's the tax-exempt one. When you sell it, any gains you make are completely tax-free. A principal residence can be any of these:

- a house, cottage, condo, duplex, apartment;
- a trailer that is "ordinarily inhabited" by a taxpayer or some family member at some time during the year;
- except where the principal residence is a share in a co-operative housing corporation, the principal residence includes the land immediately subjacent to the housing unit and up to one-half hectare of adjacent property that contributes to the use of the housing unit as a residence; or
- if the lot size exceeds one-half hectare, it may be included in the principal residence if it can be shown to be necessary for the use of the housing unit. This is most commonly the case when the farm home is sold. Additional land required because of the location of the home may also be eligible for the exemption but land and buildings used principally for the operation of the farm will not qualify.

One Per Household. The principal residence is an important concept because each household (defined as an adult taxpayer and/or that person's spouse) may choose one property as a principal residence for each year that it is owned and avoid a capital gain when that property is sold. But what happens if you own both a home and a cottage? Which one would you choose?

One Property Only. This is the simplest scenario. If the family owned only one property and lived in it in every year while they owned it, there will be no taxable capital gain on the property. But do you have to report this sale. Technically, the *Income Tax Act* requires that a taxpayer file a *"principal residence designation"* for the year in which the property is sold using form T2091 *Designation of a Property as a Principal Residence by an Individual (Other Than a Personal Trust)*, administratively CRA doesn't require this. No reporting is required when you sell a property that was your principal residence for the entire time it was owned.

No Losses. Recall that a principal residence is considered to be *"personal use property,"* and so any loss on disposition is deemed by to be nil. No reporting required here either.

No Capital Cost Allowance. There's a special rule and a trap for software users whenever a statement for rental or business income from a home-based business is prepared. Often tax software will automatically calculate capital cost allowance on the building in the background. You will want to override this to preserve that exempt status for any of your personal residences. That's very important because the claiming of *CCA* on any of your residences, even if only a small portion of the home is used in a home-based business, will compromise your tax exemption on that part of the home.

More than one residence. Where a family owns more than one property and both properties are used by the family at some time during the year, the calculation may become slightly more difficult. Back in the day, (for periods including 1971 to 1981) each spouse could declare one of the properties as their principal residence, which allowed a family to shelter gains from tax on a home and a cottage for example.

But starting in 1982, only one property per year can be designated as a principal residence for the family. This means that any accrued capital gain on one of the properties (that is not designated as a principal residence) will be ultimately subject to tax when sold.

This is where Form T2091 *Designation of a Property as a Principal Residence by an Individual (Other Than a Personal Trust)* comes in. This form may not be available in your tax software so check that out. If it's not there, print it out from the CRA website.

Form T2091 is used to calculate the exempt portion of a capital gain on a principal residence. Here's how it's done:

1. *Calculate the gain.* The capital gain on the property is first calculated, using regular rules for capital gains and losses.

2. *Calculate the exempt part of the gain.* Once this has been done, the exempt portion is calculated, and then subtracted from the capital gain. The exempt portion of the gain is calculated as follows:

Total gain x $\dfrac{\text{(Number of years designated as Principal Residence + 1)}}{\text{Number of years the property was owned}}$

3. *Note the "+ 1."* Because the numerator in the exemption formula adds 1 to the number of years that a property is designated as a principal residence, it is only necessary to designate a property for one year less than the total number of years it was owned to exempt the entire gain. This is because two residences will be owned in the year that the taxpayer moves from residence to another.

Case Study | Planning Sale of Home and Cottage

Phil and Sylvia have owned their home in the city for 20 years and their cottage at the lake for 10 years in that 20-year period. The cottage was sold for a substantial sum last year—$500,000—despite the fact that they only paid $150,000 for it. They did not report it for tax purposes, because they designated it as their tax-exempt residence for the entire ownership period.

This year they are thinking of selling their home, which cost them $225,000. They think they can get a price of $650,000. Will any part of the gain be tax exempt?

The answer is yes. That's because there was a period of time before they owned the cottage in which the exemption would qualify. Phil and Sylvia would have to complete Form T2091 to take this into account.

The calculations would look like this:

1. The capital gain on the city home is $425,000 (= $650,000 less $225,000).

2. Tax-exempt portion: Designate the city home as principal residence for 10 years, as only 10 years of the ownership period included the cottage.

To calculate the exempt portion, the number of years the house is designated as the principal residence plus 1 (10 + 1 = 11) is divided by the total number of years the house was owned (20 years).

The exempt portion of the gain: (11/20 x 425,000) = $233,750.

The taxable portion of the gain: $425,000 − 233,750 = $191,250, and 50% of this is taxable on Schedule 3 ($95,625).

Capital Gains Election. The taxable capital gain is further reduced by any capital gains election made to use up the $100,000 Capital Gains Deduction on February 22, 1994. Look for *Form T664 Capital Gains Election* from the 1994 return to find the amount of the election. Where the capital gains election was made, use Form T2091(IND)-WS *Principal Residence Worksheet* in addition to T2091. Warning: This is complicated. Best to have a tax professional help.

Change In Use of A Principal Residence. When a taxpayer starts using a principal residence for income-producing purposes (for example, as a rental, or for a home office) you'll need to take care of the following details to prepare for a future capital gain:

- *The Fair Market Value (FMV)* of the property is required as it is considered to have been disposed of at this amount and then immediately reacquired at the same amount.
- *Personal to Business Use.* The gain resulting, if any, would be nil if the home was used in each year before this as a principal residence. However, if the taxpayer owns another residence that has appreciated more in value, you'll want to value this property on change of use, as you will report a taxable disposition.
- *Business Use to Personal Use.* If the property is converted back to be used as a principal residence only in the future, the same FMV assessment must be done as there is another deemed disposition and reacquisition of the property to account for. Tax consequences are then assessed, possibly resulting in a capital gain or loss. Note that a loss would be allowed only on the land (the building is depreciable property) because during this period, the property was not personal-use property.

Elections. *Two special elections can help you avoid the tax consequences above.*

Deferral to Actual Disposition (S. 45(2) Election). When a principal residence is converted from personal use to income-producing use, an election may be made to ignore the deemed disposition normally required to be reported under the change of use rules above. You can instead choose to defer any capital gain/loss until the time of actual disposition, or at any time you choose to rescind the election.

Example: In 2012, Liam decided to make renovations and convert his basement into a rental apartment. Normally this would mean that he had disposed of part of his principal residence and acquired a rental property. However, Liam may elect to defer the recognition of the disposition until he actually sells the property.

Moving and Renting. In addition, you can choose to designate the property as a personal residence for up to four years after moving out of the house; longer if your employer requires you to relocate to a temporary residence that is at least 40 kilometres away. If you move back to your original home before the end of the calendar year in which employment is terminated, you'll avoid any capital gain.

This election is made by attaching a letter to the tax return, noting that an election is being made under S. 45(2). The election should be signed, and a description of the property should be attached. If you're filing your return electronically, send the election letter to CRA by mail. But do observe these rules:

- Capital Cost Allowance (CCA) must not be claimed.
- No other property can be designated a principal residence at the same time
- You must have been a resident or must be deemed to be resident of Canada.
- Any rental income earned on the property while you were absent is to be reported in the normal manner (See next chapter)

Rental to Personal Residence (S. 45(3) Election). It is also possible to make a special election when a taxpayer converts a rental property to a principal residence. In that case, there is a deemed disposition at fair market value, but the capital gain is deferred to be reported on the actual disposition of the property. *This is only allowable, however, if no capital cost allowance was claimed on the property since 1984.* Follow the same election procedures as described above.

No Attribution. You may wish to purchase a home for your 19-year-old son and daughter so they can have their own tax-exempt principal residence. There is no Attribution Rule because the child is an adult and there will be no tax avoidance on the subsequent tax-exempt sale. So that's a good move.

 The Bottom Line | Your home is your castle. The principal residence exemption makes it a tax exempt one if you follow proper procedures on change of use or when you have more than one personal residence. It's important to update your property values so that you can make sound decisions about the taxes you may need to pay when that great offer to sell comes along. Also remember to look for evidence of a 1994 Capital Gains Election so you don't understate your adjusted cost base on the taxable residence.

32

Rental Property

Do you collect rent? Would you like to rent out your basement suite? Newly single and thinking about taking in a university student? If so, you will want to get your documentation ready for a change in your tax filing.

Your tax software will do a great job helping you calculate the numbers you enter, but you'll need to keep your rental agreement on file, as well as back up for retrieval at tax time: income record, expenses and your valuation of the property when you changed its use from personal rental.

Look for *Form T776 Statement of Rental Income*. You can use this as a printed checklist behind which to attach your receipts.

✓ **CHECK IT OUT** | **How do you report rental income?** Here are some basic rules:
- *Use a calendar year.* Income and expenses will be reported on a calendar year basis. *Accrual accounting* (report income when receivable and expenses when payable) is supposed to be used but administratively CRA will accept cash basis accounting for most individuals so long as the cash income reporting does not differ significantly from the accrual basis.
- *Report gross rental income.* Do open a separate bank account for your rental income and expense transactions.
- *Charge rent at FMV.* You may not be able to write off losses if you can't justify that you are charging rent at fair market value. Take newspaper clippings and other proof of rentals in the area and add to your permanent records so you can make a case for what you are charging, especially if you're renting to a related person.

- Record *income reporting.* Advance payments of rent can be included in income according to the years they relate to. Lease cancellation payments received are also included in rental income.
- Record *expense reporting.* To deduct operating expenses from rental income, there must be a reasonable expectation of profit on an annual basis. Fully deductible operating expenses include maintenance, repairs, supplies, interest, taxes. Partially deductible expenses could include the business portion of auto expenses and meal and entertainment expenses incurred. But this is where many tax filers make mistakes. Take note of these traps:
  - **Trap #1** Maintenance and repairs are 100% deductible; improvements over the original condition or that extend the useful life of the asset are added to cost base because they are capital in nature. Put those expenses on the Capital Cost Allowance (CCA) statements instead.
  - **Trap #2** Land is not a depreciable asset. Separate the cost of the land from the cost of the buildings for the purpose of your CCA statement.
  - **Trap #3** The deduction for CCA is always taken at your option so if your assets, particularly the building, are appreciating in value rather than depreciating, you may wish to forego the claim to avoid Recapture in income later.
  - **Trap #4** CCA deductions cannot be used to create or increase a rental loss. This rule is applied to all rental properties you may have together. Thus, if you have more than one property, CCA may be claimed to create a loss on one property so long as you do not have a rental loss on all properties combined.
  - **Trap #5** Don't claim auto expenses for visits to collect rents if you own only one rental property. However, if you personally do the maintenance and repairs for a nearby property, and use your car to carry the tools to do so, the claim will be allowed.
  - **Trap #6** Don't deduct any personal living expenses.
  - **Trap #7** Family member rentals may be exempt. If you are renting to your youngest son, Charlie, for the cost of the groceries, there is no expectation of profit. Don't expect to be able to deduct a rental loss against other income, but in this case, unless there is a demonstrable profit motive, you don't need to report the income, either.

✓ **CHECK IT OUT** | **Are there more deductible rental expenses?** Aside from the above, common deductible operating expenses include:

- *Advertising*—Amounts paid to advertise the availability of the rental property.
- *Condominium Fees*—Applicable to the period when the rental condo was available.
- *Insurance*—If the insurance is prepaid for future years, claim only the portion that applies to the rental year, unless you are using cash basis accounting.
- *Landscaping*—Deduct in the year paid.

- *Lease Cancellation Payments By Landlord*—Deduct these amounts over the term of the lease, including renewal periods. In the case of dispositions at arm's length, a final amount may be deducted, but based on the current capital gains inclusion rate (50%). The full amount of the lease cancellation payment may be deducted on a sale if the building was considered to be inventory rather than capital property.
- *Legal, Accounting and Other Professional Fees*—Note the following:
  - Legal fees to prepare leases or to collect rent are deductible.
  - Legal fees to acquire the property are added to cost base.
  - Legal fees on the sale of the property are outlays and expenses which will reduce any capital gain on the sale.
  - Accounting fees to prepare statements, keep books, or prepare the tax return are deductible.
- *Maintenance and Repairs*—Costs of regular maintenance and minor repairs are deductible. For major repairs, it must be determined if the cost is a current expense (restoration) or capital in nature (improvement).
- *Management and Administration Fees*—If you pay a third party to manage or otherwise look after some aspect of the property, the amount paid is deductible. Note that if a caretaker is given a suite in an apartment block as compensation for caretaking, a T4 slip must be issued to report the fair market value of the rent as employment income.
- *Mortgage Interest*—Interest on a mortgage to purchase the property plus any interest on additional loans to improve the rental property may be deducted, provided you can show there is a reasonable expectation of profit from the revenue property. Note:
  - If an additional mortgage is taken out against the equity in the property and the proceeds are used for some other purpose, the mortgage interest is not deductible as a rental expense, but may be deductible as a carrying charge if the proceeds were used to earn investment income.
  - Other charges relating to the acquisition of a mortgage (banking fees, for example) are not deductible in the year paid, but can be amortized over a five-year period starting at the time they were incurred.
  - If the interest costs relate to the acquisition of depreciable property, you may elect to add the interest to the capital cost of the asset rather than deduct it in the year paid. This will be beneficial if, for example, the property generates a rental loss and you cannot use that loss to reduce your taxes owing.
- *Office and Other Supplies*—Office and other supplies used up in earning rental income are deductible as are home office expenses in situations where you use the office to keep books or serve tenants.
- *Property Taxes*—These are deductible.
- *Renovations For the Disabled*—Costs incurred to make the rental property accessible to individuals with a mobility impairment may be fully deducted.

- *Utilities*—If costs are paid by the landlord and not reimbursed by the tenant, they will be deductible. Costs charged to tenants are deductible if amounts collected are included in rental income.

Multiple Owners. When two or more taxpayers jointly own a revenue property, it is necessary to determine whether they own the property as co-owners or as partners in a partnership. If a partnership exists, all the partners are subject to the same CCA claim. Then a partnership allocation of net profits is made. If a co-ownership exists, each owner can claim CCA individually on his/her share of the capital costs.

 The Bottom Line | Rental properties can increase wealth in two ways: by providing cash flow to pay for the mortgage and building net worth with an increase in value of your investment. However, revenue properties are often audited, so be sure you stay out of the traps identified.

33

Deducting Carrying Charges

Likely the most missed tax deduction is the safety deposit box… few people remember to claim it at tax time. A small but mighty carrying charge, over a 10-year adjustment period it can amount to several hundred dollars in your pocket, so if you missed it, make the adjustment. These charges, however, are not deductible on the Quebec provincial return.

 CHECK IT OUT | **What carrying charges can be deducted on Schedule 4?** Following is a checklist of commonly missed items:

Accounting Fees. These are claimable if they relate to business income or investments. In the case of investors, the fees pertaining to the income tax schedule for investments count, unless you otherwise hire an accountant to help with accounting for your wealth management or business activities.

Canada Savings Bond Payroll Deductions. The difference between the face value of the CSB you bought at work and the total you paid is a deductible carrying charge.

Example: Monthly deduction of $35 x 12 = $420
      Face value of bond $400
      Carrying charge $ 20

Employer-Provided Loans. The interest benefit from a low- or non-interest-bearing loan is deductible if you use the money to buy investments including the employer's stock. Look to your T4 slip for the amount in Box 36.

Exploration and Development Expenses. A separate line is devoted on the return for the expenses of investment in petroleum, natural gas or mining ventures. Form T1229 *Statement of Resource Expenses and Depletion Allowance* must be completed and the total from Part III posted to Line 124. These expenses will be allocated to investors in petroleum, natural gas or mining ventures. The amounts allocated to you will be shown on a T5 slip, a T101 slip, or a T5013 (or T5013A) slip. Enter the box numbers and your software will post to the T1229 form and make the claim on Line 124.

Interest on Investment Loans—Traceable Use. Are you using your operating line to buy the kids a big screen TV and also to fund your investment activities? This may not be a good idea. It's important to keep your borrowings separate and traceable if you want to write off the interest costs as a carrying charge. The onus is on you to establish that the borrowed funds are being used for the purposes of earning income from a business (claim on business statement) or from property (claim on Schedule 4) or from for your rental (claim on your Rental Property statement).

Borrowing for Exempt or Registered Funds. No interest is deductible if the loan is made to acquire property which produces exempt income or to acquire an interest in a life insurance policy, RRSP, RESP, RDSP or TFSA.

Borrowing to Buy Stocks. In addition, if the investment does not carry a stated interest or dividend rate, which might be the case with some common shares or mutual funds, the interest costs on an investment loan may not be deductible. CRA will generally allow interest costs on funds borrowed to buy common shares to be deductible if there is a possibility of receiving dividends, whether or not they are actually received, but each case may be assessed individually upon audit.

Diminished Asset Values. If the source of income for which you borrowed no longer exists or has substantially diminished because the investment has lost significant value, you may continue to write off the interest on the loan as if the underlying asset still existed. The amount considered "not to be lost" must however be traceable to the loan you are paying off. If you dispose of the asset at a loss, you may continue to write off the interest costs so long as the proceeds were used to pay down the loan amount.

If the property was acquired by a creditor for a reduction in debt owing, this reduction in debt is subtracted from the amount of the loan on which you can make an interest deduction.

Investment Counsel Fees. Fees paid to a financial, investment or wealth advisor or advisory firm, other than commissions, are claimable if they are paid for advice on buying or selling securities or for the administration of those assets, if this is the principal business of this individual or firm. Note that fees paid to a person related to you are only deductible to the extent that they are reasonable based on the amount of work done and the time spent in doing it.

Fees paid to stockbrokers are not deductible for these purposes unless the broker also provides investment portfolio management and administration services for which a separate fee is charged. Also not deductible are fees paid for newspaper, newsletter or magazine subscriptions or fees paid to a trustee of an RRSP or TFSA.

Life Insurance Policy Loans. If you borrow against your cash value in your life insurance policy to then invest the money, you can claim the interest paid as a carrying charge. If the interest is not repaid but rather deducted from the value of the insurance, you'll need to complete form *T2210 Verification of Life Insurance Policy Loan Interest.*

Student Loan Interest. Claim this as a non-refundable tax credit on Line 319.

 The Bottom Line | If you have borrowed to invest, or paid investment counsel fees, and keep your records in a safety deposit box, chances are you'll have a deduction against all other income on Line 221 Carrying charges. This deduction will reduce net income, thereby increasing your tax credits as well as reducing your taxes payable.

34

T-Slip Entry Guide

T3 Slip

I✦I Canada Revenue Agency / Agence du revenu du Canada		Year / Année		**Statement of Trust Income Allocations and Designations** / État des revenus de fiducie (répartitions et attributions) **T3**

Actual amount of eligible dividends / Montant réel des dividendes déterminés	Taxable amount of eligible dividends / Montant imposable des dividendes déterminés	Dividend tax credit for eligible dividends / Crédit d'impôt pour dividendes déterminés	Capital gains / Gains en capital	Capital gains eligible for deduction / Gains en capital admissibles pour déduction
49	50	51	21	30

Actual amount of dividends other than eligible dividends / Montant réel des dividendes autres que des dividendes déterminés	Taxable amount of dividends other than eligible dividends / Montant imposable des dividendes autres que des dividendes déterminés	Dividend tax credit for dividends other than eligible dividends / Crédit d'impôt pour dividendes autres que des dividendes déterminés	Other income / Autres revenus	Trust year end / Fin d'année de la fiducie
23	32	39	26	Year / Année — Month / Mois

Other information (see the back) / Autres renseignements (lisez le verso)

Box / Case	Amount / Montant	Box / Case	Amount / Montant	Footnotes – Notes

Recipient's name (last name first) and address – Nom, prénom et adresse du bénéficiaire

→

Trust's name and address – Nom et adresse de la fiducie

Recipient identification number / Numéro d'identification du bénéficiaire	Account number / Numéro de compte	Report code / Code du genre de feuillet	Beneficiary code / Code du bénéficiaire	**For information, see the back. Pour obtenir des renseignements, lisez le verso.**
12	14 T	16	18	

T3 (12)

Box	Where do I put it?	What is it?	What else is relevant?
21	Schedule 3, Line 176	Capital gains	Your software will subtract the amount in Box 30 to get the amount of capital gains that are not eligible for the capital gains deduction. If any portion of this amount is foreign non-business income, a footnote will indicate the amount that is to be entered on form T2209 to calculate your Foreign Tax Credit.
22	Line 130	Lump-sum pension benefits	This amount is eligible to be transferred to the taxpayer's RRSP.
23		Actual amount of dividends other than eligible dividends	This amount is used to calculate the amount shown in Box 32. Do not include this amount on the return.
24	Line 135 and Form T2209	Foreign business income	Your software should post this to Form T2209—Federal Foreign Tax Credits, to determine the credit for taxes shown in Box 33. You will likely have to enter the source country so the foreign tax credit can be calculated.
25	Schedule 4 and Line 433 on Schedule 1	Foreign non-business income	Your software should post this to Form T2209—Federal Foreign Tax Credits, to determine the credit for taxes shown in Box 33. You will likely have to enter the source country so the foreign tax credit can be calculated.
26	Line 130	Other income	Your software should reduce the amount in Box 26 by the amount in Box 31 and enter the result on Line 130. If a footnote indicates that a portion of the amount in this box is for eligible capital property, enter that amount on Line 173 of Schedule 3.
30	Schedule 3	Capital gains eligible for the capital gains deduction	The footnotes will tell you how much is for qualified small business corporation shares—to be posted to Line 107 of Schedule 3—and the amount that is for qualified farm or fishing property—to be posted to Line 110 of Schedule 3.
31	Line 115	Qualifying pension income	This amount qualifies for the Pension Income Amount on Line 314 and thus for pension income splitting.
32	Line 120	Taxable amount of dividends other than eligible dividends	This is 125% of the amount in Box 23. This amount is added to the taxable amount of eligible dividends and the total is reported in Line 120. This amount is also reported in Line 180.

Box	Where do I put it?	What is it?	What else is relevant?
33	T2209	Foreign business income taxes paid	Your software should post this to Form T2209— Federal Foreign Tax Credits, to determine the credit for taxes shown in Box 33. You will likely have to enter the source country so the foreign tax credit can be calculated.
34	Schedule 1	Foreign non-business income taxes paid	Your software should post this to Form T2209— Federal Foreign Tax Credits, to determine the credit for taxes shown in Box 33. You will likely have to enter the source country so the foreign tax credit can be calculated.
35	Line 130	Eligible death benefits	This amount may be reduced by the $10,000 exemption. If your software posts the full amount to Line 130, subtract the $10,000 manually.
37	Schedule 3	Insurance Segregated Fund Capital Losses	Your software will post this amount as a loss (negative amount) on Line 176 of Schedule 3.
38	Line 456	Part XII.2 tax credit	This is a credit for taxes already paid by the trust.
39	Schedule 1, Line 425	Dividend tax credit for other than eligible dividends	This is the credit for the dividends reported in Box 23 (and shown grossed-up in Box 32). This amount is added to the dividend tax credit for eligible dividends reported in Box 51 and the total is reflected in Line 425.
40	T2038(IND)	Investment tax credit—cost	Use this amount in completing T2038(IND)— Investment Tax Credit (Individuals).
41	T2038(IND)	Investment tax credit	Use this amount in completing T2038(IND)— Investment Tax Credit (Individuals).
42		Amount resulting in cost base adjustment	This amount is not entered on the current year return, but is used to reduce the ACB of the mutual fund units owned by the taxpayer.
45	T1129	Other credits	Use the footnoted amount to complete Form T1129—Newfoundland Scientific Research and Experimental Development Tax Credit or the Form T1232—Yukon Research and Development Tax Credit. The credit will be transferred to Line 479.
46		Pension income qualifying for an eligible annuity for a minor	This amount is already included in Box 26.

Box	Where do I put it?	What is it?	What else is relevant?
47		Retiring allowance eligible for transfer to an RRSP or RPP	This amount is already included in Box 26.
48	Schedule 9	Eligible amount of charitable donations	This amount will be posted to the appropriate line of Schedule 9, depending on the type of donation.
49		Actual amount of eligible dividends	This amount is used to calculate the amount shown in Box 50. Do not include this amount on the return.
50	Line 120	Taxable amount of eligible dividends	This is 138% of the amount in Box 49. This amount is added to the taxable amount of other than eligible dividends and the total is reported in Line 120. This amount is also reported in Line 180.
51	Schedule 1, Line 425	Dividend tax credit for eligible dividends	This is the credit for the dividends reported in Box 49 (and shown grossed-up in Box 50). This amount is added to the dividend tax credit for other than eligible dividends reported in Box 32 and the total is reflected in Line 425.

T5 Slip

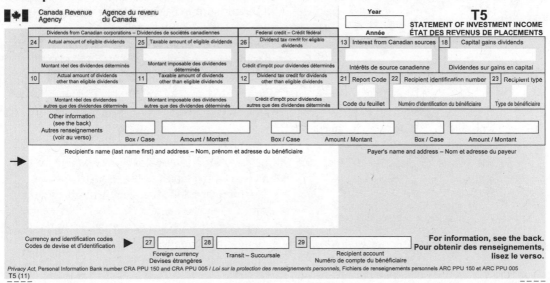

Box	Where do I put it?	What is it?	What else is relevant?
10		Actual amount of dividends other than eligible dividends	This amount is used to calculate the amount shown in Box 11. Do not include this amount on the return.
11	Line 120	Taxable amount of dividends other than eligible dividends	This is 125% of the amount in Box 10. This amount is added to the taxable amount of eligible dividends and the total is reported in Line 120. This amount is also reported in Line 180.
12	Schedule 1, Line 425	Dividend tax credit for dividends other than eligible dividends	This is the credit for the dividends reported in Box 10 (and shown grossed-up in Box 11). This amount is added to the dividend tax credit for eligible dividends reported in box 51 and the total is reflected in Line 425.
13	Schedule 4	Interest from Canadian sources	Carries forward to Line 121.
14	Schedule 4	Other income from Canadian Sources	Carries forward to Line 121.
15	Schedule 4	Foreign income	Carries forward to Line 121. Use this amount in calculating the Foreign Tax Credit on T2209. You may have to specify the country for the software to calculate your foreign tax credit.
16	T2209	Foreign taxes paid	Use this amount in calculating the Foreign Tax Credit on Form T2209 to calculate the Foreign Tax Credit. You may have to specify the country for the software to calculate your foreign tax credit.
17	Line 104 or Line 121	Royalties from Canadian sources	If the amount is from a work or invention, it will be posted to Line 104, otherwise it will be posted to Line 121.
18	Schedule 3, Line 174	Capital gains dividends	
19	Line 115 or Schedule 4	Accrued income from annuities	If the taxpayer is over 64 or received this amount as a result of the death of the spouse, it will be included on Line 115. It is eligible for the Pension Income Amount on Line 314. Otherwise, it should be included on Schedule 4, Section II as interest.
20		Amount eligible for resource allowance deduction	This amount is already included in Box 17 so do not report it again.
21		Report code	Indicates whether the slip is Original, Amended or Cancelled.

Box	Where do I put it?	What is it?	What else is relevant?
22		Recipient identification number	For an individual, this is the taxpayer's SIN.
23		Recipient type	Indicates "1" for an individual or "2" for a joint account.
24		Actual amount of eligible dividends	This amount is used to calculate the amount shown in Box 25. Do not include this amount on the return.
25	Line 120	Taxable amount of eligible dividends	This is 138% of the amount in Box 24. This amount is added to the taxable amount of other than eligible dividends and the total is reported in Line 120. This amount is also reported in Line 180.
26	Schedule 1, Line 425	Dividend tax credit for eligible dividends	This is the credit for the dividends reported in Box 24 (and shown grossed-up in Box 25). This amount is added to the dividend tax credit for other than eligible dividends reported in Box 32 and the total is reflected in Line 425.
27		Foreign currency	ISO country code if amounts not in Canadian dollars. If you have a code in this box and your software does not include this box, you will have to convert the amounts on your slip manually to Canadian dollars.
28		Transit	Recipient's transit code or branch identification number if a bank or similar institution.
29		Recipient account	Recipient's account or policy number.

<hr />

PART 5

Pensioners—Where the Action is!

There is, no doubt, this is where the action is when it comes to the future of tax preparation in Canada. The baby boomers are moving into the pension profile, together with their parents, and both groups are living longer. An increasing number of people in Canada are centenarians—in fact the rate of growth for those who reach 100 is the second highest of all age groups in Canada-after those who turn 60-64.

What's New

The age of eligibility for Old Age Security (OAS) and Guaranteed Income Supplements (GIS) will be gradually increased to 67 from 65, starting in April 2023, with full implementation by January 2029. But, starting in 2013, you can elect to defer taking your OAS income for up to five years to build a bigger pension for later. OAS income will get clawed back when net income exceeds $69,562 in 2012. So, you'll want to plan your income streams to come in under this number if possible.

Hard Copy

It's possible you will need to make quarterly tax instalment remittances for the first time as your income profile changes from employed to pensioner. That means your relationship with CRA will change: you'll get new hard copy reminding you to pay, regularly. Also, collecting receipts for new costs, like medical expenditures, can become more daunting, as they increase with age. This may all happen as you travel more, so organizing yourself around new tax compliance will become more important. You may also be a Power of Attorney or Executor for others, which means you'll be in charge of their hard copy, too.

Software Tips

While reporting pension income sources on the tax return is easy—just enter the numbers off the slips in your software program—there can be lots of them: The T4(OAS), the T4A(P) for CPP Benefits, the T4(A) for private periodic pensions, T4RSP for RRSP withdrawals, the T4RIF for Registered Retirement Income Fund withdrawals. You need to find software that "optimizes" pension income splitting opportunities, which can save you tens of thousands of dollars each year.

Tax Sleuthing

The devil is in the details for pensioners. Statistically, as people age, they give more to charity, they look after others in their home, and they gain access to new tax credits like the Amount for Eligible Dependant, the Caregiver Amount and, of course, medical expenses. Seniors who go back to school will find new rewards in the claiming of non-refundable tax credits, too.

Tax Pro Alert

Saving money on income taxes and the capital you have accumulated is critical, especially when returns on investments are lower than the rate of inflation. You'll want somebody who specializes in tax planning for boomers. Because most of the 50Plus crowd will live off a combination of actively and passively earned income sources, their tax returns can be complicated. This is about paying the least taxes on each income source and planning to preserve capital with tax efficiency. See a tax pro before withdrawing large amounts from your accounts or transferring assets.

36

OAS Pension Reforms

People can retire at any age, but it is increasingly rare for people to simply go from earning income from employment or self-employment directly to withdrawing income from investments and other sources including pensions. After the financial crisis, and as a result of changing demographics, most people will continue to work well into their 60's and possibly 70's, if they can maintain their health.

Close to five million Canadians are reporting Old Age Security (OAS) income today, and over six million tax filers are reporting Canada Pension Plan (CPP) benefits. But recent pension reforms are providing important new planning opportunities that started in 2012. This has been bewildering to some, who confuse the "univcrsal" OAS benefits (everyone who is age 65 may qualify for OAS so long as they've been resident in Canada 10 years) with benefit payments from the CPP, which come from contributions by the individual and their employer throughout a working life.

How much is the OAS pension? OAS amounts are paid monthly but they are adjusted for inflation every quarter. At the time of writing, the monthly benefit was just under $545 and the annual OAS pension for the full year was $6,510.60 for the year.

The average life expectancy in Canada is 78.5 years for men and 83.1 years for women. Assuming retirement at age 65 when OAS becomes payable, men will receive OAS for 13.5 years and women for 18.1 years. Therefore, OAS is worth, on average, $88,000 for men and $118,000 for women. For an average couple, that means $206,000.

The OAS income is taxable, reported on a T4 (OAS) slip and on Line 113 of your tax return. However, it is offset by the Age Amount on Line 301 of Schedule 1.

CHECK IT OUT | **What is the Age Amount?** The Age Amount is a non-refundable tax credit found on Line 301 of Schedule 1. It is $6,720 in 2012 and is phased out when net income on Line 236 exceeds $33,884, by 15% for every dollar over this. If your income exceeds $78,684, your age amount will be zero. Your tax software will automatically calculate this for you:

Example: Rupert is 66. His net income in 2012 was $65,000. His federal Age Amount will be: $6,720 – [($65,000 – $33,884) x 15%] = $2,052.60. In real dollar terms, this saves him $307.89, assuming he lives in Ontario (where his provincial age amount was zero because his income is too high).

Why do you need to know this? You're often in control of the timing of new taxable income sources. If, for example, your income is largely comprised of dividends from your small business corporation, remember they will be "grossed up" for tax purposes, which means you may lose your Age Amount sooner than if you planned to earn interest or capital gains from your investments, for example.

Example: Helen is 68. If she earned $50,000 in interest income (in addition to $6,510 OAS and $10,890 CPP) her net income would be $67,400 so her federal Age Amount would be $6,720 – [($67,400 – $33,884) x 15%] = $1,692.60.

If, instead of the interest, she earned $50,000 in dividends from public corporations, her net income would be $86,400 (it's much higher because the $50,000 is grossed up by 138% to $69,000). She would not qualify for an Age Amount now and her taxes would rise by $6,600, mostly because she is now in the clawback zone for Old Age Security.

Age Amount Transfers. In addition, if you have a spouse who has a low income, you'll be able to transfer the Age Amount to your return, doubling up your tax benefits. Your tax software will do this for you automatically on Schedule 2 and Line 326. That will save you over $1,000.

Example: Eunice's income is $15,000, consisting of OAS and RRIF income. Her husband Gerald's income is $45,000, including CPP, OAS and RRIF income. Because Eunice does not need her full Age Amount to reduce her taxes to zero, she can transfer the unused amount ($4,542) to Gerald. This saves Gerald $681 federally, plus $15 provincially (assuming they live in Ontario).

Managing the OAS Clawback. Here is another important fact: The OAS pension is income-tested; that is, you will repay some or all of it if your net income exceeds another "clawback" limit. Similar to the Age Amount clawback, this time, you'll have to repay the OAS, if your net income is just over $69,562 in 2012. The OAS is completely lost when net income exceeds $112,966.

Software Tips. Your tax software takes care of all the clawback calculations for you, but you still need to be aware of them because this *Social Benefits Repayment* is a tax that can be avoided if you structure your income properly. There's also a lot of entries, which may confuse you. First, you will find the calculation of the clawback is entered on Line 235 as a deduction, which reduces net income. The actual repayment is entered on Line 422 and is added to your federal and provincial taxes payable on Line 435.

Worse, any repayment you make on your tax return this year will reduce the OAS monthly benefit you will qualify to receive in July. Finally, the reduction in your OAS will be shown on your T4A(OAS) as a "recovery tax," which is entered on Line 437 Income Tax Deducted.

 Case Study | **Planning to Maximize OAS and Minimize Instalment Payments**

Joanne is a single, senior manager who makes $85,000 from her employment. She will continue to work well into the future even though she turned 65 last December. This year she is unsure how much OAS she will retain after taking into account withdrawals from her RRSPs and earnings in her non-registered savings accounts. She also wants to stay invested. She would prefer to minimize the amount of quarterly instalment taxes she must pay. Here is how it stands for Joanne:

If Joanne continues to earn $85,000 salary plus $6,510 OAS in 2012, she'll have to repay $3,292 of the OAS, leaving her with a net amount of $3,218 on which she would pay an additional $1,380 in income taxes (assuming she lives in Ontario). This is an equivalent tax rate of more than 72% on her OAS income.

To avoid the clawback, Joanne would have to arrange her affairs so her net income is less than $69,500. If she wishes to continue earning $85,000 salary then she could reduce her net income by making an RRSP contribution of $15,500 (she is earning $15,300 of contribution room each year).

OAS Pension Benefit Deferral Reforms. The recent tax changes for pensions are summarized in Appendix 2. You will note that starting in July 2013, OAS recipients can elect to defer taking their OAS pension for up to five years. This would provide for a larger pension then.

However, keep in mind that those five years will represent 37% of the life expectancy of a male after 65 and 27.6% of the life expectancy of a female. Therefore, for the average man, the bump in the OAS needs to be at least 59% to make up for the lost earnings in postponement. For the average woman, the bump needs to be at least 38%. The maximum OAS deferral of five years will result in a 36% increase in benefits received at that time so the average person would not benefit from deferral unless clawbacks are involved. If you beat the odds and live beyond your 79th birthday, you will receive a larger lifetime OAS benefit if you have deferred one year for each year you live beyond 79.

If you are a woman or if you are a high-income earner who is required to repay the full amount of OAS received, it may work in your favor to defer. For high-income earners, the deferral will have no current year loss of income and could increase future cash flows.

The postponement might also work to your advantage to reduce taxes on other income, particularly if you are single and can't split income with a spouse. By creating this "*untaxed retirement income room*" you could generate tax on other sources, such as RRSP or RRIF savings, that would otherwise attract higher tax rates if OAS were taken at the same time, or at death.

Example: Barbara will turn 65 in June 2013. She is a widow with $500,000 in her RRSP that was transferred to her when her husband passed away. Her income from her husband's pension, CPP survivor benefit and investment income will total $88,000 in 2013. If she begins receiving OAS in July, she'll have to repay all of it so she should elect to defer the pension.

Since Barbara is currently in the 26% federal bracket and her income at death will be in the highest bracket, she might consider removing some funds from her RRSP to pay taxes now at a lower rate than she would if the funds remain in her RRSP when she dies. The funds could be put into a TFSA so the earnings outside the RRSP are not taxed. Or, they could be invested in some other non-registered investment.

OAS Age Eligibility Deferral Reforms. If you were under age 54 in 2012, you should take note that your OAS Pension will begin later—age 67 instead of age 65—starting in 2023. This amounts to a potential loss of over $13,000 in current dollars. These changes will be phased in as follows:

- If you are born on or after Feb. 1, 1962, you will be eligible for OAS at 67.
- If you are born between April 1, 1958, and Jan. 31, 1962, your OAS will start between 65 and 67.
- If you are born in April 1960—one year and one month after the minimum eligibility age of March 31, 1958—you will be eligible for OAS at age 66 and one month—one year and one month later than the age 65 start date in place today.
- If you are a low-income earner, the ages at which the *Guaranteed Income Supplement (GIS)* Allowance and the Allowance for the Survivor are provided will also gradually increase from 60 and 64 today to 62 and 66 starting in April 2023. This change will not affect anyone who is age 49 or older on March 31, 2012.

Low-income earners. Low-income pensioners may receive the GIS as noted above. The Supplement is included in total income and net income, but is deducted in computing taxable income. In other words, it will reduce any tax preference—such as refundable and non-refundable tax credits that are based on net income, while it does not itself attract tax.

 The Bottom Line | When planning for retirement, recent pension reforms require some strategizing. To maximize the OAS pension benefit, which can amount to well over $200,000 for a senior couple, you'll need to keep your eye on the clawback zones for the Age Amount and the OAS itself because this will make a difference to your cash flow all year long.

37

The New Canada
Pension Plan Benefits

The Canada Pension Plan (CPP) is paid to Canadian residents who have contributed to the plan through employment or self-employment. The amount of the CPP pension depends on the level of contributions made and the number of years on contributions. See Appendix 3 for details of changes to benefits and premiums.

Normally recipients begin receiving the CPP retirement pension when they reach age 65 but they may apply for an early (reduced) pension once they reach age 60 or they may defer starting CPP and receive an enhanced pension beginning at any age up to age 70.

Prior to 2012 it was possible to apply for early CPP benefits at age 60, but you had to stop working or reduce the hours you worked. This is no longer necessary, but now there are changes in how you contribute when you receive benefits:

- *For CPP recipients under the age of 65*, contributions will be **required** (by both the employee and the employer) even though they are receiving the CPP retirement pension.
- *For CPP recipients age 65 to 69*, contributions will be optional but if an employee does not opt not to contribute, then their employer will also be required to contribute. Employers will automatically deduct CPP contributions for these employees unless the employee completes form *CPT30 Election to Stop Contributing to the Canada Pension Plan, or Revocation of a Prior Election* with the employer.
- *For CPP recipients over the age of 69:* You may no longer contribute to the CPP and you must take your pension.

The additional contributions will increase the amount of CPP pension possibly above the "maximum" pension payable. See later discussion on CPP Reforms under Pooled Retirement Income Benefit.

Reporting CPP on the T1. CPP retirement benefits are reported on a T4(A)P Slip and it's important to show how many months of the year you received your CPP benefits, because in some cases, the premiums are prorated, giving you a bigger tax return.

> **CHECK IT OUT** | **Are my CPP premiums prorated when I start to draw benefits from my CPP?** If you're over age 64 when you begin receiving your CPP retirement pension and you opt not to continue contributing, your required contributions will depend on the month that you begin receiving your pension. The calculation of the required contribution will be made by your software on Form T2204.

Example: Lawrence began receiving his CPP retirement pension in July 2012 when he turned 65 and opted not to continue to contribute. His required CPP contributions for 2012 will be prorated so he will make one-half of the contributions he would have had to pay had he not opted out of making additional contributions.

Splitting CPP Income. If your spouse is at least age 60, it may be advantageous to apply for an assignment of benefits. That splits the CPP credits earned during the marriage by one or both spouses equally between the two and can save tax dollars, particularly if one spouse's income is significantly higher than the other's. Do the returns in your software both ways to be sure whether or not to apply. An application to split CPP benefits must be made through Service Canada.

Example: Robert receives $10,000 in CPP retirement benefits. His wife of 40 years, Mary, did not contribute to CPP so she is not entitled to any CPP benefits. The couple did not make any RRSP contributions and neither is eligible for an employer pension. Luckily, Robert did accumulate significant non-registered investments. His investment income is $50,000 annually. Mary's only income is $6,510 in OAS.

For 2012, the couple's tax bill is $12,355. The couple is eligible to apply to split Robert's CPP pension equally between them giving each $5,000 per year. If they split the CPP, their tax bill will reduced to $11,631, saving them $724 in income taxes each year.

Other CPP Benefits

- *Disability Benefits*—These are reported in Box 16 of the T4A(P) slip and are posted to both Line 152 and Line 114 of the return. No CPP contributions are required once a taxpayer begins receiving a CPP disability benefit. In addition, these benefits are considered to be "earned income" for RRSP purpose.
- *Disabled Contributor Child Benefit*—Children of taxpayers who receive a CPP disability pension are eligible to receive a child benefit if they are under age 18 or are under age 25 and are attending school at a recognized financial institution on

a full-time basis. This child benefit is reported in Box 17 of the T4A(P) slip and is posted to Line 114 on the return for the child.

- *Survivor's Benefits*—When a taxpayer who has contributed to CPP dies, his spouse may be eligible for a survivor pension. The amount of that pension depends on a number of factors:
  - Age of the survivor at the time of death
  - Amount of pension to which the deceased was entitled
  - Whether the deceased was disabled
  - Current age of the survivor
  - Whether or not the survivor is receiving a CPP retirement pension

The survivor pension is reported in Box 15 of the T4A(P) slip and is posted to Line 114 of the survivor's return.

- *Deceased Contributor Child Benefit*—Children of taxpayers who contributed to the CPP may be eligible to receive a child benefit if they are under age 18, or are under age 25 and are attending school at a recognized financial institution on a full-time basis. This child benefit is reported in Box 17 of the T4A(P) slip and is posted to Line 114 on the return for the child.

- *Combined Retirement and Survivor Benefit*—When the recipient of a CPP survivor's benefit begins receiving their own CPP disability or retirement benefit the amount of the survivor benefit may be reduced because the maximum CPP pension that can be received is limited. For 2012, the maximum CPP retirement pension (or combined retirement and survivor pension) is $986.67 per month. The maximum disability pension (or combined disability pension and survivor pension) is $1,185.50 per month).

- *CPP Death Benefit*—When a CPP contributor dies, a one-time death benefit is paid to the deceased's estate. The maximum CPP death benefit is $2,500 but this amount is reduced if the deceased was not entitled to a retirement pension of at least $416 per month. The death benefit is income of the recipient (or the deceased estate). It is not income of the deceased. The amount is reported in Box 18 of a T4A(P) slip and is posted to Line 114 of the recipient's return.

Post Retirement Benefit (PRB). An adjustment to your "regular" CPP benefits will occur if you choose to start your benefits either before or after the normal age 65 start date. The adjustment is 0.52% for each month before the taxpayer's 65th birthday and 0.64% for each month after the taxpayer's 65th birthday (for pensions starting in 2012). The pension may be decreased as much as 31.2% for those who opt to receive their pension at age 60 or increased by as much as 38.4% for those who opt to receive their pension at age 70.

- Beginning in 2011, the augmentation for late pension take-up will be increased to 0.7% per month, phased in over a period of three years.

- Beginning in 2012, the reduction for early pension take-up will be increased to 0.6% per month, phased in over a period of five years.

So what's the right thing to do? Increasing the new PRB may work in your favor, depending on how long you think you'll live after starting the CPP.

Example: Paul will turn 60 in 2013. Per his CPP Statement of Contributions, he will be eligible for a CPP retirement pension of $950 when he turns 65. If Paul decides to start the CPP retirement pension early at age 60, his pension entitlement will be reduced by 0.54% per month x 60 months or 32.4% to $642.20 per month.

If, instead, he opts to defer receiving her CPP retirement pension until he turns 70 in 2023, his pension will be increased by 0.7% x 60 months or 42% to $1,349 per month.

Quebec. Quebec has gone forward earlier, with plans of their own to bolster the pension benefits system with similar plans. Quebec Pension Plan (QPP) contributions will also rise, as explained below, to encourage workers to stay at work longer:

- the monthly increase in the QPP pension applied for after age 65 will rise from 0.5% to 0.7% as of January 1, 2013;
- the monthly reduction in a pension applied for prior to age 65 will be raised, in proportion to the amount of the QPP pension, from 0.5% to 0.6% in the case of a maximum pension; and
- the adjustment will be phased in over three years beginning January 1, 2014; the increase will be proportional to the amount of the pension to limit the impact on lower-income.

 The Bottom Line | Deciding when to take your CPP retirement benefit requires planning under the new reforms which are designed to encourage you to work longer and defer taking your benefits. Use your tax software to do "what if" scenarios to plan the layering of private pension sources if you defer the CPP. Or check out the CPP Income Calculator at www. knowledgebureau.com/calculators for help with this decision.

38

Benefits From Private Pensions

You've been saving all your life for this time: the golden years of retirement. Yet for some actually taking the money out seems wrong. For others, doing it without paying attention to the tax erosion can prematurely wipe out too much capital. That's why you need to carefully report and plan your private pension sources.

Private pension income can come from a couple of different sources. Commonly, those who participated in an employer-sponsored Registered Pension Plan (RPP) will receive a periodic monthly pension on retirement. Other employees may have been members of a Deferred Profit Sharing Plan (DPSP). Still others, who may not have had the opportunity to participate or who were largely self-employed, may have accumulated their own tax-assisted retirement saving through a Registered Retirement Savings Plan (RRSP). New on the horizon is the Pooled Retirement Pension Plan (PRPP) that provides pension savings opportunities for those who work for small employers. See Appendix 2 for an explanation of the contribution rules and recent changes to these and other private pension plans.

 CHECK IT OUT | **How do I report private pension income?** Private pension income will be reported to you on a variety of T-Slips if from Canadian sources, as detailed below; you will usually have to self report any foreign sources.

T4A—The T4A slip is used to report income from a Registered Pension Plan—a pension generally set up by an employer or a union. Periodic payments from these pensions (Box

016) are eligible for the pension income amount and pension income splitting (see Chapter 39). Lump sum payments (Box 018) will be posted to Line 130.

T4RSP—Amounts withdrawn from your RRSP will be reported on a T4RSP slip. Annuity payments (Box 16) from a matured RRSP are eligible for the pension income amount and for pension income splitting (see Chapter 39) if you are over age 65 or if they are received as a result of the death of a former spouse. Most RRSP withdrawals (except HBP and LLP withdrawals) will be reported on Line 129 of your return.

T4RIF—Amounts withdrawn from your RRIF will be reported on a T4RIF slip. Amounts withdrawn from your RRIF are eligible for the pension income amount and pension income splitting if you are over 65 or if they are received as a result of the death of a former spouse. RRIF withdrawals that are eligible for the pension income amount and pension income splitting (see Chapter 39) will be reported on Line 115 of your return and amounts that are not will be reported on Line 130.

Others—You may also receive a T3 slip eligible (Box 31) or lump sum (Box 22) pension benefits or a T4ARCA slip if you're a member of a Retirement Compensation Arrangement. Eligible pension amounts reported in Box 31 of a T3 slip are posted to Line 115 and are eligible for the pension income amount and pension income splitting (see Chapter 39). Lump sum payments and Retirement Compensation Arrangements (RCA) income are reported on Line 130.

Retiring Allowances. Retirement often begins with a termination from employment. Employees who retire after long service may receive a retiring allowance. For some this is the largest lump sum of money they will receive in their lifetime so it needs to be carefully managed. Retiring allowances are also sometimes paid in instalments over a period of years.

A retiring allowance is taxable and is reported on Line 130. Simply key in the amounts shown on your T4A slip and the software will post them automatically.

The amounts received may qualify for an RRSP rollover—that is, they can be contributed to an RRSP over and above the normal RRSP contribution room, thereby deferring taxation. Amounts that qualify for transfer to an RRSP are reported as "eligible" on the T4A (Box 026). Amounts that do not qualify are reported as "non-eligible" (T4A Box 027). These rules were discussed under RPP Contributions in Part 2.

Do work to minimize tax on this income distribution. If you are going to receive it late in the year, for example, ask whether your employer will consider paying it in two lump sums: in the current year and the balance in the new year. That will help you defer the tax to another tax year and also, could save you several percentage points in your marginal tax rate.

Case Study | Splitting Severance

Tom, who is 58 and single, earns $65,000 at his job at the local manufacturing plant where he has been a supervisor for 10 years. He received a layoff notice from his employer on November 15. He is has decided to take an early retirement and to begin receiving a periodic pension ($4,000 per month) from the company-sponsored pension plan. His employer will also pay him a severance package of $50,000. Tom has asked that this be paid to him half on December 1 and half on January 2. Using his tax software he has computed this will save him thousands of dollars:

Had Tom received both his salary and the full severance in one year, his taxable income would have been $115,000 in the year of retirement and $48,000 in the next year. This would have resulted in tax bills of $33,290 and $8,350 in the two years. The total tax bill would be $41,640.

By splitting the severance into two $25,000 amounts his income in the year of retirement would be $90,000 and $73,000 in the following year. This would result in tax bills of $22,440 and $16,500 respectively. The strategy reduces his tax bill from $41,640 to $38,940 or $2700.

Pre-Retirement Counseling. Employer-provided pre-retirement counseling is considered to be a tax-free benefit, so taxpayers should be sure to take advantage of this before leaving their employment.

Starting Your Superannuation Benefit. Reporting this income is straight forward. You will receive a T4A slip, the amount will be shown in Box 016. When you key this into your software, it will be reported on Line 115 *Other Pensions or Superannuation* and your software will claim the pension income amount on Line 314 of Schedule 1. If you have a spouse with a lower income than you, this amount will be eligible for pension income splitting which will not happen automatically. Look for a way to split pension income with your spouse using Form 1032 *Joint Election to Split Pension Income*.

Make sure your tax withholdings from this pension are adequate, if you are uncomfortable with making quarterly instalment remittances yourself. Otherwise, if you have the choice, you may wish to take and use the gross pension, saving money for your tax instalments as required.

Generating a Pension from an RRSP. It can be sad to see people live frugally for many years in their late 50's and 60's, fearing they will run out of money during their golden years. The big unknown, of course, is how long we will live and whether long-term care to ensure the dignity we desire will be a part of the final stages of life. However, often it is the taxman who gets the biggest piece of the pie if couples don't plan effectively. RRSP accumulations are a common example. They can be withdrawn before or after maturity with varying tax results.

Age Eligibility. Before the end of the year in which the taxpayer turns 71, RRSP accumulations must be either cashed out in full (not generally a good idea), transferred to a Registered Retirement Income Plan (RRIF) or used to purchase an annuity, so periodic taxable pension payments can begin. Taxpayers may no longer contribute to an RRSP after the end of the year in which they turn 71, unless they have unused RRSP contribution room and a spouse who is age-eligible—under 72, in which case a spousal RRSP contribution can be made.

Example: Edward is 72 so he is no longer eligible to make contributions to his own RRSP. However, he has unused RRSP contribution room and his wife Edith is only 69, he can make a spousal RRSP contribution using his own contribution room and taking deduction for that contribution.

RRSP Withdrawals Before Maturity. Individuals can make withdrawals at any time and in any amount but in the year that they do the full amount of principal and earnings will be added to their income. Your lump sum withdrawals will be reported in Box 22 of your T4RSP slip along with the required income tax withholding in Box 30. Your software will post the amount from Box 22 to Line 129 and claim a credit for the withholding tax on Line 437.

RRSP Withdrawals After Maturity. Once your RRSP has matured, it will pay you a pension which will be shown in Box 16 of your T4RSP slip. Your software will post this to Line 129 and, if you're over age 65 the software will claim the pension income amount on Line 314. If you're over age 65, this pension will also be eligible for pension income splitting using Form T1032.

> ✓ **CHECK IT OUT** | **How do I report RRSP withdrawals on my return with tax efficiency?** RRSP withdrawals are reported on a T4RSP slip and on Line 115 or on 129 *RRSP Income* in the following instances:

- pensions paid out of a matured RRSP (Box 16) will be posted to Line 115, will trigger the pension income amount on Line 314 if you're over age 64 and are eligible for pension income splitting (if you're over age 64)
- lump-sum payments withdrawn from your RRSP (whether before or after maturity and no matter what your age) are reported on Line 129 and are not eligible for the pension income amount or pension income splitting.

Income Equalization. Unless the taxpayer has equalized RRSP contributions with a spousal RRSP throughout the accumulation period, it is not currently possible to split RRSP retirement income until the taxpayer is 65 (when the RRSP income becomes eligible for the pension income amount). Withdrawals must be reported as income by the plan annuitant.

In the case of a spousal RRSP, the withdrawals are taxed in the hands of the "annuitant spouse," that is, the spouse whose name is on the account rather than the contributing spouse, if three years from the last contribution to a spousal plan have passed.

Example: Jerry made spousal RRSP contributions of $6,000 for his wife Frances in 2009 and again in 2010. If Frances removes $5,000 from her spousal RRSP in 2012, Jerry will have to report the income because it was not left in the plan for three years. If she waits until 2013, the income will be reported on her return.

Where the annuitant spouse transfers the RRSP savings to his or her own RRIF, the minimum payments required under the plan will be taxed in his or her hands. But any amounts over this will be taxed in the hands of the contributor spouse until the restriction period has passed.

Example: If Frances (previous example) had transferred her spousal RRSP to a RRIF and then withdrew the same $5,000, a portion of the withdrawal will be taxed in her hands and the remainder in Jerry's. If the full balance in the RRIF was $12,000 (Jerry's contributions) and Frances was 60 years old at the time of the withdrawal, then she would be required to withdraw $12,000 x 1/(90-60) = $400. The $400 minimum withdrawal is her income and the excess withdrawal ($4,600) is reported on Jerry's return.

Pension Income Splitting. Seniors with eligible pension income and a spouse or common-law partner may elect annually to split up to 50% of pension income on their income tax returns. In the case of an RRSP, you must wait to be age 65 or receive the amounts as the result of a spouse's death. See the next chapter for details.

If your plan is to retire earlier, withdrawing from a Spousal RRSP first may be a good idea. Before you withdraw, do some "what if scenarios" in your tax software to anticipate how much tax will be payable. Also bear in mind you could be setting your spouse up to pay quarterly tax instalment amounts. How can you avoid this? By ensuring that taxes payable at the end of the year are not over $3,000.

Single Taxpayers or Surviving Spouses. If you are single with RRSP accumulations or if a couple, when the first spouse dies, the full amount of RRSP accumulations is included in income on the final return and taxed, but it is possible to transfer (or "roll over") any RRSP accumulations on a tax-free basis to an RRSP, RRIF or RDSP for a surviving financially dependent child.

When RRSP accumulations are left to a financially dependent child (someone who earns less than the Basic Personal Amount), two rules apply:

- For children who are not disabled, RRSP accumulations must be used to buy a term annuity to age 18.
- For infirm children, accumulations can be transferred to their own RRSPs, RRIFs or RDSPs, or to a life annuity thereby further deferring taxes.

Average Income Down over Time. Should you withdraw your RRSP contributions before this? It can make sense to "average down" the taxes you will pay on the RRSP accumulations over a longer period of time, especially if you are in a lower tax bracket when you choose to do this than at the end of life.

When the second survivor passes on, all remaining accumulations in the RRSP must be added to income and will be taxed at the marginal tax rate of the final survivor. For these reasons it's very important to plan to "average down" the tax on your RRSP accumulations over a longer period of time. If you are not going to spend the money, simply reinvest it—perhaps to your TFSA, which will produce tax-exempt income in the future.

Example: Margaret is a 73-year-old widow. She has $750,000 in her RRIF. Her taxable income in 2012 was $52,000, including her required RRIF withdrawal, so her marginal tax rate is 32% (she lives in Alberta). When Margaret dies, the remaining balance in her RRIF will be added to her income putting her into the highest possible tax bracket of 39%. By withdrawing enough out of her RRIF each year to bring her income to just below the OAS clawback threshold, she can have that income taxed at her current marginal rate (32%) rather than 39% when she dies. Even if she lives to use up her RRIF funds, this method will not increase her taxes paid on these funds or the earnings from them.

Foreign Pension Income. Self-reported pension sources can include amounts received from foreign pension sources. Depending on the terms of the tax treaty between Canada and the country in question, some or all of that income may be deductible, as illustrated by the examples below.

- *German Social Security.* Certain social security pensions from Germany are added into pension income on Line 115, and qualify for the $2,000 *Pension Income Amount* but qualify for a partially offsetting deduction on Line 256. See Appendix 2 for a discussion of recent new tax filing requirements in Germany.
- *U.S. Social Security* income is recorded in full at Line 115, qualifies for the $2000 pension Income Amount but also for a 15% deduction on Line 256 Other Deductions. (15% rate in effect from 1996 to date). For seniors who began receiving U.S. Social security before 1996, the deduction is 50% of the amount received. All foreign income sources must be reported in Canadian funds. The taxable portion of U.S. Social Security is eligible for the pension income amount and pension income splitting.
- *IRAs and Roth IRAs.* Similar to our RRSPs, these plans are reported in Canada as follows: So long as no contributions are made to a Roth IRA after 2008 while the

taxpayer is resident in Canada, income from a Roth IRA will be considered as pension income in Canada. This means that the taxpayer may elect that income earned within the Roth IRA is not taxable as it is earned. If the election is not made or contributions are made while the taxpayer is resident in Canada (after 2008), then the Roth IRA is treated like any other investment and earnings are taxable as foreign investment income. Distributions from a Roth IRA are not taxable. Income from an IRA (not a Roth IRA) is taxable when received if it would be taxable in the U.S. This means withdrawals are taxable except when transferred from one IRA to another.

Claiming the Foreign Tax Credit. When there are withholding taxes on foreign pensions, you can offset them with the Foreign Tax Credit, which is calculated on Form T2209 and then ends up on Schedule 1, Line 405. This credit can be confusing even if you use tax software. Here are some tips to help you get it right:

- The calculation must be done for each foreign country so be sure to specify what country the taxes were paid to so that the software can make the calculations and claim the credits.
- A foreign tax credit is only available if Canada has a tax treaty with the foreign jurisdiction to eliminate double taxation. Be sure that the taxes paid are eligible.
- When your Canadian tax rate is low, you may not be able to recover all of the foreign taxes paid using the foreign tax credit. If so, your software should take a deduction for the excess foreign taxes paid.

Withdrawing Other Investments. Most taxpayers supplement their pension income with income from investments held in non-registered accounts. Their filing profile is therefore often layered in with an investor's profile and the way that income from investments is realized has important consequences for their overall tax position.

Certain amounts included in investment income and, therefore, in net income do not represent cash income available for spending. The taxable amount of a dividend from a publicly traded corporation is normally 38% greater than the cash amount of the dividend, for example.

In another example, compounding interest income must be reported annually even though cash is not received until maturity. While interest rates have been low recently, those planning retirement for the future when interest rates may be higher will want to take this into account in their retirement income planning now.

Together with the start of superannuation benefits including withdrawals of RRSP deposits, earnings from investments can be quickly eroded, especially when income reaches the thresholds at which the clawbacks of the Age Amount and OAS benefits begin. When net income is too high, the amount that is spent for long-term care (if based on net income levels) will increase too.

Benefits from insurance products—disability and long-term care insurance or life insurance policies—can ensure prosperity is maintained on disability without taxation and, for surviving family members, after death. Income earned in these plans is usually tax deferred and the total benefits received by beneficiaries are generally not taxable.

Software Tips. If a taxpayer will be in a lower-tax bracket during life than at death, it may make more sense to withdraw money now, and if not needed, to make gifts to loved ones during life. This can be easily illustrated using your tax software. Consider withdrawing enough money to "top income up" to the end of the lowest tax bracket:

Example: Joyce, age 80, is a widow. She has $350,000 in her RRIF. Her annual income is $44,000 which she is comfortable living on. She lives in Ontario and has a marginal tax rate of 31.15%. When she dies, her remaining RRIF balance will be added to her income and will be taxed at more than 46%. If she draws $25,000 additional funds from her RRIF she will both stay in the 31.15% tax bracket and avoid the OAS clawback. That money will then be taxed at 31.15% rather than the 46% rate applicable when she dies.

This results in a tax savings of $3,700 for each year that she makes the extra withdrawal. If she does not need to spend the money, she can leave it to her heirs without CRA taking 46% of it.

 The Bottom Line | Deciding when to take your CPP retirement benefit requires planning under the new reforms which are designed to encourage you to work longer and defer taking your benefits. Use your tax software to do "what if" scenarios to plan the layering of private pension sources if you defer the CPP. Or check out the CPP Income Calculator at www.knowledgebureau.com/calculators for help with this decision.

39

Splitting Pension Income
With Your Spouse

Taxpayers who receive pension income that is eligible for the pension income amount may elect to split up to 50% of that income with their spouse or common-law partner. The transferee reports the split income reports it on Line 116. The taxpayer who received the income reports the full amount received on Line 115 and claims a deduction on Line 210 for the elected amount.

 CHECK IT OUT | **How do I elect pension income splitting?** The amount to be split is to be set out annually in an election which will accompany the return of both taxpayers. The election will be made on Form T1032, *Joint Election to Split Pension Income.*

The split pension amount:

- is deemed to be income of the transferee;
- is deductible by the transferor; and
- is deemed to be qualified pension income of the recipient, for purposes of claiming the Pension Amount credit. Thus, the transferee can claim the credit (limited to $2,000 a year).

Both the transferee and the transferor must be residents in Canada at the end of the taxation year in which income is to be split or, in the case of a transfer, in the year of death of either, at the time of death.

Eligible Pension Income

For taxpayers who are under 65, eligible pension income includes:

- payments in respect of a life annuity from a superannuation or pension plan, and
- amounts received from the following *because of the death of the taxpayer's spouse*:
  - RRSP annuity;
  - RRIF payment;
  - DPSP annuity; and
  - amounts accrued under certain life insurance policies and annuities.

For persons over 65, eligible pension income includes:

- payments in respect of a life annuity from a superannuation or pension plan;
- RRSP annuity;
- RRIF payment;
- DPSP annuity;
- the interest portion of annuity payments; and
- amounts accrued under certain life insurance policies and annuities.

Impact of Splitting on Tax Payment. Where pension income that is split was subject to tax withholding at source, the portion of the withholding tax that relates to the split amount is deemed to have been tax withheld from the transferee, not the transferor. What this means is that the withholding tax follows the income. The transferee and transferor are jointly and severally liable, however, for the tax due on the split amount.

Example: Gary and Virginia are a retired couple. Each receives Old Age Security and Gary has RRIF income of $40,000 from which $4,000 in income taxes was withheld. Gary and Virginia can elect to transfer $20,000 of Gary's pension to Virginia by each filing the T1032 form. If the election is not made, Gary would owe $1,253 while Virginia would owe nothing. If they make the election, their total tax bill would decrease by $1,430 and because $2,000 of the income tax withheld would also be transferred to Virginia, each would have a refund of $89.

Splitting eligible pension income involves balancing potentially conflicting outcomes on the tax return, as shown below. Your software will help you optimize these effects?

	Potential Conflicts of Pension Income Splitting	
Transfer from	Higher income spouse to	Lower income spouse
OAS	May reduce clawback	May increase clawback
Age amount	May reduce clawback	May increase clawback
Spousal amount	Will reduce claim	
Age amount transferred	Will reduce claim	
Pension amount	No effect	May increase availability
Federal tax rate	May be reduced	May be increased

Case Study | Optimizing Pension Income Splitting

Colin is a teacher who recently retired at age 62 with superannuation of $35,000. He decided to take CPP early to travel with his wife, Aimee, who is 65 and has never worked out of the home. How can pension income splitting help this couple? For these purposes, we will assume there is no other income or deductions.

Before pension income splitting, Colin's income (including $6,000 CPP) is $41,000. Aimee's only income is her Old Age Security. Aimee is not taxable, but Colin's tax bill is $4,518. By electing to split half of his pension with Aimee, Colin's tax bill is reduced to $2,458, but Aimee's tax bill becomes $1,351. Still, the net savings in taxes payable as a result of the election to split Colin's pension is $709.

Deductions and Credits to Offset Private Pension Income. There are no deductions specific to pension income. However, there are some important tax credits. As you have learned, when you start receiving qualifying periodic pension income, you'll qualify for the $2,000 Pension Income Amount, as explained above. However, before leaving this topic, you need to understand other credits specific to seniors that can help to average down income in retirement.

Transfers from Spouse or Common-law Partner. When the lower-income earning spouse has insufficient income to absorb the following non-refundable tax credits, the balance of the unused amounts may be transferred to the higher income earner, using Schedule 2 (which carries up to Line 326 on Schedule 1):

- Age Amount
- Pension Income Amount
- Disability Amount
- Tuition, Education and Textbook Amounts

Once again, prepare both spouses' returns in a couple of different ways to ensure the best benefit is achieved using these options.

Supporting Other Infirm Adults. Additional credits are available where a taxpayer supports an adult dependant, other than a spouse. An infirm adult is someone who lives in Canada, age 18 and over, who is mentally or physically disabled and related to the taxpayer by blood, marriage or adoption. A credit for the care of infirm adults may be claimed under one of three different provisions, using Schedule 5.

Schedule 5 is used to report the dependant's income and identification information, so credits can be claimed on Line 305, 306 and 315, as explained in the following paragraphs.

Line 305 Amount for Eligible Dependant. If the supporting person is single and living with the infirm adult dependant, this credit may be claimed if the infirm dependant is a parent or grandparent and lives with that taxpayer. Formerly known as the Equivalent-to-Spouse Amount, this claim provides for a credit based on an amount of $10,822 in 2012 if the dependant is not infirm; $12,822 if the dependant is infirm. The claim is reduced dollar for dollar by the net income of the eligible dependant and so is phased out completely when the dependant's net income exceeds $10,822 if they are not infirm or $12,822 if they are.

Line 306 Amount for Infirm Adults age 18 or Older. The credit is calculated on $6,402 for 2012 and is reduced by the dependant's net income over $6,420 and so is phased out completely when the dependant's net income exceeds $12,822 in 2012.

The net income thresholds for the Eligible Dependant Amount and the Amount for Infirm Dependants usually result in no claim under these provisions for the care of dependant seniors, because often their income level, based on the receipt of OAS (including supplement) and CPP, is too high.

Line 315 Caregiver Amount. This is a non-refundable tax credit of $4,402 in 2012 if the dependant is not infirm and $6,402 if the dependant is infirm to those supporting individuals who care for elderly parents or grandparents or other infirm adults in that supporting person's home. The dependant's net income threshold is higher $15,033 in 2012, so the Caregiver Amount credit is often available when the other credits are not. It therefore makes a better claim. The claim is phased out completely when the dependant's net income exceeds $21,435 if the dependant is infirm or $19,435 if the dependant is not.

Example: Anna is a widow who supports her brother Charles in her home. Charles is confined to a wheelchair, is 60 and his only income is a CPP disability pension of $1,100 per month. Although Anna is eligible to claim any of these credits for her brother, his $13,200 income eliminates the Amount for an Eligible Dependant and the Amount for Infirm Adults. Anna can claim the Caregiver Amount of $6,402.

Note: In certain circumstances, a taxpayer may qualify to claim the Amount for Infirm Dependants Age 18 or Older or the Caregiver Amount. Where both are available, the Caregiver Amount must be claimed. Note that the Caregiver Amount requires that care be provided in the claimant's home while the Amount for Infirm Dependants does not. Either of those amounts is reduced by any claim made under the Amount for Eligible Dependant.

Disability Amount. As people age, disabilities begin, as discussed in Chapter 25. It bears repeating here that this lucrative tax credit should claimed if the taxpayer or spouse has:

- a disability that is severe and prolonged, which is expected to last for a continuous period of at least 12 months, starting in the tax year.
- markedly restricted basic activities of living. Marked restrictions include the following conditions:
  - Permanent blindness (a CNIB number is usually available)

  - Severe cardio-respiratory failure
  - Inability to feed or dress oneself
  - Inability to perceive, remember or think
  - Inability to walk
  - Inability to speak
  - Inability to hear
  - Inability to contain bowel or bladder functions
- Taxpayers who must receive therapy like kidney dialysis may claim this credit if a doctor certifies that at least 14 hours per week are taken for such therapy.
- Form T2201 *Disability Tax Credit Certificate* must be completed and signed by a medical doctor, optometrist, psychologist, occupational therapist, audiologist or speech-language pathologist and so on. Generally, the CRA requires that the form be filed in the first year that the credit is claimed.
- The Disability Amount may be claimed if there is a claim for Attendant Care Expenses elsewhere on the return. However, the Disability Amount may not be claimed if the costs of a full-time attendant or care in a nursing home or institution are also claimed as a medical expense unless the amount claimed is less than $10,000.

Medical Expenses. See Chapter 24 for a list of allowable medical expenses.

 The Bottom Line | Pension income splitting is lucrative. Be sure you do it if you qualify!

40

T-Slip Guide for Seniors

T4A

You will receive this slip if you receive a pension or annuity, a retiring allowance, and often if you are self-employed but provide services to another business.

Payer's name – Nom du payeur		Canada Revenue Agency	Agence du revenu du Canada	**T4A** STATEMENT OF PENSION, RETIREMENT, ANNUITY, AND OTHER INCOME ÉTAT DU REVENU DE PENSION, DE RETRAITE, DE RENTE OU D'AUTRES SOURCES

Year / Année

061	Payer's account number / Numéro de compte du payeur

	Pension or superannuation – line 115 Prestations de retraite ou autres pensions – ligne 115		Income tax deducted – line 437 Impôt sur le revenu retenu – ligne 437
	016		022

Social insurance number Numéro d'assurance sociale	Recipient's account number Numéro de compte du bénéficiaire	Lump-sum payments – line 130 Paiements forfaitaires – ligne 130	Self-employed commissions Commissions d'un travail indépendant
012	013	018	020

		Annuities Rentes	Fees for services Honoraires ou autres sommes pour services rendus
		024	048

Recipient's name and address – Nom et adresse du bénéficiaire

Last name (in capital letters) – Nom de famille (en lettres moulées)   First name – Prénom   Initials – Initiales

Other information (see over)
Autres renseignements (voir au verso)

Box – Case	Amount – Montant	Box – Case	Amount – Montant
Box – Case	Amount – Montant	Box – Case	Amount – Montant

Box – Case	Amount – Montant	Box – Case	Amount – Montant	Box – Case	Amount – Montant	Box – Case	Amount – Montant
Box – Case	Amount – Montant	Box – Case	Amount – Montant	Box – Case	Amount – Montant	Box – Case	Amount – Montant

T4A (11)

Box	Where do I put it?	What is it?	What else is relevant?
016	Line 115	Periodic Payments From a Pension Plan	This amount will generally qualify for the pension income amount on Line 314 of Schedule 1.
018	Line 130	Lump Sum Payments From an RPP or DPSP	Generally these lump sum payments may be transferred directly to an RRSP. The amount in Box 18 is included in Boxes 102, 108, 110, 158, 180 and 190. Refer to those boxes to determine how much can be transferred.
020	Line 166 Line 139	Self-employed Commissions	Generally complete Form T2125—*Statement of Business Activities* to report gross commissions on Line 166 and net commissions on Line 139.
022	T1 Line 437	Income Tax Deducted	
024	T1 Line 115	Annuity Income	This amount is generally eligible for the Pension Income Amount on Line 314 if the taxpayer is over 65 or received this amount as a result of the death of a spouse. Amounts in Boxes 111 and 115 are included in Box 024.
026	T1 Line 130	Eligible Retiring Allowance	This box is not used for 2012. Retiring allowances should be reported on a T4 slip.
027	T1 Line 130	This box is not used for 2012.	This box is not used for 2012. Retiring allowances should be reported on a T4 slip.
028	T1 Line 130	Other Income	Income not reported in any other box on the T4A slip.
030		Patronage Allocations	This amount is taxable only if it is received as a rebate for goods claimed as a business expense. If so, report it on Line 130.
032	Line 207	RPP Contributions For Past Service	Some restrictions may apply if the claim on Line 207 exceeds $3,500.
034	Line 206	Pension Adjustment	This amount will reduce the taxpayer's RRSP contribution room for the following tax year.
036		Pension Plan Registration Number	Do not enter on the return.
040	Line 130	Registered Education Savings Plan Accumulated Income Payments	Complete Form T1172—Additional Tax on Accumulated Income Payments from RESPs. The amount in Box 122 is included in Box 040.
042	Line 130	Registered Education Savings Plan Education Assistance Payments	

Box	Where do I put it?	What is it?	What else is relevant?
046	Schedule 9	Charitable Donations	Treat as any other donation. May be claimed on the spouse's return if more beneficial or carried forward for up to five years.
048		Fees For Services	Report as income on T2125 or applicable Self-Employment form
102		Lump-sum Payments— non-resident services transferred under paragraph 60(j)	Included in Box 018
104	T1 Line 104	Research Grants	Deduct related expenses and report the net amount on Line 104.
105	T1 Line 130	Scholarships, Bursaries or Fellowships	Reduce by $500 if the student does not qualify for the Education Amount. If the student does, the amount is not taxable.
106	T1 Line 130	Death Benefits	May qualify for $10,000 exemption.
107	T1 Line 104	Wage Loss Replacement plan	Reduce by premiums paid since 1968.
108		Lump-sum Payments From a Registered Pension Plan (RPP) that you cannot transfer	Included in Box 018
109	T1 Line 130	Periodic Payments From an Unregistered Pension Plan	
110		Lump-sum Payments accrued to December 31, 1971	Included in Box 018.
111		Income Averaging Annuity Contracts (IAAC)	Included in Box 024.
115		Deferred Profit-sharing Plan (DPSP), Annuity or Instalment Payments	Included in Box 024.
116		Medical Travel Assistance	Do not report. May qualify for the Northern Residents Deduction (Form T2222).
117	T1 Line 130	Loan Benefits	

Box	Where do I put it?	What is it?	What else is relevant?
118	T1 Line 104	Medical Premium Benefits	These may qualify as a medical expense.
119	T1 Line 104	Group Term Life Insurance Plan Premiums	
122		RESP Accumulated Income Payments Paid to Other	Included in Box 040.
123	T1 Line 130	Revoked DPSP Income	
124		Board and Lodging at Special Work Sites	Do not report.
125	T1 Line 130	Disability Benefits From a Registered Pension Plan	
127	T1 Line 104	Veterans' Benefits	
129	T1 Line 130	Tax-deferred Corporate Share	
130	T1 Line 130	Apprenticeship Incentive Grant or Apprenticeship Completion Grant	
131	T1 Line 125	RDSP Income	
132	T1 Line 104	Wage Earner Protection Program	
133	T1 Line 115	Variable Pension Benefits	
134	T1 Line 130	Tax-Free Savings Account taxable amount	
135	Line 330	Recipient-paid Premiums for Private Health Services Plans	
135	T1 Line 330	Recipient-paid Premiums for Private Health Services Plans	
142		Status Indian (exempt income)—Eligible Retiring Allowances	Do not report.

Box	Where do I put it?	What is it?	What else is relevant?
143		Status Indian (exempt income)—Non-eligible Retiring Allowances	Do not report.
144		Status Indian (exempt income)—Other Income	Do not report.
146		Status Indian (exempt income)—Pension or Superannuation	Do not report.
148		Status Indian (exempt income)—Lump-sum Payments	Do not report.
150	T1 Line 130	*Labour Adjustment Benefits Act* and *Appropriation Acts*	
152	T1 Line 130	SUBP Qualified Under the *Income Tax Act*	
154	T1 Line 130	Cash Award or Prize From Payer	
156	T1 Line 130	Bankruptcy Settlement	
158		Lump-sum Payments not From an RPP or a DPSP That You Cannot Transfer	Included in Box 18.
180		Lump-sum Payments From a Deferred profit-Sharing Plan (DPSP) That You Cannot Transfer	Included in Box 18.
190		Lump-sum Payments From an Unregistered Plan	Included in Box 18.

T4A(OAS)

You will receive this slip if you receive the Old Age Security pension.

| Canada Revenue Agency | Agence du revenu du Canada | STATEMENT OF OLD AGE SECURITY RELEVÉ DE LA SÉCURITÉ DE LA VIEILLESSE | T4A (OAS) |

| Year Année | 18 Taxable pension paid / Versement de pension imposable | 19 Gross pension paid / Versement brut de pension | 20 Overpayment recovered / Paiement en trop recouvré | 21 Net supplements paid / Versement net des suppléments | 22 Income tax deducted / Impôt sur le revenu retenu | 23 Quebec income tax deducted / Impôt sur le revenu du Québec retenu |

Issued by: Service Canada
Émis par : Service Canada

12 Social insurance number / Numéro d'assurance sociale

13 Old Age Security number / Numéro de la Sécurité de la vieillesse

T4A (OAS) (06)
ISP-0137nat-10-03B

Keep this copy for your records
Conservez cette copie pour vos dossiers

Canadä

Box	Where do I put it?	What is it?	What else is relevant?
18	Line 113	Taxable OAS paid	Be sure to claim the Age Amount on Line 301 of Schedule 1. If income exceeds a base amount (the taxpayer may be required to repay a portion of this amount).
19		Gross OAS	This is the total amount of OAS received. The taxable portion is included in Box 18.
20	Line 232	OAS Overpayment Recovered	This is the amount of OAS repaid in the year. Deduct it on Line 232.
21	Line 146 and Line 250	Net Spouse's Allowance or Guaranteed Income Supplement Paid	Enter the income on Line 146 and deduct it again on Line 250. This amount is not taxable, but increases the taxpayer's net income in calculating some credits and benefits.
22	Line 437	Income Tax Deducted	
23		Quebec Income Tax Deducted	If the taxpayer lives in Quebec, report this on the Quebec income tax return. If not, include this amount in Line 437.

T4A(P)

You will receive this slip if you receive benefits under the Canada Pension Plan.

	Canada Revenue Agency	Agence du revenu du Canada	STATEMENT OF CANADA PENSION PLAN BENEFITS ÉTAT DES PRESTATIONS DU RÉGIME DE PENSIONS DU CANADA		T4A (P)

Year	20 Taxable CPP benefits	21 Number of months	22 Income tax deducted	12 Social insurance number	13 Onset or Effective date	14 Retirement benefit
Année	Prestations imposables du RPC	Nombre de mois	Impôt sur le revenu retenu	Numéro d'assurance sociale	Date de début ou d'entrée en vigueur	Prestation de retraite

15 Survivor benefit	16 Disability benefit
Prestation de survivant	Prestation d'invalidité
17 Child benefit	18 Death benefit
Prestation pour enfant	Prestation de décès

Issued by: Service Canada
Émis par : Service Canada

0910

Benefit number
N° de prestation

RC-06-946

T4A (P) (06)
ISP-0136nat-10-06

Canada

Box	Where do I put it?	What is it?	What else is relevant?
13		Effective Date	
14		Retirement Benefit	Included in Box 20.
15		Survivor Benefit	Included in Box 20.
16	Line 152	Disability Benefit	Included in Box 20. This amount qualifies as earned income for RRSP purposes
17		Child Benefit	Included in Box 20. This amount should be reported on the return for the child. It will increase the child's net income and may affect credits claimed with respect to the child.
18		Death Benefit	Included in Box 20. This amount may be reported by the surviving spouse or on a return for the estate of the deceased taxpayer.
20	Line 114	Taxable CPP Benefits	This amount includes all the amounts in Boxes 14 to 18. It also includes any recovery of CPP or payments for arrears.
21		Number of Months	This is the number of months the taxpayer received CPP benefits in the year. Use this number if you need to prorate CPP contributions for the year the taxpayer begins to receive CPP retirement or disability benefits.
22	Line 437	Income Tax Deducted	

T4RSP

You will receive this slip if you received income from a Registered Retirement Savings Plan.

Box	Where do I put it?	What is it?	What else is relevant?
16	Line 129	Annuity Payments	This amount qualifies for the Pension Income Amount on Line 314 of Schedule 1 if the taxpayer is over 64 or if they received these payments as a result of the death of their spouse. As such, these amounts are eligible for pension income splitting.
18	Line 129	Refund of Premiums	This is the amount paid to the partner because of the death of the RRSP holder. This amount may be rolled over to the recipient's RRSP during the year or within 60 days after the end of the year.
20	Line 129	Refund of Excess Contributions	This amount refunded was never deducted. Complete Form T3012A—*Tax Deducted Waiver on the Refund of Your Unused RRSP Contributions Made in* _____, to qualify for a corresponding deduction on Line 232.
22	Line 129	Withdrawals and Commutation Payments	If the amount withdrawn was not deducted from income as an RRSP contribution you may be able to claim a deduction using form T746.
24		Contributor Spouse or Common-law Partner	This box indicates if this is a spousal RRSP. See Box 36.

Box	Where do I put it?	What is it?	What else is relevant?
25	Schedule 7 Line 17	LLP Withdrawals	This is the amount of withdrawals from the RRSP under the Lifelong Learning Plan.
26	Line 129	Amount Deemed Received on Deregistration	This is the fair market value of all property in the RRSP just before it was deregistered.
27	Schedule 7 Line 15	HBP Withdrawals	This is the amount of withdrawals from the RRSP under the Home Buyers' Plan.
28	Line 129 or Line 232	Other Income or Deductions	If the amount is shown in brackets, it is a deduction—claim it on Line 232. If it is not shown in brackets it is income—report it on Line 129.
30	Line 437	Income Tax Deducted	
34	Line 129	Deemed Receipt on Death	This is Fair Market Value of the deceased RRSP at the time of his or her death and the amount deemed to have been received immediately before death. Report it on the final return for the deceased. A qualified beneficiary may designate any part of this amount as a Refund of Premiums by filing Form T2019—*Death of an RRSP Annuitant—Refund of Premiums*. The designated amount may be rolled over to the beneficiary's RRSP.
35		Amount Directly Transferred on Breakdown of Marriage or Common-law Relationship	Direct transfers on relationship breakdown are not taxable.
36		Social Insurance Number	This is the SIN of the spouse or common-law partner who made the contributions. If contributions were made to the RRSP in the tax year or the preceding two years, a portion of the income may have to be reported by the contributor. Complete Form T2205—*Amounts From a Spousal or Common-law Partner RRSP or RRIF to Include in Income for* _____ to determine the amount.
40		Tax-paid Amount	This is the amount to be included on the final return of a deceased taxpayer. It represents income earned in the RRSP after the end of the year of death.

T4RIF

You will receive this slip if you received income from a Registered Retirement Income Fund.

| | | Canada Revenue Agency   Agence du revenu du Canada | | STATEMENT OF INCOME FROM A REGISTERED RETIREMENT INCOME FUND
ÉTAT DU REVENU PROVENANT D'UN FONDS ENREGISTRÉ DE REVENU DE RETRAITE | | | | | **T4RIF** |

Year	16 Taxable amounts	Amounts deemed received by the annuitant			22 Other income or deductions	24 Excess amount	26 Spousal or common-law partner RRIF
		18 Deceased	20 Deregistration				
Année	Montants imposables	Personne décédée	Annulation de l'enregistrement		Autres revenus ou déductions	Excédent	FERR au profit de l'époux ou conjoint de fait
		Montants réputés reçus par le rentier					

28 Income tax deducted	30 Year	Month	Day	35 Transfers on breakdown of marriage or common-law part.	32 Spouse's or common-law partner's social insurance number*
Impôt sur le revenu retenu	Année	Mois	Jour	Transferts après rupture du mariage ou de l'union de fait	Numéro d'assurance sociale de l'époux ou conjoint de fait*

*If your social insurance number is not shown, see the back of this slip.
Si votre numéro d'assurance sociale n'est pas indiqué, lisez le verso de ce feuillet.

Recipient's name and address – Nom et adresse du bénéficiaire

Last name (print)
Nom de famille (en lettres moulées)

First name
Prénom

Initials
Initiales

12 Social insurance number*	14 Contract number
Numéro d'assurance sociale*	Numéro de contrat

60 Name of payer (carrier) of fund
Nom du payeur (émetteur) du fonds

61 Account Number	36 Tax-paid amount
Numéro de compte	Montant libéré d'impôt

Privacy Act, Personal Information Bank number CRA PPU 005
Loi sur la protection des renseignements personnels, Fichier de renseignements personnels ARC PPU 005

T4RIF (11)

Box	Where do I put it?	What is it?	What else is relevant?
16	Line 115 or Line 130	Taxable amounts	This amount qualifies for the Pension Income Amount on Line 314 of Schedule 1 if the taxpayer is over 64 or if they received these payments as a result of the death of their spouse. If so, enter it on Line 115. Such amounts are eligible for pension income splitting. Otherwise, enter the amount on Line 130.
18	Line 130	Amounts Deemed Received by a Deceased Annuitant	This is the fair market value of the RRIF at the time of death and the amount deemed to have been received by the deceased at that time. Report it on the final return for the deceased. A qualified beneficiary may designate any part of this amount as a Refund of Premiums by filing Form T1090—*Death of an RRIF Annuitant—Designated Benefit*. The designated amount may be rolled over to the beneficiary's RRSP or RRIF.

Box	Where do I put it?	What is it?	What else is relevant?
20	Line 115 or Line 130	Amount Deemed Received on Deregistration	This is the fair market value of all property in the RRIF just before it was deregistered. It qualifies for the Pension Income Amount on Line 314 of Schedule 1 if the taxpayer is over 64 or if the payments were received as a result of the death of the spouse. If so, enter it on Line 115. Otherwise, enter the amount on Line 130.
22	Line 115 or Line 130 or Line 232	Other Income or Deductions	If the amount is shown in brackets, it is a deduction—claim it on Line 232. If it is not shown in brackets it is income—report it on Line 115 if over 64 or if the amount is received as a result of the spouse's death. Otherwise, enter the income on Line 130.
24		Excess Amount	This is the amount (already included in Box 16) that exceeds the minimum amount for the year. If the RRIF was created from a Spousal RRSP, these amounts may be attributed back to the contributor if deposited within the prior three years (use T2205 to determine the amount).
26		Contributor Spouse or Common-law Partner	This box indicates if this was a spousal RRSP. See Box 32.
28	Line 437	Income Tax Deducted	
30		Date of Death	This is the deceased annuitant's date of death.
35		Amount Directly Transferred on Breakdown of Marriage or Common-law Relationship.	Direct transfers on relationship breakdown are not taxable.
36		Tax-paid Amount	This is the amount to be included on the final return of a deceased taxpayer. It represents income earned in the RRIF after the end of the year of death.

PART 6

Special Situations

What's New

Just about everything we talk about in this part of the book will be new to most people. Understanding how to do taxes for an immigrant will expose you to the concept of "part-year residency." Understanding emigration will expose you to a whole new level of taxation—departure taxes. And, of course most of us will want to avoid talking about end of life—but the special rules that apply to returns in the year of death can save your family thousands of dollars. It may be news to you, but the time to manage your affairs for end of life, is now.

Hard Copy

Newcomers to Canada will have to file the T1 General *Income Tax and Benefit Return* for the first time. Those who leave Canada may be filing T1159—*Income Tax Return for Electing Under Section 216* or Schedule C—*Electing Under Section 217 of the Income Tax Act for Non-Resident and Deemed Residents of Canada* or a host of other new forms for elections upon emigration. Those filing returns for deceased taxpayers may need Form T2075 *Election to Defer Payment of Income Tax, Under Subsection 159(5) of the Income Tax Act by a Deceased Taxpayer's Legal Representative or Trustee* as well as a TX19 *Clearance Certificate,*

Software Tips

Upon emigration, be sure that you have established yourself as a resident of another jurisdiction before entering a date of departure in your software. The software will apply the rules for emigrants (such as proration of personal amounts) based on this date. Returns in the year of emigration can be expensive, because you'll need to report the fair market value of taxable assets at the time of emigration.

Returns in the year of death can also be tricky as some rules that apply to the living are applied differently in the year of death (capital losses, medical expenses and charitable donations, for example). Your software will only be able to apply the rules properly if you enter the date of death and choose the options for reporting yourself. Remember that the deceased's marital status on the return does not change—but the surviving spouse's does, as of the date of death.

Tax Sleuthing

If you're new to Canada, there's a lot to become familiar with. Take the time to explore the parts of this book that are relevant to your entire family unit. Remember that once you're a resident of Canada you're taxable on your world income in Canadian funds. Make sure you take advantage of the foreign tax credits so you don't pay tax on that same income twice!

If you're leaving Canada, be sure to document the fair market value of all assets on which you'll be paying a departure tax. That fair market value will be the new adjusted cost base of those assets when you enter a new country for the purposes of future capital gains tax in your new country. If the departure taxes pose hardship, check out the election to provide security for the taxes owing rather than having to come up with the cash before leaving.

When filing a final return, one of the most difficult tasks is determining the adjusted cost base of assets owned by the deceased—especially if they've been owned for a long time. Be sure to track down the Form T664 from 1994 to determine if an election was made on any of the assets to increase their cost base. Also be sure you've determined any carry forwards that the deceased may have from prior years. Capital losses, for example, can be used to reduce income from other sources in the year of death and the immediately prior year. Carried forward charitable donations are valuable too.

Tax Pro Alert

Most taxpayers who have recently immigrated to Canada are not at all familiar with the Canadian income tax system. So professional help, especially with that first tax return, is recommended.

When you're leaving Canada, get help both with the intricacies of the departure taxes and what obligations you will continue to have with CRA after you emigrate (if any). Remember, finding an expert on Canadian taxes while you're in a foreign country is not necessarily going to be as easy from there.

In the year of death, a deceased taxpayer will be in the higher income tax bracket due to the deemed disposition of capital assets and the deregistration of RRSPs and RRIFs. In Canada today, we have punitive provincial surtaxes on high incomes. You want to try to income split and average down taxes on those types of deposits well before death, if possible. And, as a survivor, this is not the best time to be trying to make difficult financial decisions. Get the professional help you need to make elections and asset transfers at the most appropriate cost bases to minimize the CRA's claim on the estate of the deceased.

41

Immigration and Emigration

Did you immigrate to or emigrate from Canada during the year? If so, you are required to file a Canadian tax return to report your world income in the time you were considered to be a resident in Canada. That makes you a part-year resident for tax purposes, and there will be some interesting implications for the reporting of your taxable assets, as well as the tax breaks you'll be able to offset your taxes with.

Returns for part-year residents must be filed on paper—they do not qualify for NETFILE.

 CHECK IT OUT | **When am I considered to have left Canada for tax purposes?**
A taxpayer who leaves Canada may or may not be considered a non-resident for tax purposes. There are a number of categories to consider, depending on circumstances, as Canada will want to retain its taxing authority in particular instances. Likewise, the rules that follow can guide new entrants to Canada, as well.

Factual Residents. Factual residents are those who have sufficient ties here to be considered a resident, even if they have physically left the country. This includes those who are teaching or attending school abroad, commuting to a work or business location in another country (generally the U.S.), those vacationing abroad, or those conducting missionary work abroad.

Factual residents are taxed as residents of Canada for the full year. This means world income is reported in Canadian funds and the taxpayer is eligible to claim all deductions and tax credits normally available to Canadian residents. The taxpayer would pay provincial taxes in the province in which the taxpayer would normally be considered to be resident as of December 31 of the tax year. Federal and provincial refundable tax credits would be claimed as usual.

Some factual residents qualify for the *Overseas Employment Tax Credit*, for example, if they are working on an oil rig in the middle of the ocean for a Canadian employer. However, this credit is being phased out. See part 2.

Deemed Residents. Deemed residents are those visitors to Canada who are considered to be residents for tax purposes, because they have "sojourned" here for a period of 183 days or more, or those Canadians who have left Canada for several years because they serve in the armed forces or as a representative of Canada.

Deemed residents must report world income in Canadian funds and are entitled to all federal tax provisions. Rather than pay federal and provincial taxes, they pay a federal non-resident surtax of 48% of federal taxes.

Non-Residents. Non-residents are not required to file a tax return in Canada unless they have income from specific sources in Canada like employment or business income, or if they choose to make an election to be taxed on income in Canada. However, a non-resident can generally only elect to be taxed on rental income and timber royalty income (under Section 216 of the *Income Tax Act*), certain acting service income, and certain deferred income plan benefits (under Section 217).

To be considered non-resident, a former resident must demonstrate that the departure is permanent. This means that residential and other personal ties have been severed. In the year of departure, the taxpayer is considered to be a non-resident for tax purposes in the period after emigration.

In general, then, taxpayers who leave Canada must continue to file Canadian income tax returns as residents of Canada unless they sever all ties with Canada or become a resident in another country. In the year of departure, income can be reported both as a resident (for the period before departure) and a non-resident (for the period after departure). Where the place of residency is not obvious, certain "tie breaker rules" are used to determine where the closer connection is, based on a number of factors including the location of your permanent home, family, banking and social circles.

Reporting Income in the Non-Residency Period. During the period in which you were a non-resident, that is, before immigration or after emigration, different rules will apply. At issue will be the avoidance of double-taxation between international jurisdictions, when you have been a resident in two countries in the same year.

Non-residents must file an income tax return and pay taxes on the following taxable income sources earned in Canada:

- Income from employment in Canada
- Income from a business in Canada
- Income from the disposition of *Taxable Canadian Property*. This is the property of any taxpayer—who may be resident in Canada or a non-resident—upon which Canada reserves the right to levy and collect tax on its actual sale in the future. This could present double taxation problems for non-residents, depending on the rules in their new country of residence. This topic will be revisited later in this chapter.

Employment income earned by a non-resident is allocated to the province where the individual's duties are carried out. Self-employment income is reported in the province where the individual has a permanent establishment—a fixed place of business. Income that cannot be allocated attracts the federal surtax described above.

For investors, reserves for debt forgiveness, recovery of exploration and development expenses, and recaptured depreciation from the sale of a business interest will be reported as well. Professional help is advised in these cases.

Part-Year Residents. When a Canadian resident leaves Canada permanently (emigrates) and becomes a non-resident, or when someone immigrates to Canada and becomes a permanent resident, it will be necessary to file a tax return for the period of residency.

 CHECK IT OUT | **What income do I have to report for the period of Canadian residency?** Part-year residents are required to report income, deductions and credits from two periods: residency during part of the year and non-residency during part of the year on the same tax return.

Reporting For Residency Period. Report all income calculated in the normal manner, but only for the residency period. Here's what that means:

- Count the number of days of residency. If you arrive on July 1, 2012, for example, that will be 184/366 days or if you leave the country on July 1 it will be 183/366 days.
- Report income earned while in Canada in full in this period.
- Report the value of assets on the day of immigration/departure.
- Personal amounts are prorated according to the residency period fraction.
- Provincial taxes are due to the province of residence on the last day of residency for emigrants and the last day of the *year* for immigrants.
- Generally refundable tax credits (GSTC, CTC, and provincial credits) are not available to emigrants.
- *Asset Valuation on Immigration*. Those who immigrate to Canada must determine the Fair Market Value (FMV) of their assets at time of immigration. Canada is not able to tax any accrued capital gains before this. Nor will Canada recognize accrued

losses. This value on entry will be the Adjusted Cost Base (ACB) of those assets at that date. Keep that information in your Permanent File. It will be used in the future to calculate capital gains and losses.

Those who have previously emigrated and now return to Canada to re-establish permanent residency will follow the same rules and provide FMV of their assets upon re-entry. They will essentially have had a tax holiday on any gains but will not be able to recognize losses accrued in the non-residency period. They will, however, be able to reach back and use any unabsorbed capital loss balances they had before they emigrated. This will be discussed in more detail later.

Case Study | Emigration

John is 58 years old. He left Canada to live in another country on September 30, 2012. What are the tax consequences?

In your tax software, mark the date of departure into the details of identification area. John's personal amounts will automatically be prorated according to the number of days he was resident in Canada (274/366 = 74.9%). World income must be reported during this period. John will also have to value his taxable assets as of September 30 so he can calculate any potential departure tax.

After emigration, John will not be entitled to personal amounts and need not report world income in Canada as he will have no Canadian employment or business income. In John's case, there is no Taxable Canadian Property to sell after departure.

Later, when he retires, John can make a special election to file under S. 217 of the *Income Tax Act* to report his Old Age Security and Canada Pension Plan income so that he will qualify for full personal amounts for the year.

Deductions in the Residency Period. Allowable deductions taken to reduce income in this period include everything you would normally be entitled to, including:

- RRSP contributions made within the calendar year or the normal 60-day period after year end. Amounts may also be transferred out of an RPP, DPSP or RRIF to an RPP, RRSP or RRIF. Complete form NRTA1 *Authorization for Non-Resident Tax Exemption* so the payor does not have to withhold non-resident taxes. You will want to seek assistance from a tax and financial advisor with these transactions.
- Tax-deductible support payments made to an estranged spouse.
- Child care expenses.
- Carrying charges: interest on loans incurred will continue to be tax deductible by a non-resident but only if they offset business income. For investment loans, interest

is generally deductible only to date of emigration, unless paid to maintain Taxable Canadian Property. You'll want to get an interest "cut off" statement from your financial institution for the date of emigration or from the date of immigration.

- Other employment expenses
- Clerics' residence deduction
- Other deductions on Line 232
- Stock Options Deduction
- Other deductions on Line 250
- Losses on Lines 251, 252, 253
- Capital gains deduction
- Northern residents deduction

In each case, it must be shown that these amounts are linked to income earned in the period of Canadian residency.

Non-Refundable Tax Credits. The following non-refundable tax credits, which apply to the residency period, can be claimed in full:

- CPP and EI premiums paid in the residency period
- Canada Employment Amount
- Public Transit Amount
- Children's Fitness Amount
- Children's Arts Amount
- Home Buyers' Amount
- Adoption Expenses
- The Pension Income Amount
- Interest on Student Loan Amount
- Tuition and Education Amounts
- Medical Expenses
- Charitable Donations
- Spousal transfers for income earned in the residency period
- Amounts transferred from child (tuition/education for residency period and a prorated disability amount)

Departure Taxes. When you leave Canada permanently and become a non-resident you are deemed to have disposed of, and immediately reacquired all your capital assets at their fair market value. This will increase your cost base for the purposes of reporting your asset values on entry in your new country of residence.

However, in Canada, emigrants must pay a departure tax (i.e. capital gains tax on gains that accrued while a resident). But not all properties are included for these purposes. These are known as Excluded Personal Property and Reportable Property:

Excluded Personal Property. This is property that is excluded from the departure tax rules. You will not have to pay the taxes on:

- Canadian real estate, Canadian resource property, and timber resource property*
- Canadian business property (including inventory) if the business is carried on through a permanent establishment in Canada*
- Pensions and similar rights including Registered Retirement Savings Plans, Registered Retirement Income Funds and Deferred Profit-Sharing Plans
- Rights to certain benefits under employee profit sharing plans, employee benefit plans, employee trusts, and salary deferral arrangements
- Trust interests that were not acquired for consideration
- Property owned at the time he last became a resident of Canada, or property inherited after he last became a resident of Canada, if he was a resident of Canada for 60 months or less during the 10-year period before emigrating
- Employee stock options subject to Canadian tax
- Interests in life insurance policies in Canada (other than segregated fund policies)

* The taxpayer may elect to declare a deemed disposition on these types of properties, however, any deemed losses may not exceed gains on the deemed disposition of other property.

Reportable Property (Asset values under $25,000). If, upon emigrating, the fair market value of all property owned by the taxpayer (excluding personal use property with a value of less than $10,000) is more than $25,000, Form T1161 *List of Properties by an Emigrant of Canada* must be filed with the tax return for the year. It's important that you do this because the penalty for filing it late is a minimum of $100, and calculating at $25 per day to a maximum of $2,500.

Reportable property is property other than:

- money that is legal tender in Canada
- personal use property (like a sailboat or car) with a fair market value of less than $10,000
- life insurance policy interests
- interests in employee trusts, amateur athlete trusts, cemetery care trusts, trusts governing eligible funeral arrangements

Tax Free Savings Accounts. The TFSA is not caught by the departure tax rules. No TFSA contribution room is earned for those years where a person is non-resident and any withdrawals while a non-resident cannot be replaced. The U.S. (and other foreign jurisdictions) does not recognize the TFSA therefore any realized income ought to be non-taxable when removed after emigration. However, any capital appreciation will be taxable. Therefore it will make sense to remove capital properties from the TFSA on a tax-free basis immediately prior to emigrating and then trigger the deemed disposition on a nominal gain on departure.

Capital Gain on Deemed Disposition at Departure. The capital gain that may arise on departure is calculated in the normal manner (See Part 4) on Form T1243 *Deemed Disposition of Property by an Emigrant of Canada* and included on Schedule 3 *Capital Gains (or Losses).*

However, the payment of the tax itself, which could produce financial hardship in many cases, may be deferred until actual disposition. You can do this by election and with the posting of security. Security is not required if the federal taxes owing on the gains is $14,500 or less. For most taxpayers this would mean the capital gain is less than $100,000.

Case Study | Deemed Sale of Shares in Private Corporation

When Tamara left the country last year, she held shares in a corporation that she started several years earlier. She had previously sold her majority interest in the company and retained only a minor interest as an investment. Although Tamara did not dispose of the shares, she is deemed to have disposed of them on departure. What are the tax consequences of such deemed disposition?

The fair market value of the shares at the time of emigration was $160,000 and the ACB for the shares was $50,000. The deemed gain on the departure was therefore $110,000. To get some relief, Tamara may defer the taxes on the deemed gain until such time as she actually disposes of the shares.

Election to Defer Departure Taxes. Taxpayers like Tamara may elect to defer paying the taxes on the deemed dispositions by filing Form T1244 *Election, Under Subsection 220(4.5) of The Income Tax Act, to Defer the Payment of Tax on Income Relating to the Deemed Disposition of Property* by April 30 of the year following emigration. The payment of the taxes may be deferred until the asset is disposed of.

Where the amount owing exceeds $14,500, acceptable security must be provided to CRA. No penalty or interest is applicable to the amount owing as long as sufficient security has been provided.

Canada has been negotiating with other countries to adopt the same deemed disposition rules to avoid double taxation when the property is later sold.

Such co-operation was announced between Canada and the U.S. on September 18, 2000. It ensures that no additional tax will be paid in the country of destination on the deemed gain at the time of emigration from the resident country. In addition, the new cost base of the asset will be recognized.

Capital Losses on Departure. Losses on the deemed dispositions that cannot be applied against capital gains in the current or previous three years will be lost unless the taxpayer becomes a resident at some time in the future, or makes an election to reduce the proceeds of disposition of Taxable Capital Properties in the future.

Case Study | Loss on Deemed Disposition

When Jillian emigrated from Canada, she owned 1,000 shares of ABC Corp. (a publicly traded corporation), which had an ACB of $85,000 and a fair market value of $5,000. Her deemed gain on other capital property on emigration was $10,000, so she has a net loss of $70,000. What are the tax consequences of this deemed disposition?

This capital loss could be applied against any other capital gains that Denise reported on her return as a Canadian resident in the year of emigration or the prior three years and the resulting capital loss can be carried forward, so it is valuable, however, it can only be applied against capital gains reported on a Canadian tax return. Should Jillian return to Canada at some future date, she will be reporting all capital gains on a Canadian return again and can apply this carried forward capital loss against those gains, as described below.

Returning Former Resident. In general, returning residents will be deemed not to have disposed of the property they reported on departure when becoming a resident of Canada again. This person may, upon making an election, receive security back or apply for a refund of departure taxes paid.

The election is made in writing and must be made no later than the filing due-date of the tax return for the year in which residency is re-established.

If the election is made for *Taxable Canadian Property (TCP),* the deemed disposition that applied on departure is treated as though it never occurred and the deemed reacquisition on returning to Canada is equally ignored. The taxpayer's cost base in the TCP is what it was before departure.

If the election is made for property that is not TCP, the taxpayer is allowed to choose an amount that adjusts both the proceeds of disposition on departure and the deemed reacquisition cost on returning to Canada. The purpose of this rule is to allow the taxpayer to shelter from Canadian tax any gain that accrued while the taxpayer was not resident in Canada.

If the departure tax was paid, the election allows the year to be re-opened and reassessed so the tax paid can be refunded. If the departure tax was not paid so that only security was provided for the tax (which would be the preferred choice if the departing taxpayer thought he or she might return to Canada), no reassessment is required.

 Case Study | **Returning to Canada**

David emigrated from Canada in 2002. At the time he owned shares in a U.S. corporation with an adjusted cost base of $45,000 and a fair market value of $92,000. On departure, he reported a gain of $47,000. When David returned to Canada, the fair value of these shares was $108,000. Absent an election, David is deemed to have reacquired the shares for $108,000 on his return. David can elect to reduce both the proceeds of disposition on departure and the cost of the shares on re-entry by the least of three amounts:

• The gain reported on the departure tax return—$47,000;
• The fair value of the shares on return—$108,000; and
• Any other amount he chooses.

In this case, David would choose $47,000. This choice eliminates the gain on departure and establishes his cost base on returning to Canada as $61,000 ($108,000 – $47,000), thereby increasing his tax cost by the gain that accrued while he was outside Canada. David might choose a lower amount if he had capital losses to apply on his departure tax return.

The Bottom Line | Immigration and emigration signify the start or end of your relationship with CRA. Income will be reported for the part year in which you begin residency or depart; there will be a proration of credits and a valuation of your assets. Seek professional help, even if you have prepared your own return, because a review of your valuations and results could save you a lot of money and make you audit-proof.

42

Death of a Taxpayer

Thinking beyond the anguish of tax season is nature's annual bonus: the joy of late spring and the upcoming season at the lake. For many boomers and their parents this is a good time to think about the future. Specifically, who should inherit the cottage? Who should own the business shares? How will the proceeds of significant gains, after taxes, be distributed?

These can be difficult questions for even the most harmonious families. Extra cocktails don't always help, either. In fact, the subject of death, succession and estate planning is a touchy subject for many families.

When is the right time to discover and discuss strategies for accrued gains in various assets, including personal residences and businesses, as well as when to sell or transfer those significant assets to better manage your tax risks? It might be now. Consider the following tax and estate planning checklist as a starting point in discussions with your family and consider doing so before you pack away your tax returns for another year:

Make decisions about the family cottage. If the cottage is the principal residence, it is possible future gains could be tax-exempt even if you own more than one residence. To qualify each property as the exempt one you simply need to "ordinarily inhabit" each one at some time in the year. Later, when one is sold or transferred, you will have the option to decide which property will be the tax exempt one. You'll want to pick the one that has appreciated in value the most, of course.

Consider buying more insurance. There can be a significant tax implication upon the sale of a taxable personal residence. This can also happen on the death of the owner, if there is no surviving spouse to transfer the property to. You may in fact wish to increase your insurance coverage to make sure your heirs are covered and the property stays in the family.

Obtain valuations. Post-tax season is a good time to obtain valuations of family properties, because most people find this to be tremendously stressful if they have to do so under pressure, for example, if someone dies suddenly. Also, if you are planning significant improvements this year, remember to keep all receipts to increase the cost base of the property next tax season. This will reduce future capital gains.

Business owners have more tax options. A tax-free capital gain is the best kind, and that's exactly what you might have when you dispose of your qualifying small business corporation, qualifying farm or fishing properties. Every resident taxpayer in Canada is allowed a lifetime Capital Gains Exemption of $750,000 when these types of properties are sold or disposed of.

This is a big advantage and a happy acknowledgement of the risks of funding and working in a family business. A family of four adults, for example, could be eligible to claim a maximum of three million in tax-free capital gains, if the company's share structure is properly planned.

Sharing your good fortunes. Many Canadians are extremely generous; their family philanthropy provides an opportunity for community leadership and to make a real difference. Often, this is also the one thing even warring family members can agree on: doing good for the vulnerable in the community is so rewarding. Strategic philanthropy is a great way to start a family succession plan and teach wealth management principles, relationship management, tax and financial literacy.

Select your executor(s) carefully. This is important, because they are the ones personally responsible for filing your final tax return and paying the final tax bill. You'll want them to know about where to find your will, power of attorney and tax filing history, especially the carry forward provisions around capital losses, medical expenses, and charitable donations, to name a few. This is a big job. It helps, too, if you introduce your executor to your tax, investment, legal and insurance specialists as you plan your estate.

Preparing the Final Return. A final return must be filed in the year of death. This return is for the period from January 1 to the date of death. Note that the final return must be filed on paper as it does not qualify for NETFILE.

In addition to the final return, several optional returns may be filed to report specific types of income, such as income from a business or partnership and certain investments. Any income reported on an optional return may be excluded from the final return.

If the forms for the year of death are not available, file using a form from the prior year, but be sure to write the correct tax year in the top right corner of page 1 of the return. Such a return will likely be assessed based on the rules applicable to the prior taxation year, and they may not be filed electronically.

On certain types of income the deceased's representative may elect to pay the taxes due in up to 10 equal annual instalments. To make this election, file Form T2075 *Election to Defer Payment of Income Tax, Under Subsection 159(5) of the Income Tax Act by a Deceased Taxpayer's Legal Representative or Trustee* with the first instalment by the balance due date of the return (see below). CRA may require security for the amount owing. Income types eligible for this election are:

- Capital gains and recapture on deemed dispositions of capital property on death;
- Gains on resource properties or land inventories; and
- Rights or things on an elective return.

 CHECK IT OUT | **Who is recognized as the deceased's legal representative?** The legal representative of the deceased is the person responsible for the tax preparation and form filing.

According to CRA, a legal representative of a taxpayer is "the executor in a will, administrator of the estate by a court, or the liquidator for an estate in Quebec." In addition to preparing and filing the tax returns of the deceased, the legal representative must also pay the taxes owing and disclose the taxable portion of the deceased's estate to the beneficiaries.

CPP/QPP Death Benefits. Canada or Quebec Pension Plan death benefits are not considered to be income of the deceased. These amounts may be reported either on a T3 *Trust Income Tax and Information Return* for the estate created on the death of the deceased or by the recipient beneficiary. If there is no other income to be reported by the estate, the estate will pay tax at the lowest rate on the income. There may be some tax savings by reporting the death benefit on a T3 return if the recipient is in a higher tax bracket.

Investment and Other Periodic Income. Interest, rents, royalties, salary, and other amounts that are paid periodically, if not paid prior to the taxpayer's death, are deemed to accrue on a daily basis. That means that all income that is due but not paid must be calculated and reported on the final return, prorated to the date of death. In the case of joint investments or investments that pass to a survivor, it is necessary to allocate the applicable portion of the income earned prior to death to the deceased and the income received for the rest of the year to the appropriate person.

In the case of Canada Savings Bonds (CSBS), interest shown on the T5 *Statement of Investment Income (slip)* is calculated on the bond year (which depends on when the bonds were issued) rather than the calendar year.

before death but not paid at the time of death, and dividends that were declared before death but not paid will qualify to be excluded from the final return and included on a return for Rights or Things.

Tax Free Savings Accounts at Death. If a surviving spouse or common-law partner is designated as a successor holder of the TFSA either in the TFSA contract or in the deceased taxpayer's will, the successor becomes the owner of the TFSA. The successor holder acquires all the rights to the TFSA, including the right to remove funds from the account on a tax-free basis or to transfer those funds to their own TFSA without using TFSA contribution room.

A surviving spouse or common-law partner may receive the TFSA fund on a tax-free basis by transferring those funds to their own TFSA without using TFSA contribution room. Use Form RC240 *Designation of an Exempt Contribution Tax-Free Savings Account (TFSA)* to designate the amount to be transferred.

A designated beneficiary (other than a surviving spouse or common-law partner or qualified donee) may receive the TFSA proceeds on a tax-free basis but may not transfer those funds to their own TFSA unless they have available TFSA contribution room.

Capital Assets. Capital property owned immediately prior to death is deemed to be disposed of for proceeds equal to the fair market value (FMV) of the asset at that time. The recipient of the property is deemed to have acquired it at the time of the taxpayer's death at a cost equal to its fair market value.

However, if the recipient is the taxpayer's surviving spouse, then the transfer is deemed to be made at the deceased's adjusted cost base (ACB). But an election is available to deem the proceeds to be at any amount between the ACB and FMV of the assets at death. This can have advantages, depending on income levels and whether there are capital losses to be used up on the final return.

It is most important for the taxpayer's representative to look for and provide to the tax practitioner a copy of the 1994 tax return and, in particular, Form T664 upon which a *Capital Gains Election* was made. This will affect the calculation of the deemed disposition of capital properties on the final return.

Capital Losses. Normally, capital losses may only be deducted against capital gains in the year, the prior three years, or subsequent years. In the year of death, capital losses from the current year and capital losses carried forward can be applied to reduce any type of income. Specifically, the capital losses must be used in this order; your tax software will have applied these in this way:

- apply capital losses to reduce capital gains in the year of death
- apply remaining capital losses against capital gains in the year prior to death

- reduce remaining unapplied losses by the amount of capital gains deductions claimed in prior years

Uncashed matured bond coupons, bond interest earned to a payment date apply any remaining loss against other income in the year of death or immediately preceding year.

Example: Trevor passed away in 2012. His taxable income for the year was $35,000 plus an allowable capital loss of $10,000. In 2011, Trevor had a taxable capital gain of $6,000.

The $10,000 allowable capital loss may be applied to reduce his $6,000 capital gain in 2011 (use Form T1A to apply the loss) and the remaining $4,000 loss may be used to reduce taxable income in 2012 to $31,000.

Other Losses. Other losses in the year of death and losses carried forward must be applied according to the normal rules. Any unapplied losses that cannot be applied in the year of death expire.

Some Tax Relief. The legal representative may elect to pay the taxes on the capital gains as a result of the deemed dispositions in up to 10 equal annual instalments. Use Form T2075 *Election to Defer Payment of Income Tax, Under Subsection 159(5) of the Income Tax Act by a Deceased Taxpayer's Legal Representative or Trustee.* Interest, however, will be payable on the deferred amounts.

RRSPs and Other Pensions. A taxpayer is deemed to have received the fair market value of all assets in his RRSP or RRIF immediately prior to death. If there is a surviving spouse or common-law partner then the assets may be transferred tax-free to that person. Similar provisions allow for the transfer of Deferred Profit Sharing Plans, Registered Pension Plan Benefits, and Registered Retirement Income Fund (RRIF) assets. In certain circumstances, the RRSP can be transferred to a financially dependent child or grandchild, even when there is a surviving spouse.

Beginning in 2009, if the value of RRSP or RRIF assets decreases before those assets are distributed to the beneficiaries, a deduction may be claimed (at Line 232) on the final return of the deceased for the decrease in value of the assets. The T4RSP issued will include the fair market value of the RRSP assets at death. The RRSP issuer completes form RC249 which may be used as backup for the deduction. If the final return has already been filed by the time the RC249 form is received, an adjustment may be made to the final return (using form T1-ADJ).

RRSP Rollovers to RDSPs. As of March 5, 2010, the rollover rules for RRSPs at death are extended to allow tax-free rollovers from the deceased taxpayer's RRSP to the RDSP of a surviving child or grandchild. Such rollovers are limited to the recipient's RDSP contribution room and will not generate a Canada Disability Savings Grant.

RPP Past Service Contributions. In the year of death, you may deduct 100% of unclaimed past service contributions without limit.

Pension income splitting. If there is a surviving spouse and either the spouse or the decreased had pension income that was eligible for splitting while the deceased was alive, then the election to split pension income may be made even though one of the spouses is deceased. The maximum amount that qualifies is prorated by the number of months that the couple was married (and both alive) during the year.

Deductions. All deductions you would normally claim can be claimed on the final return.

Personal Amounts. You can claim personal amounts on each of the returns filed on behalf of the deceased, with exception of the Schedule 2 Amounts Transferred to Spouse, which can only be used on the final return. In computing the amount for a spouse or other dependant, the dependant's income for the full year must be used in the computation of the amount of the credit.

Medical Expenses. In years other than the year of death, medical expenses may be claimed for any 12-month period ending in the taxation year. In the year of death, medical expenses may be claimed for the 24-month period, which includes the date of death. This includes medical expenses paid after death. Where the legal representative pays medical expenses in respect of the deceased after the return is filed, the return may be adjusted to include such expenses. When medical expenses for the deceased are claimed by the surviving spouse or other supporting individual, the 24-month period applies to the expenses paid for the deceased but claimed by that person.

Charitable Donations. Deduct charitable donations up to 100% of net income, both in the year of death and the immediate preceding year. Bequests (i.e. gifts made in the will) are deemed to have been made immediately prior to death. Donations to a registered charity as the beneficiary of a life insurance policy, RRSP, RRIF or TFSA, is also possible.

Minimum Tax. Minimum tax carryovers may only be applied against taxes on the final return. Minimum tax does not apply in the year of death.

Refundable Tax Credits. Deceased taxpayers are not eligible to receive the Goods and Services Tax Credit (GSTC) or the Child Tax Benefits (CTB). If the taxpayer died after June 30, and would otherwise qualify, the Working Income Tax Benefit (WITB) may be claimed on the final return.

Income After Death. Most payments received by the deceased after death will have to be returned. For example, GST, CTB, OAS, and CPP Disability or Pension cheques should be returned if they relate to a period after the death of the taxpayer. The following types of income earned or paid after death should be reported by the estate on a T3 return:

- Salary or wages paid for the period after death
- Severance pay received because of death (as a death benefit, the first $10,000 may be non-taxable). If this amount is paid on the employee's death to recognize service in an office or employment, it can be received by the deceased's testamentary trust, in which case the trust may exclude up to $10,000 from income; the same is true if the amount is received by a single beneficiary. If it is received by several beneficiaries the $10,000 exempt income amount must be shared proportionately.
- Future adjustments to severance pay

Clearance Certificates. The legal representative should acquire a clearance certificate before distributing any property to beneficiaries. A clearance certificate certifies that all amounts for which the deceased is liable to CRA have been paid, or that CRA has accepted security for the payment. Legal representatives who do not obtain a certificate may be liable for any amount owed to CRA by the deceased. A certificate covers all tax years to the date of death. It is not a clearance for any amounts a trust owes. If there is a trust, a separate clearance certificate is needed for the trust.

To request a certificate, complete Form TX19 *Asking for a Clearance Certificate* and send it to the Assistant Director, Verification and Enforcement Division, at the tax services office to which the return is filed. Do not include Form TX19 with a return. Send it only after the notices of assessment for all the returns filed have been received and all outstanding amounts paid or security provided for amounts to be paid by instalments.

Funeral Arrangements. The costs of funeral arrangements are not deductible. However, amounts received from an eligible funeral arrangement for the provision of funeral arrangement is not income of the deceased or the estate.

Filing Due Dates for Final Return. The due date for final returns depends on the circumstances as shown below. Note that the due date for the surviving spouse is the same as the due date for the deceased. It is recommended that you seek the help of a professional tax advisor if there is income that qualifies for elective returns.

Date of Death	Filing Due Date	Balance Due Date
Before Nov. 1	April 30 of following year	April 30 of following year
After Oct. 31	Six months after date of death	Six months after date of death
Before Nov. 1 if SE*	June 15 of following year	April 30 of following year
After Oct. 31 if SE*	Six months after date of death	Six months after date of death

*Self-employed or spouse self-employed.

Prior Year Returns. The legal representative of the deceased should ensure that all prior-year returns have been filed to carry forward all unused capital losses, non-capital losses, etc. If it is to the advantage of the taxpayer, the survivors, or the estate, the deceased's representative may request adjustments to returns for up to 10 prior years under the Taxpayer Relief Provisions (formerly known as the Fairness Package). However, as a minimum, at least those returns for the prior three taxation years must be filed.

 The Bottom Line | The greatest eroder of wealth can be the taxes you pay on the final return. Planning ahead can insure more of your financial legacy remains intact once you've continued on with your journey. Preparing the final tax return is an important financial document and professional help is a good idea especially if the deceased was self-employed or an investor. If you're the surviving spouse remember that it's often difficult to make sound financial decisions in the year following the loss of a spouse so be sure to get proper advice during this difficult time.

PART 7

Be Sure

You've worked hard on your tax return and now better understand all the nuances. You also have improved questions to ask your tax professionals. Before putting all that paperwork to bed, however, you need to be sure.

By "being sure," we mean that you've double-checked your work and have taken every precaution to avoid possible tax penalties. You'll learn more about how to do just that in this part of the book.

The first step in being sure is leaving yourself enough time to complete your taxes. Filing your tax return on time is paramount. For most individuals, the filing due date is April 30. You and your spouse can wait to file on June 15 if you are reporting income from an unincorporated small business, but you will pay interest on outstanding amounts starting on May 1, so it's a good idea to file by April 30. If you owe money to CRA but fail to file on time, you will be subject to late filing penalties, and in some cases, gross negligence or even tax evasion if you have willfully committed fraud. In severe cases, jail terms are possible. CRA also has the power to garnishee wages (or seize your assets), so as mentioned, it's important to stay onside.

As you've learned, the focus of tax preparation is not only on what you earn, but what you keep. Knowing more about your tax filing rights, obligations and milestones will help you better plan your investments and work-life activities.

43

Double Check

Wow, you made it! You got to the end of another tax filing year, and using the knowledge you've gained in reading this book and the power of your tax software, you're ready to hit the "send" button and NETFILE your return. If for some reason you don't qualify (see Part 1), you can print and mail in your taxes or drop them off at the nearest Tax Services Office. Be sure to do so on time to avoid late filing penalties.

But before you do this, check everything over once more, carefully. With any luck and an accurate tax return, the waiting time won't be long, especially if you have completed the request for direct deposit.

 CHECK IT OUT | **What can I do to double-check my tax returns in a consistent process?** Besides reading carefully the checklist of errors and notes your tax software will generate, use our checklist below. Have your documents and calculator handy for a manual process check:

- All numbers are entered into the right screens from all the slips and there are no transposition errors (78 instead of 87, for example).
- The income information is on the right return (18-year-old Suzie is not reporting dad's early benefits from the Canada Pension Plan).
- The investments are right: income from property appears on Schedule 4 (interest, dividends and limited partnership income) together with the carrying charges, while capital gains and losses are on Schedule 3 and rental property Iicome on Form T776.

- Pension income amounts are separated properly to report periodic income received on Line 115 and lump sums or those amounts received by those under 65 on Line 130 or on Line 125 (RDSP benefits) or Line 129 (RRSP benefits).
- Net Income From a Proprietorship appears on Line 135 and the *Statement of Business Activities* Form T2125.
- The right auxiliary tax forms are completed for discretionary deductions like child care on Line 214 (Form T778), moving expenses on Line 219 (Form T1M) and employment expenses on Line 229 (Form T777 and T2200).
- The RRSP contribution and repayments into the Home Buyers' Plan and Lifelong Learning Plan are properly reported.
- The Schedules for Tax Credits are perfect: Schedule 1 for all the non-refundable tax credits, Schedule 2 for Transfers from the Spouse, Schedule 5 (for Infirm Adult Dependants and the Caregiver Amount), Schedule 9 (for Donations), Schedule 11 (for Tuition, Education and Textbook Amounts).
- You got the tax withholdings right: off all the slips on Line 435, and from quarterly instalments on Line 476.
- You've optimized all income splitting opportunities: perks and benefits from the employer have been claimed with all offsetting deductions (like carrying charges, Northern residents amounts or stock options deductions), pension income has been split with your spouse and investment income sources follow the Attribution Rules.
- You've transferred all the deductions and non-refundable credits to the optimal advantage of the family unit.

Then, print your returns and use Appendix 4, our T1 line-by-line tax guide.

 The Bottom Line | Before you finish your tax files, print a copy of your tax filing summaries for your permanent file, your working copy file and your CRA audit file, remembering to print schedules and forms that support your receipts, as well as the carry forward summaries for use next year. If your hard disk crashes for some reason, or you change software and lose data in the process, finalizing the files you learned about in Part 1 is a smart move.

44

Avoid Penalties

Balance Due? If you have been shocked to find a balance due rather than a refund, file your return anyway to avoid late filing penalties. This is an important first step in keeping more money, even if you can't pay your bill immediately. You may wish to have a pro look over your return (or prior returns) to see if they can find something you missed. Otherwise, pay what you can, then make arrangements to pay over time. You'll be charged interest, but not penalties.

Penalty Alert. You will avoid expensive *gross negligence* or possibly *tax evasion* penalties if you avoid the temptation to rework the numbers to get a refund instead of a balance due. Know the difference between tax avoidance and tax evasion, especially if you are doing your own return by computer.

Do you know which is legal and which is a criminal offence—tax evasion or tax avoidance? The latter is okay. Here's a true-to-life example to make the point:

Example: A group of pre-retirement tax seminar attendees were asked by their instructor to consider this scenario:

An estimation for a basement renovation is in progress. The contractor says, "The fee is 'X' with a receipt, and 'Y' (substantially less) for cash…"

Which quote would you take?

Many in the audience thought it was perfectly acceptable to take the Y option, turning a blind eye to their active participation within the underground economy. Few were outraged by the fact that the contractor, assuming he would not report the cash received, would be doing so at the expense of honest suppliers and taxpayers as a whole.

Consider other common scenarios: a babysitter refuses to take on care for a new baby because the working mother wants a receipt… "I give no receipts," she says, and in apparent justification, "It costs my husband too much on his taxes." Or perhaps your domestic cleaning help wants cash too?

Is this *tax evasion*? The answer in all cases is yes. Tax evasion is the act of making false or deceptive statements in a return, certificate, statement or even an answer filed or verbally given to the Canada Revenue Agency, with the intent to willfully evade the payment of your taxes. You'll also be caught if you willfully make deceptive entries or omissions in your books. A person who destroys, alters, mutilates or otherwise willfully disposes of the records or books of account to evade the payment of tax is also asking for prosecution.

Inadequate bookkeeping can attract harsh penalties. Prime candidates are those who carry on a business or who are required to pay or collect taxes or other amounts under the *Income Tax Act*. But people who claim carrying charges, moving expenses, medical and charitable donations are at risk, too. So are waiters and waitress who don't declare their tips or anyone who refuses to file a tax return, or the people who overstate their refundable or non-refundable tax credits by claiming a single status to avoid counting in their common-law spouse's net income.

Record Retention. Know that you must keep records and books of account for at least six years after the end of the taxation year to which those records relate. However, CRA has the right to demand that records be kept longer.

What's a "record?" This includes anything that contains information, whether in writing or in any other form, including electronic forms. If books and records are inadequate the penalties can be steep:

- a fine of not less than $1,000 and not more than $25,000
- both a fine and imprisonment for up to 12 months.

You may request permission to destroy records before the six-year period is up. By filing a special form—T137. But we don't recommend it: such a request invites the taxman to consider verifying those records prior to destruction.

But, it gets worse for tax evaders. Most people don't know that there are, in fact, several layers of punishment for tax evaders. There are administrative penalties CRA can levy and criminal penalties that can be imposed by the courts. What's important to note is that both the penalties can apply to the same crime.

Take, for example, the *gross negligence penalties.* Every person who knowingly makes false statements or omissions can be subject to a penalty of the greater of $100 and 50% of the tax sought to be evaded or tax credits sought to be received. This penalty relates specifically to the taxpayer, rather than his or her advisors. In addition, the grossly negligent taxpayer may be subject to late filing penalties if the return did not get in on time and interest on any outstanding balance owing, compounding daily.

Taxpayers who are found to participate in *tax evasion* will face more penalties by being charged with an offense. When a taxpayer is guilty of an offense, a criminal prosecution takes place. While in the case of gross negligence, the *burden of proof* is on the taxpayer; in tax evasion cases, the burden is on CRA to show that there was willful evasion and that there is no reasonable doubt of the crime.

Those convicted of tax evasion face a series of penalties, the most common of which is a fine of not less than 100% and not more than 200% of the tax sought to be evaded or credits sought to be gained. This penalty could also be accompanied by a prison term of not more than five years.

Voluntary Compliance. The good news for those who may have uncomfortable consciences, is something called "*voluntary compliance.*" If you initiate an adjustment of your tax returns to report the correct income and deductions or credits for the tax year, you'll avoid the major penalties, but not interest. And of course, you always have to pay the tax you properly owe.

 The Bottom Line | Tax avoidance—arranging your affairs within the framework of the law to pay the least taxes legally possible—is your right and it's legal. It's only a criminal offence if you evade taxes, mess with the books, or stick your head in the sand and don't file at all.

Common Administrative Penalties Levied by CRA

Circumstance	Penalty
Failure to file a return on time	5% of unpaid taxes plus 1% per month up to a maximum of 12 months from filing due date, which is June 15 for unincorporated small businesses
Subsequent failure to file on time within a three-year period	10% of unpaid taxes plus 2% per month to a maximum of 20 months from filing due date
Failure to provide information on required form	$100 for each failure
Failure to provide Social Insurance Number	$100 for each failure unless the card is applied for within 15 days of the request
Failure to file a return or comply with a duty	For each such failure, the greater of $100 and the product obtained when $25 is multiplied by the number of days, not exceeding 100 during which the failure continues.

Circumstance	Penalty
Gross negligence: false statement or omission of information in the return	50% of tax on understated income with a minimum $100 penalty. This penalty will also apply to a false statement relating to the GSTC.
Late or insufficient instalments	50% of interest payable exceeding $1,000 or 25% of interest payable if no instalments were made, whichever is greater.
Misrepresentation by a third party: penalty for tax planning arrangements or valuation activities	$1,000 and the total of gross entitlements from the plan or in all other cases, $1,000
Third-party participation in make of false statements	$1,000 and lesser of the penalty to which the taxpayer is liable to under S. 163(2) and the total of $100,000 plus the person's gross compensation
Failure to deduct or remit source deductions	10% of amount not withheld, or remitted
Second such failure in same year	20% of amount not withheld or remitted if this was done knowingly or through gross negligence.

Offences and Punishment. Convictions result from criminal prosecution. The taxpayer's advisors can also be found guilty and charged.

Offence	Punishment
Failure to make or file a return as required	A fine of not less than $1,000 and not more than $25,000 or both fine and imprisonment for a term not exceeding 12 months
Tax evasion, including making of false, deceptive statements in a return, certificate, statement or answer, destroying, altering, mutilating, books or records, or otherwise willfully evading tax or fraudulently claiming refunds or credits	A fine of not less than 50% and not more than 200% of the amount of tax sought to be evaded or both the fine and imprisonment of not more than two years.
Prosecution on indictment: any person charged tax evasion may be prosecuted at the election of the Attorney General of Canada to a further penalty—in addition to any other penalty.	A fine of not less than 100% and not more than 200% of the amount of tax sought to be evaded or credits sought to be obtained.
Communication of confidential information by government official	A fine of not more than $5,000 or imprisonment of up to 12 months or both.
Communication of taxpayer's SIN	A fine of not more than $5,000 or imprisonment of up to 12 months or both.

45

Exercise Your Rights: It's About What You Keep

Filing a tax return is about what you keep.

If you are an individual employee, the objective is to get the biggest refund possible—in other words, get the government to give back to you as much of the withholding taxes taken from your paycheque as possible. It's your first step to incredible wealth.

Think about it… if you are financially focused and invest that average tax refund of $1,659 you'll get back every year over the course of your working lifetime—let's say that's 40 years—you will have $66,360 more in savings to live your dreams with.

Invested at a 4% interest rate, that tax refund will grow to $160,770 in a TFSA, or $131,600 in a non-registered account, assuming a tax rate on income of about $45,000. (Remember your tax calculations will change depending on your province of residence.) Either way, this is a six-figure lump sum you are turning over to the government to use every year of your working life, interest-free. You could be paying down your mortgage instead.

More financial power comes your way when you take a family focus. If there are four adults in the family, for example, each making roughly the same amount of money, the family capital saved in a TFSA would grow to hundreds of thousands of dollars: over $643,000 using our example above!

You make economic decisions as a family; you earn refundable tax credits based on family income, and you can now accumulate large sums of money—tax free—to fund your family members' retirements in the future. If you plan well, you can split pension income sources with your spouse and transfer assets between families because you know how to avoid the Attribution Rules.

Because you understand your tax-filing right better, you can make better investment decisions. You'll put your savings into the right "buckets" to grow in, and this is extremely smart because you will need to be more tax astute to get ahead in the near future.

Today it's in vogue for debt-ridden governments to "tax the rich," with surtaxes on incomes over $130,000, $150,000, $250,000, etc. We even hear of proposed increased income inclusion rates on capital gains, in the case of the province of Quebec. Make no mistake—these are taxes on inheritances of private pension accumulations left by grandparents to their heirs. Governments, which position themselves to grab more on the increasing value of your dividends or capital assets, reap rewards exponentially as inflation rises because they get to tax gains due to inflation. Good for the government but not so good for you because you end up with less purchasing power.

It's been a decade of markets with nil or negative returns but some investors have done extremely well because they have a secret insight. They simply stay the course in their investment strategies and refuse to bolster a period of negligible returns with the insult of tax erosion. It's impossible to control inflation or government policies, but we absolutely can arrange our affairs within the framework of the law to pay the least amount of taxes possible over time.

By learning to prepare your family's taxes and using the fast convenient electronic filing methods, you have taken a sound first step in proactively increasing the returns you get from your two precious resources: time and money. That's one of the important tax secrets of rich people: by investing their precious resources of time and money to their best tax advantage, they manage risk better, with family net worth that keeps growing no matter what the taxman or the economy throws at them.

I hope this book has helped you find new ways to "pay yourself first." When you slash away at all the wealth eroders—expensive user fees, interest costs and MERs, tax withholdings and instalment payments—you can invest with an eye to keeping more for your own future. I hope you had some "aha" moments around:

- Tax deductions and credits you may have missed or not known about.
- Splitting retirement and investment income with your spouse.
- Structuring net income (Line 236 of your return) to come in under the "clawback zones" for Child Tax Benefits, GST/HST Credits, Working Income Tax Benefits, Employment Insurance and OAS Repayments, as well as the many provincial tax credits available.
- Avoiding net income "spikes" with investment income diversification. (Dividends, for example, can artificially gross up net income, which in turn can increase per diem fees at nursing homes, and public pharmacy care plan deductibles, while reducing monthly social benefits like OAS and other tax credits found on your tax return). Tax, investment and retirement planning, in other words, work hand in hand.

In volatile times, it can also pay handsomely to work with a team of tax-astute advisors who can crunch the numbers to verify your tax planning and investment decisions. I hope the "Tax Pro Alerts" have helped you to ask better questions of your professional financial advisors. Remember, you can also look back to recover errors and omissions on prior-filed returns (up to 10 years back) and then use that new money to fund your TFSA, RRSP or emergency funds. A pro can help make that process easier for you, too.

Tax-efficient wealth planning is an important bi-product of astute family tax preparation. Filing an accurate tax return every year for each family member and the family as a whole is absolutely critical to your financial health—consider it your annual "Vitamin T."

I know you'll make better financial decisions because you have made the effort to learn how to do your returns with more tax savvy. Congratulations! You're well on your way to affluence… the peace of mind that comes with knowing you'll have enough when you really need it.

Yours in tax savings,
Evelyn

Appendices

Consider our appendices your very own Jacks on Tax guide.

Not sure of the important dates? Appendix 1 keeps you abreast of the tax milestones all year long that require your attention.

Appendix 2 is your guide to what items you can carry forward on your tax return. It's important to know these specifics since they may reduce your taxes in the future, and some in prior years, too.

Keeping more money in your pocket is the emphasis of Appendix 3. It focuses on all the tax credits available to you—make sure you don't miss any that you directly qualify for. Clawback zones are summarized as well.

Appendix 4 is the T1 line-by-line tax guide, which goes through the actual tax return in more detail and what's most relevant about specific line items.

Finally, look to Appendix 5 for Knowledge Bureau books and courses for more information. Check out our new releases from our highly sought-after experts, and get connected to ongoing tax and economic updates by reading *Knowledge Bureau Report*.

Appendix 1. Tax Filing Milestones

January
- **Jan. 2:** Reduce your tax withholdings at source: file your TD1 form to claim tax credits and a T1213 form.
  - Make your TFSA contribution.
- **Jan. 30**: Interest payment on inter-spousal loans.

February
- **End of Month:** You'll receive T4, T5 slips
- Federal Budget (dates vary)

March
- **March 1:** RRSP filing deadline (60 days after year end)
- **March 15** Quarterly Instalment due
- **March 31:** T3 slips due
  - File "Advantage" Tax Returns for TFSA, RRSP due 90 days after year-end.
  - File form T1-OVP to pay RRSP Excess Contributions Penalty of 1% per month due 90 days after year-end.

April
- **April 15:** U.S. Tax filing date
- **April 30:** Individual tax filing deadline
  - Late elections for 2009 pension income splitting expires

May
- Update will, powers of attorney and health care directives

June
- **June 15**: Quarterly instalment due
  - Tax deadline for self-employed individuals and their spouses
- Closer Connection Exception Statement for Aliens (IRS Form 8840)

July
- Portfolio and cash flow review
- Review RRSP meltdown strategies
- Instalment payment review: Did you have to pay more than $3,000 when you filed your T1 return? If so, you may be required to make quarterly tax instalments starting September 15!

August
- Back-to-school expense planning review
- File for WITB prepayment

September
- **September 15:** Quarterly Instalment due
- Book medical appointments, dental appointments, glasses, etc. to claim expenses before December 31.
- Review asset purchase strategies—cars, computers, buildings, equipment, etc. to acquire before year-end to increase Capital Cost Allowance claims.
- Review donations strategies and give before December 31.

October
- **Thanksgiving:** Review family income splitting, cottage valuation, plan inter-spousal loans and asset transfers
- **October 15:** IRS Form 4868 Extension of filing time

November
- CSB, CPB, investment portfolio review

December
- **December 15:** quarterly instalment due
  - Tax Loss selling
- **December 31:** Make RESP, RDSP contributions; transfer RRSPs to RRIF if you turned 71; make 2012 TFSA contribution
  - Adjust T1 returns for errors or omissions to prior filed returns (2002 to 2011)
  - Annual instalment for farmers and fishers

Appendix 2. Carry Forward Information

You can adjust returns	Significance
The preceding ten years	• To correct errors and omissions for most federal provisions. • To correct errors and omissions for GST/HST Rebates (Line 457).
The preceding three years	• To apply capital losses to capital gains in those years. • To apply non-capital losses to income of prior years. • To adjust most provincial tax credits.
Over a 24-month period	• Medical expenses can be claimed over this period ending on and including the date of death.
The current and immediately preceding year	• To apply previous net capital losses carried forward against other income in the year of death, after their application to capital gains in current and prior three prior years. • To claim charitable donations in year of death.
The preceding 11 months	• To recover unpaid Child Tax Benefits and GST Credits. Note: late applications may be allowed with sufficient documentation.
The following year	• To use unclaimed medical expenses of the previous year to make a claim for the best 12-month period ending in the tax year.
The next three years	• To make or amend a joint election to split pension income. • To recover overpaid EI premiums in cases where employee did not qualify (e.g. significant or majority owner of a corporation).
The next five years	• To use any charitable donation tax receipts. • To deduct student loan interest.
The next seven years	• To minimum tax carry forwards. • To claim legal fees in excess of RRSP contributions in respect of job termination payments.
The next 10 years	• To apply allowable Business Investment Losses (BIL) against other income. Thereafter, unabsorbed loss becomes a capital loss.
The next 20 years	• To apply unused non-capital losses to other income (previously: seven years for non-capital losses incurred before 2004, 10 years for losses incurred in 2004 and 2005).
Indefinite time	• To use RRSP deduction when there is RRSP room (individual or if no longer age-eligible, to spousal RRSP if spouse is under age 71). • To use capital losses against capital gains up to and including year of death. • To use unclaimed RRSP deductions, up to & including year of death. • To use tuition, education and textbook amounts.

Appendix 3. Refundable and Non-Refundable Tax Credits Summary

The Benefit Year. The GST Credit and Child Tax Benefit are based on a July to June benefit year. Income levels quoted are for net income from the previous taxation year. Rates for the specified time period are indexed based on CPI for prior December.

Split Child Benefits. Note that after *June 2011*, each parent who lives with the child can receive 50% of any GST Credit and Child Tax Benefits. Each parent will want to invest these benefits in the name of the child to build up a great education fund, but also to avoid tax on resulting investment earnings.

GST/HST Credit

	July 2012 to June 2013	July 2011 to June 2012
Adult maximum	$260	$253
Child maximum	$137	$133
Single supplement	$137	$133
Phase-in threshold for the single supplement	$8,439	$8,209
Family net income at which credit begins to phase out	$33,884	$32,961

Child Tax Benefit

	July 2012 to June 2013	July 2011 to June 2012
Base benefit	$1,405	$1,367
Additional benefit for third child	$98	$95
Family net income at which base benefit begins to phase out	$42,707	$41,544
NCB: First child	$2,177	$2,118
NCB: Second child	$1,926	$1,873
NCB: Third child	$1,832	$1,782
Family income at which NCB begins to phase out	$24,863	$24,183
Family net income at which NCB supplement phase-out ends	$42,707	$41,544
CDB Maximum benefit	$2,575	$2,504
Family net income at which CDB begins to phase out	$42,707	$41,544

Working Income Tax Benefit

2012 Rates	Most Provinces		British Columbia		Alberta		Nunavut	
Working Income Tax Benefit	Single Taxpayer	Family (or Single Parent)	Single	Family	Single	Family	Single	Family
Minimum earned income	$3,000	$3,000	$4,750	$4,750	$2,760	$2,760	$6,000	$6,000
Credit rate	25%	25%	21%	21%	20%	20%	5%	10%
Maximum credit	$970	$1,762	$1,206	$1,914	$1,059	$1,589	$608	$1,216
Clawback of income begins at	$11,011	$15,205	$12,059	$16,254	$11,535	$15,730	$20,973	$26,740
Clawback rate	15%	15%	17%	17%	15%	15%	4%	8%
Income for maximum credit	$6,880	$10,048	$10,493	$13,864	$8,055	$10,705	$18,160	$18,160
Credit fully clawed back	$17,478	$26,952	$19,153	$27,513	$18,595	$26,323	$36,173	$41,940

Clawback Zones for 2012

The following table shows clawback zones for personal amounts for 2012.

Credit	2012 Reduction Begins	2012 Credit Eliminated
Old Age Security	$69,562	$112,966
Employment Insurance	$57,375	Varies with EI amount
Age Amount	$33,884	$78,684
Spouse or Common-Law Partner Amount (not infirm)	$0	$10,822
Spouse or Common-Law Partner Amount (infirm)	$0	$12,822
Amount for Eligible Dependants (not infirm)	$0	$10,822
Amount for Eligible Dependants (infirm)	$0	$12,822
Amount for Infirm Dependants	$6,402	$12,822
Caregiver Amount (not infirm)	$15,033	$19,435
Caregiver Amount (infirm)	$15,033	$21,435

Summary of Personal Amounts for 2010 – 2012

Personal Amounts		2010	2011	2012
Basic Personal Amount	Maximum Claim*	$10,382	$10,527	$10,822
Age Amount	Maximum Claim*	$6,446	$6,537	$6,720
	Reduced by net income over*	$32,506	$32,961	$33,884
Spouse or Common-Law Partner Amount	Not infirm*	$10,382	$10,527	$10,822
	Infirm*	$10,382	$10,527	$12.822
Eligible Child under 18	Not infirm*	$2,101	$2,131	$2,191
	Infirm	$2,101	$2,131	$4,191
Amount for Eligible Dependants	Not infirm*	$10,382	$10,527	$10,822
	Infirm*	$10,382	$10,527	$12,822
Amount for Infirm Dependants	Maximum Claim*	$4,223	$4,282	$6,402
	Reduced by net income over*	$5,992	$6,076	$6,420
Pension Income Amt.	Maximum Claim	$2,000	$2,000	$2,000
Adoption Expenses	Maximum Claim	$10,975	$11,128	$11,440
Caregiver Amount	Not infirm	$4,223	$4,282	$4,402
	Infirm	$4,223	$4,282	$6,402
	Reduced by net income over	$14,422	$14,624	$15,033
Disability Amount	Basic Amount	$7,239	$7,341	$7,546
	Supplementary Amount*	$4,223	$4,282	$4,402
	Base Child Care Amount*	$2,473	$2,508	$2,578
Tuition and Education Amounts +Textbook Tax Credit	Minimum Tuition	$100	$100	$100
	Full-time Education Amt. (per month)	$400 +$65	$400 +$65	$400 +$65
	Part-time Education Amt. (per month)	$120 +$20	$120 +$20	$120 +$20
Medical Expenses	3% limitation*	$2,024	$2,052	$2,109
	Maximum claim for other dependants	$10,000	N/A	N/A
Refundable Medical Expense Credit	Maximum*	$1,074	$1,089	$1,119
	Base Family Income*	$23,775	$24,108	$24,783
	Minimum earned income*	$3,116	$3,179	$3,268
Canada Employment Amount	Maximum*	$1,051	$1,065	$1,095
Children's Fitness Amount	Maximum	$500	$500	$500
Home Buyers' Amount	Maximum	$5,000	$5,000	$5,000
Children's Arts Amount	Maximum	N/A	$500	$500

*Indexed.

Provincial Refundable Tax Credits

AB AB Family Employment Tax Credit (AFETC)

BC Basic Family Bonus
BC Earned Income Benefit
BC HST Credit (BCHSTC)
BC Low Income Climate Action Tax Credit (BCLICATC)
BC Venture Capital Tax Credit
BC Mining Exploration Tax Credit
BC Training Tax Credit

MB Advance Tuition Fee Income Tax Rebate
Fertility Treatment Tax Credit
Education Property Tax Credit
School Tax Credit for Homeowners
Personal Tax Credit
Primary Caregiver Tax Credit
MB Book Publishing Tax Credit
Green Energy Equipment Tax Credit
Cultural Industries Printing Tax Credit

NB NB Child Tax Benefit (NBCTB)
NB Working Income Supplement
NB School Supplement

NL NL and Labrador Child Benefit
Mother Baby Nutrition Supplement
NL and Labrador harmonized sales tax credit (NLHSTC)
NL and Labrador seniors' benefit (NLSB)

NT NT Child Benefit (NWTCB)
NT Cost of Living Tax Credit

NS NS Child Benefit (NSCB)
NS Affordable Living Tax Credit (NSALTC)

NU NU Child Benefit (NUCB)
Cost of Living Tax Credit
Political Contribution Tax Credit
Basic Training Tax Credit

ON ON Child Benefit (OCB)
ON Children's Activity Tax Credit
ON Political Contribution Tax Credit
ON Focused Flow-Through Share Tax Credit
ON Apprenticeship Training Tax Credit
ON Co-operative Education Tax Credit
ON Trillium Benefit

PE None

PQ Child Assistance
Supplement for Handicapped Children
Adapted Work Premium
Property Tax Refund
Property Tax Refund for Forest Producers
QST Rebate for Employees and Partners
Solidarity Tax Credit
Supplement to the Work Premium
Tax Credit for a Top-Level Athlete
Tax Credit for Adoption Expenses
Tax Credit for an On-the-Job Training Period
Tax Credit for Caregivers
Tax Credit for Childcare Expenses
Tax Credit for Home-Support Services for Seniors
Tax Credit for Income from an Income-Averaging Annuity for Artists
Refundable Tax Credit for Medical Expenses
Tax Credit for Respite of Caregivers
Tax Credit for Scientific Research and Experimental Development
Tax Credit for Taxi Drivers and Taxi Owners
Tax Credit for the Acquisition of Pig Manure Treatment Facilities
Tax Credit for the Acquisition or Lease of a New Energy-Efficient Vehicle
Tax Credit for the Income Tax Paid by an Environmental Trust
Tax Credit for the Repayment of Benefits
Tax Credit for the Reporting of Tips
Tax Credit for the Treatment of Infertility
Tax Credit for Volunteer Respite Services
Work Premium

SK SK Low-Income Tax Credit (SLITC)
Graduate Retention Program Tuition Rebate
Active Families Benefit

YT YT Child Benefit (YCB)
YT Research and Development Tax Credit

Appendix 4. T1 Line-By-Line Tax Guide

Line	Tax Tips for Double Checking Your Data Entries
Page 2	
101 Employment Income	• Only report Box 14 amount from T4 slip. Do not report any taxable benefits or commission in other boxes. One exception is Box 87 for volunteer firefighters. If the volunteer firefighters' amount is claimed on Line 362 is claimed, the excluded income shown in Box 87 must be included on Line 101. • **Offsetting Deductions**. Income may be offset with employment expenses on Line 229 and the GST/HST Rebate on Line 457 should be claimed. • **Canada Employment Credit**. Taxpayers reporting employment income are eligible for the Canada Employment Credit claimed on Line 363. • **Taxable Benefits**. Do not report taxable benefits noted elsewhere on the T4; they are already included in Box 14. If taxable benefits include a standby-charge for auto expenses, it may be possible to claim offsetting deductions for costs incurred on Line 229 Employment Expenses and to claim a GST/HST Rebate on Line 457. • **Tax-Free Benefits** (not reported) could include tuition for training taken by the employee that is of benefit to the employer, discounts on merchandise, subsidized meals, recreational facility memberships, employee counseling, uniforms, transportation provided for security reasons. • **If no T4 slip received**, report employment income based on pay stubs if available or an estimate. • **Clerics** will be taxed on housing allowance, report the employment earnings without this allowance on Line 101. Report allowance on Line 104. • **Salary Deferral Arrangements.** Where the employee defers the receipt of compensation to a future tax year that compensation must normally be included in income in the year earned, not received. Exceptions include income deferred by certain temporary residents of Canada and plans under which a bonus can be paid within three years after the end of the tax year in which it was earned. Also included are self-funded leaves of absence of a minimum of six months, especially for teachers and professors. Income can be deferred up to six years for not more than 1/3 of salary. Also eligible for deferral is salary of professional hockey officials working for the NHL.
102 Commissions Earned	• Complete Form T777 Employment Expenses and have the employer complete Form T2200 Declaration of Conditions of Employment in order to claim expenses against commissions on Line 229 and the GST/HST Rebate on Line 457. • Do not report commissions again on Line 101; they are already included in Box 14. • Advances against commissions are taxed in the year received.

Line items are in the order as they appear on the tax form.

Line	Tax Tips for Double Checking Your Data Entries
104 Other Employment Income	• Report other income from employment, including casual employment here: • Clerics housing allowance—claim offsetting deduction at Line 231(included in T4 Box 14) • Employment income from working in foreign country • Director's fees • Net research grants (T4A Box 104 less expenses) • Wage Earner Protection Plan (WEPP) payments (T4A Box 132) • GST/HST Rebates received in the year by employees who filed a GST/HST 370 in the prior year • Employment income not reported on a T4 slip, such as casual labour, tips, executor's fees • Royalties from work or invention • Wage Loss Replacement Plan benefits (T4A Box 107 if taxable) • Supplementary Unemployment benefits (T4A Box 152) • Group life insurance premiums (T4A Box 119) • Medical premium benefits (T4A Box 118) • Veterans benefits (T4A Box 127)
113 OAS Benefits	• Check T4A (OAS) for any tax withholding and claim this on Line 437. • Claim the Age Amount on Schedule 1, Line 301. • Do not report the spouse's OAS here; however note that spouse's Age Amount may be transferable to the taxpayer at Line 326. See Schedule 2. • High-income earners may have to repay some of their OAS benefits. Social Benefits Repayment: Line 235. Net income can be reduced—and the repayment possibly avoided—with an RRSP contribution if age eligible.
114 CPP Benefits	• **Report CPP benefits here**: retirement, disability, death and survivor's benefits from T4A(P). • CPP retirement benefits can be split between spouses if an assignment request has been made with Service Canada and the spouses are at least 60 years of age. • Disability benefits qualify as earned income for RRSP purposes. Lump sums over $3,000 are averaged by CRA over the period of years in which the benefits should have been paid after the return is filed, and an additional refund may result. • Child's survivor benefits are reported on the child's return. This could affect Amounts for Eligible Dependant claims. • Reinvestments of CPP benefits by lower income earners in the family generate investment earnings, which are taxed at their lower rates.

Line	Tax Tips for Double Checking Your Data Entries
115 Other Pensions, Superannuation	• **Report pension income received periodically here**: from private company pensions, annuities or deferred profit sharing plans. These will qualify for the Pension Income Amount on Line 314 if the recipient was over 64 or receiving the amounts as a result of their spouse's death. • Foreign pensions are reported here too, in Canadian funds, and may qualify for the Pension Income Amount if paid periodically. Certain pensions (like U.S. Social Security or certain German pensions) qualify for offsetting deductions on Line 256. • Foreign retirement arrangements are exempt from income here in Canada if they are not taxable in their originating country. • Do not report income from RRSP withdrawals here. See Line 129. • RRIF withdrawals on a T4RIF are reported here if the taxpayer was 65 or older or in receipt of the payments as a result of the spouse's death. Otherwise report the income on Line 130. • Spousal RRIFs: when amounts originally contributed to a spousal RRSP are transferred to a RRIF, the contributor must report any income over the minimum amounts required to be withdrawn, if the rollover occurred within three years from the last spousal contribution.
116 Elected Split- Pension Amount	• For transferors, enter the amount (up to 50% of eligible pension income) that is jointly elected on Form T1032. • This amount is deemed to be income of the transferee and is deductible by the transferor on Line 210.
117 Universal Child Care Benefit	• UCCB amounts received by the family must be reported by the taxpayer who has the lower net income (Line 236) before reporting the UCCB. For single parents, beginning in 2010, the UCCB may be included in income of the child that is claimed as an eligible dependant rather than in the parent's income. Report the designated amount on Line 185.
119 EI Benefits	• Report amounts from T4E slip here; the income is fully taxable. • High-income earners who have received EI benefits in the prior 10 years may be subject to the Social Benefits Repayment on Line 235 if net income on Line 236 is over $57,375 (for 2012). • Net income can be reduced—and the repayment possibly avoided—with an RRSP contribution, provided the taxpayer has RRSP room. • If EI was repaid due to ineligibility, an offsetting deduction can be claimed for the repayment on Line 232. File documentation to support repayment. • When tuition is paid by EI for programs designed for workforce re-entry, the amounts will not be included in income. • If EI pays tuition for education programs approved by HRDC, EI or provincial Labour Market Development Agreements, the taxable amounts will qualify for the tuition/education/textbook tax credits.

Line	Tax Tips for Double Checking Your Data Entries
120 Taxable Canadian Dividends	• **Use taxable amount.** Report the "taxable" not the "actual amounts" here and then take the offsetting Dividend Tax Credit on Line 425 of Schedule 1. For eligible dividends, the taxable amount is 138% of the actual dividends received (for other dividends—usually from a small business corporation—the taxable amount is 125% of the actual dividends received). • **Attribution.** Dividends resulting from money transferred to the spouse or minor child must be reported by the transferor, unless the dividends received by a minor child attract the tax on split income. • **Tax on split income.** When minors earn dividends and certain other income from a corporation owned by a relative the amounts received must be reported on Form T1206 Tax on Split Income. The dividends, first reported on Line 120, are deducted on Line 232 Other Deductions, and are subject to tax at the highest marginal tax rates on Form T1206 and Schedule 1. Beginning in 2011, capital gains on the disposition by a minor of shares in a corporation owned by a relative are deemed to be dividends and subject to tax on split income. • **Stock dividends and stock splits** increase number of shares held but do not affect adjusted cost base. They are not reported until shares are sold. • **Dividend Transfer.** If the lower-income spouse is not taxable, dividends and the dividend tax credit can be transferred to the higher earner if by doing so an amount for spouse or common-law partner is created or increased. • **Patronage dividends** paid to customers of credit unions or other co-ops are not considered to be taxable and should not be reported, even if a T4A is received, as long as the related purchases were not deductible. If the amounts are received in respect of deductible goods and services of a business, the patronage dividends are added to business income. • **Capital dividends** paid out of a corporation's Capital Dividend Account are not taxable, as they can represent the non-taxable portion of capital gains received by the company, or receipts such as tax-exempt life insurance policy proceeds.
121 Interest & Other Investment Income	• **T-slips.** Interest income will be reported on T3 or T5 slips if amounts earned in the year are over $50. If not, it is necessary to self-report by looking at bank statements or books for the interest earned. • **Compound interest** must be reported on the tax return every year as it accrues. Be careful that only the final year's amount is included in the year of maturity. • **Interest received from CRA** due to a refund of income taxes is reported as income but can be used to offset interest costs owed by the taxpayer on a prior year's balance. Interest paid on balances owing to CRA is not tax-deductible. • **Other interest** earned from holding mortgages, notes, receiving annuity payments or foreign income (which must be reported in Canadian funds) are all reported first on *Schedule 4 Statement of Investment Income* and then on Line 121.

Line	Tax Tips for Double Checking Your Data Entries
121 Interest & Other Investment Income (continued)	• **Interest costs and other carrying costs** (like a safety deposit box or the interest paid to buy a Canada Savings Bond on a payroll plan), resulting from loans taken to acquire interest-bearing non-registered investments are deductible on Line 221 Carrying Charges. • **T-Bills**. Discounts received on the purchase of treasury bills are considered to be interest income, as are the amounts received on maturity, if those amounts exceed the cost. • **Spouse and minor child**. Interest earned on money transferred to minor children or to a spouse or common-law partner must be reported by the transferor, unless the money was received by the child from non-resident grandparents. Exception: Interest earned on Child Tax Benefits saved in an untainted account in the name of the child will be taxed in the hands of the child (as will salary paid to a child who works in his/her parents' business). • **Other income** reported here includes income from royalties from resource property production or licensing of a patent, foreign investment income and self-reported interest on mortgages or other loans held by the taxpayer.
122 Net Partnership Income	• This income results from an investment in a limited partnership by an inactive partner. It is reported on a statement or a T5013 slip. • Unapplied partnership losses from prior years may be used to offset partnership income reported on this line but show losses on Line 251. • Interest costs resulting from loans taken to make these investments are deductible on Line 221 Carrying Charges.
125 RDSP Income	• Report amounts received from a RDSP in the year. The amount will be reported on a T4A slip in Box 131.
126 Rental Income	• **Rent** received from use of the taxpayer's home, office, boat, or other asset or from sharecropping is generally required to be reported as income, unless there is no profit motive (e.g. child pays parents' room and board but costs exceed income received). • **Interest expense can be capitalized**, rather than deducted, on loans used to acquire capital property, if this is to the taxpayer's advantage. However, this election is not possible if the costs are part of the "soft costs" of construction in the period prior to its completion, in which case the costs **must** form part of the cost base of the property. Landscaping costs, maintenance and repairs, including modifications for the disabled are deductible, but not capital additions like a new roof, new carpets or a fence (these costs are added to the cost base and reduce future capital gains). • **Interest and property taxes on undeveloped land** are deductible only if rental income is earned. It is not possible to create or increase a loss on such property with interest and property tax costs. If the property is classified as capital or inventory, these costs can be added to the cost base.

Line	Tax Tips for Double Checking Your Data Entries
126 Rental Income (continued)	• **Legal fees** are deductible, except if legal fees are incurred to buy or sell property, in which case they form part of the capital cost as outlays and expenses. • **Prepaid expenses** are generally deductible if matched to the year to which they relate. In the case of mortgage penalties, the rules are complex and unclear but penalties to pay down the mortgage are deductible in the year paid up to the present value of the interest not paid. • **Auto expenses** if the taxpayer does repairs to the rental personally; otherwise these expenses are only available to those who have two or more rental properties. • **Capital cost allowance**. There are numerous special rules to note: – Rental losses cannot be created or increased with a CCA claim. – Land is not a depreciable asset. – Each rental property with a cost of $50,000 or more must be included in a separate class on the CCA schedule. This includes two or more condos in the same building with an individual cost of $50,000 or more.
127 Taxable Capital Gains	• Only a portion of the gain is taxable. Since October 2000, this is 50%. • Capital gains on Qualified Farm Property, Qualified Fishing Property or Qualified Small Business Shares are eligible for a Capital Gains Deduction of up to $375,000. • When a taxpayer disposes of a depreciable asset at a loss, the loss is a "Terminal Loss" and must be deducted in full on the business or rental statement where CCA is claimed. Do not list losses on depreciable assets on Schedule 3. • If the taxpayer suffers a loss on shares or debt to a Small Business Corporation, the loss is considered to be a Business Investment Loss and the allowable 50% may deduct against other income in the year. • Capital losses of prior years that have been carried forward may be claimed up to the total taxable capital gains in the current year. Deduct these losses on Line 253. • Gains on the sale of a personal residence are not taxable unless it has been claimed as a business asset. • If the taxpayer has a taxable capital gain on a disposition but will not receive all of the proceeds of the sale in the current year, they may claim a reserve for the proceeds not yet due and spread the gain over a period not exceeding five years. • Taxpayers may have reported capital gains on their 1994 income tax return on assets disposed of in the current year. If so, the adjusted cost base of the property includes the gain reported in 1994. • Special valuation rules apply to property owned on January 1, 1972. • Beginning in 2011, capital gains on the disposition by a minor of shares in a corporation owned by a relative are deemed to be dividends and subject to tax on split income.

Line	Tax Tips for Double Checking Your Data Entries
128 Support Payments	• Spousal support payments made, or child support payments pursuant to a court order or agreement made before May 1, 1997 will be reported by the recipient. • This amount qualifies for the purposes of RRSP earned income. • The payor receives a tax deduction on Line 220 and must reduce RRSP contribution room by the amount of the deduction taken. • For agreements signed after April 30, 1997, child support is not included in income by the recipient and the payor will not receive a tax deduction. • The lower-net income of the recipient of tax-exempt child support may increase amounts payable under the Child Tax Benefit or GST/HST Credit programs.
129 RRSP Income	• RRSP withdrawals are reported on Line 129, but if the taxpayer is over 64 or receiving the amounts as a result of the spouse's death, the Pension Income Amount on Line 314 will be available if the payments are part of a life annuity (shown in Box 16 of the T4RSP slip). • Withdrawals can be made at any time, but are taxable in the year received. • When contributions exceed RRSP room, but are less than $2,000 over that room, they are known as "over-contributions." These may remain in the plan and a deduction taken in the future, so long as there is RRSP room. They can also be withdrawn on a tax-free basis, if withdrawn in the year the Notice of Assessment is received or in the following year. • Excess contributions—investments over the $2,000 over-contribution limit—are subject to a penalty tax of 1% per month until they are withdrawn. File Form T1-OVP. • Plan to withdraw funds to minimize taxes. Taxpayers withdrawing RRSP amounts towards the end of the calendar year should consider doing so in January of the New Year to defer income reporting to the next calendar year. If funds are withdrawn from a spousal plan, they are taxed in the hands of the annuitant spouse and not in the hands of the contributor spouse, so long as no spousal RRSP contributions were made in the current or preceding two taxation years. • Unfortunately, taxpayers who did not take advantage of the opportunity to split RRSP accumulations by contributing to a spousal RRSP during their accumulation years, cannot split income with the spouse until they are at least 65. Beginning at age 65, taxpayers may elect, using Form T1023, to split up to 50% of eligible pension income with their spouses. • Withdrawals under the Home Buyers' Plan or Lifelong Learning Plan are not taxable unless they are not repaid on schedule.

Line	Tax Tips for Double Checking Your Data Entries
130 Other Income	• Report death benefits received from employer. Beneficiaries may claim a deduction of up to $10,000 if amount was in recognition of deceased employee's services or unused sick leave. • Retiring allowances or severance including damages for loss of office. • RRIF payments that do not qualify for the $2,000 Pension Income Amount; that is, those received by taxpayers who are under 65 and not receiving amounts as a result of a spouse's death. • Scholarships, fellowships and bursaries. If the student is eligible to claim the Education Amount on Line 323 of Schedule 1 then this income is exempt from taxation. If not, the first $500 is not taxable. • Payments from an RESP. These are not eligible for the scholarship exemption. • Interest income from bona fide loans made to the spouse. • Payments for serving on a jury. • Certain lump sums received from pensions or deferred profit sharing plans. • Apprenticeship Incentive Grant or Completion Grants • Saskatchewan Pension Plan payments (T4A Box 109) • Payments from a trust (T3 Box 26) • Taxable TFSA amounts
135 to 143 Self-Employment	• Report net income from the business. This is gross revenues, reduced by sales taxes remitted, returns or discounts, cost of goods sold, operating expenses, capital cost allowance, and the business portion of auto and home office expenses. • Restricted expenses include meals and entertainment; only 50% is deductible. • Home office expenses cannot be deducted to create or increase a business loss. • Business losses are used to offset other income of the year. If those losses create a loss on Line 236, the excess non-capital loss becomes available for carry-back. Use Form T1A *Request for Loss Carry Back* to apply these losses to income in any of the prior three tax years, or to any of the twenty years in the future.
144-146 Assistance Payments	• These amounts are reported as income for the purposes of increasing Line 236 Net Income, the figure on which refundable and non-refundable tax credits are based. • A tax deduction for the full amount of these receipts is taken on Line 250 Other Payments Deduction.
150 Total Income	• Divide this figure into Total Taxes Payable on Line 435 to arrive at the taxpayer's effective tax rate on income.

Line	Tax Tips for Double Checking Your Data Entries
Page 3	
Net And Taxable Income	• **Net income** appears on Line 236. This figure is used in the calculation of refundable and non-refundable tax credits, so reducing it with all available deductions on Lines 207 to 232 can provide benefits in addition to reduced taxable income. • **Taxable income** appears on Line 260. This is the figure that provincial and federal income tax calculations are based on.
206 Pension Adjustment	• This figure is used to reduce the available RRSP contribution room. It is based on contributions to a Registered Pension Plan by the taxpayer's employer. • A pension adjustment reversal (PAR) may be reported on Form T10 and restores RRSP room.
207 RPP Deduction	• This is a deduction for employer-sponsored pension plan contributions by the employee. Contributions can be made to either a defined benefit or money purchase plan. • Current year contributions made within limits of your RPP are deductible. • When past service contributions are made, they may be deducted, but only to a maximum of $3,500 for both current and past service contributions. Any unused past service contributions can be carried forward and deducted in future years, again subject to the same maximum. • Instalment interest paid to make past service contributions over time may either be deducted on Line 232 or as an additional past service contribution subject to the $3,500 maximum.
208 RRSP Deduction	• Based on Contribution Room of prior years in which a return was filed. Check Notice of Assessment for taxpayer's "earned income" calculation. Contribution is 18% of earned income to a maximum of $22,970 for 2012. • Deductible contributions may be made to either the taxpayer's own RRSP or to an RRSP for their spouse. After three years with no spousal contributions, the withdrawals from the spousal RRSP are taxable to the spouse. • RRSPs may hold many different types of investments but there are some restrictions, for example, RRSPs may not own land.
210 Deduction for Elected Split-Pension Amount	• For transferors, enter amount from Line E on form T1032 which is the *Joint election to Split Pension Income.*
212 Union/ Professional Dues	• Amounts paid to maintain professional status, as well as amounts paid to a trade union, are deductible. • If dues include GST or HST, the taxes may qualify for rebate on Form GST/HST 370. • Make sure that if union dues reported in Box 44 of the T4 are not the same dues shown on receipts.

Line	Tax Tips for Double Checking Your Data Entries
213 UCCB Repayment	• Person who reported the UCCB income in the prior year may deduct. • Box 12 of the RC62 slip.
214 Child Care	• Child care expenses paid to a qualified babysitter for an eligible child so the parent may work or attend school are normally deductible. • Child care expenses must be claimed by the supporting person with the lower net income unless that person was unable to care for the child because of confinement to a bed or wheelchair for at least two weeks, was permanently disabled, was in prison or an institution for at least two weeks, was separated from the higher-income person for at least 90 days or was attending a designated educational institution. • The maximum claim for each child is limited to two-thirds of the taxpayer's earned income for the year • For students, the maximum claim for child care is $250 per week for each disabled child; for other children, it is $100 per week for each child between 7 and 16, plus $175 per week for children under 7. • For others, the maximum claim for child care is $10,000 for each disabled child; for other children, it is $4,000 for each child between 7 and 16, plus $7,000 for children under 7.
215 Disability Supports Deduction	• If the taxpayer is disabled and pays an unrelated attendant who is over 18 for assistance to enable them to work or study, they may claim these expenses as well as other supports expenses on Line 215. • The deduction may not exceed the taxpayer's earned income. If the taxpayer attends a designated educational institution, the limit is increased to the lesser of the taxpayer's other income, $15,000, and $375 per week in attendance at the educational institution. • Claims for Disability Support reduce the claim for the supplementary disability amount claimed on Line 306 or claimed by a supporting person on Line 306.
217 Business Investment Losses	• One half of the losses on shares or loans to a Canadian Small Business Corporation are deductible against other income on this line. • Business Investment Losses that exceed other income are treated as non-capital losses and may be carried back three years or forward 10 years to reduce other income in that period. • Business Investment Losses that are not absorbed in the 10-year carry forward period are treated as capital losses and may be applied against capital gains until they are used up.

Line	Tax Tips for Double Checking Your Data Entries
219 Moving Expenses	• If the taxpayer moves more than 40 km within Canada to start a new job or attend college or university, their moving expenses are deductible against income earned at the new location. • Moving expenses include costs of selling the former residence, costs of acquiring a new home, temporary living expenses for up to 15 days, costs of moving household belongings, costs of transporting the taxpayer and their family to the new home, costs of revising legal document to the new address, and costs of keeping the vacant old residence up for sale (to a maximum of $5,000). • If moving expenses exceed the taxpayer's income at the new location, the unused amount may be carried to the following taxation year. • Taxpayers may not deduct any of the following: costs of making the old home more saleable, losses on the sale of the old home, expenses to find the new job or new home, value of goods that could not be moved, losses on or replacement of carpets, drapes, firewood, tool sheds, etc., or expenses that are reimbursed (unless the reimbursement is included in their income).
220 Support Payments	• See Line 128 above.
221 Carrying Charges	The following are deductible (on Schedule 4) as carrying charges: • Safety deposit box charges • Accounting fees relating to investments • Investment counsel fees • Taxable benefit from employer-provided loans (if used for investment purposes) • Canada Savings Bond interest paid by payroll deduction • Management and safe custody fees • Foreign non-business income taxes that are not claimed as a foreign tax credit • Interest paid on loans to invest, including amounts paid on life insurance policy loans The following may **not** be deducted: • Student loan interest (claim credit on Line 319) • Interest paid to contribute to an RRSP, RESP, or RRIF • Brokerage fees (these for part of the cost of the asset or proceeds of disposition) • Exploration and Development expenses (claim these at Line 224)
222 CPP Deduction for Self-Employment	• One half of the Canada Pension Plan (or QPP) contributions payable by a self-employed taxpayer is deductible on Line 222. • The other half of the CPP or QPP payable is claimed as a credit on Line 310.

Line	Tax Tips for Double Checking Your Data Entries
224 Exploration And Development Expenses	• If the taxpayer invests in a petroleum, natural gas or mining venture, a portion of the Exploration and Development expenses incurred may be deducted. These are normally reported on a T5013 slip or a T101 slip. • Enter the deduction on Schedule 4 and transfer the total to Line 224.
229 Employment Expenses	Employment expenses include: • Apprentice mechanic's tools expense • Artists' expenses • Board and lodging expenses or transport employees (Form TL2) • Board and lodging for commission salespersons (Form T777). • Contributions to a Retirement Compensation Arrangement (RCA) • Entertainment expenses for commission salespersons (50% of amounts not reimbursed—claim on Form T777) • Forfeitures under an Employee Profit Sharing Plan • Legal expenses to collect or establish a right to a retiring allowance or pension benefits • Motor vehicle expenses if the taxpayer is ordinarily required to carry out duties away from their place of employment and doesn't receive reimbursement or a tax-free allowance • Musician's expenses, including capital cost allowance on musical instruments (claim on Form T777). • Power saw expenses • Repayment of salary or wages previously reported as income • Salaries paid to an assistant if required under the taxpayer's contract of employment • Supplies used in employment if required under the contract of employment • Tradesperson's tools expense • Travelling expenses if the taxpayer is ordinarily required to carry out duties away from their place of employment and don't receive reimbursement or a tax-free allowance If the taxpayer paid GST/HST on expenses deductible on this line, the GST/HST paid may be eligible for the GST/HST Rebate on Form GST 370.
231 Clerics Residence	• If the taxpayer receives a cleric's residence allowance which is reported on Line 104, they may claim a deduction for the lesser of: • the actual amount of the housing allowance received; and • the greater of $10,000 and one-half of their ordinary remuneration as a cleric.
232 Other Deductions	Other deductions include: • CCA on Canadian motion picture or videotape investments • Accounting and legal costs for appealing income tax, Employment Insurance, or CPP decisions • Teachers exchange fund contributions

Line	Tax Tips for Double Checking Your Data Entries
232 Other Deductions (continued)	• Repayments of any of the following (to the extent they were included in income): – Allowances under the National Training Act – CPP benefits – EI benefits – life insurance policy loans – OAS – Overpayments received from the Program for Older Workers Adjustment, Plant Worker's Adjustment, Labour Adjustment Benefits, or the Atlantic Ground Fish Strategy – scholarships, fellowships, bursaries – shareholder loans – refund interest from CRA – research grants – retiring allowances • Depletion Allowances • Legal fees to collect taxable support payments, • Reserve for amounts added to income under the Debt Forgiveness Rules • Refund of undeducted RRSP contributions and received in the tax year (attach Form T3012A or T746) Income subject to tax on Split Income.
235 Social Benefits Repayment	• If the taxpayer received EI benefits for the second time in ten years and their net income exceeds $57,375 for 2012 or OAS and their net income exceeds $69,562 for 2012, they will be required to repay a portion of the EI and/or OAS received. • Complete the calculation on the back of the T4E slip and the Worksheet included with the income tax return package or in your tax software.
236 Net Income	• This is the figure that is used to calculate eligibility for refundable and non-refundable tax credits, such as the Age Amount, GSTC, Child Tax Benefit and many provincial credits. It is also used by any supporting individual in the calculation of credits for the taxpayer.
244 Canadian Forces Personnel and Police Deduction	• Members of the Canadian Forces or a Canadian police force serving on a deployed operational mission that is assessed for risk allowance pay at level three or higher may claim a deduction here for their earnings related to the mission (to the maximum rate of pay earned by non-commissioned members of the armed forces—approximately $6,000 per month). The deductible amount is shown in Box 43 of the T4 slip.
248 Employee Home Relocation Loan	• If the taxpayer received a taxable benefit for an employee home relocation loan, it will be included in Box 36 of the T4 slip. Deduct it here.

Line	Tax Tips for Double Checking Your Data Entries
249 Security Options Deduction	• If the taxpayer received a taxable benefit for employee stock options, the deduction will be shown in Box 39 or 41 of the T4 slip. The deduction is equal to 50% of the benefit. It is designed to put employees on the same tax basis as those who have a capital gain shares purchased on the stock market. Claim the deduction here. • For options exercised prior to March 5, 2010, taxpayers may apply to defer the benefit by filing Form T1212 with the employer if they did not dispose of the shares purchased under the Employee Stock Option Plan. The benefit (and resulting deduction) will be deferred until they dispose of the shares.
250 Other Payments Deduction	• If the taxpayer included income from Social Assistance, Workers Compensation or Net Federal Supplements on Lines 144, 145, or 146 of their return, deduct those amounts here. • This line is designed to ensure that social benefits are included in Net Income for the calculation of credits, but are not included in Taxable Income.
251 Limited Partnership Losses of Other Years	• Limited Partnership Losses that are carried forward may be claimed against Limited Partnership Income in the current year. • Claim Limited Partnership Losses incurred in the current year on Line 122. Losses not deductible in the current year are normally reported in Box 31 of Form T5013. Carry these forward and apply them to Limited Partnership Income next year.
252 Non Capital Losses of Other Years	• If the taxpayer has non-capital losses carried forward from a prior year, claim them on this line. The original carry forward amount is shown on Form T1A in the year the loss was incurred. Keep track of the amount claimed each year and the remaining amount available for future years. • Losses incurred prior to 2004 were carried forward for seven years and expired prior to 2012. Losses incurred in 2004 and 2005 may be carried forward 10 years. Losses incurred after 2005 may be carried forward 20 years. • Non-capital loss balances may be reduced if the taxpayer's commercial debt is forgiven by their creditors.
253 Net Capital Loss Of Other Years	• Net capital losses carried forward from a prior year may be claimed against capital gains in the current year. • A special rule applies to net capital losses carried forward from before 1986. Up to $2,000 of such losses may be claimed against income from other sources each year.
254 Capital Gains Deduction	• If the taxpayer has taxable capital gains on the disposition of Qualified Farm Property, Qualified Fishing Property or Qualified Small Business Corporation shares, the gains may be eligible for a Capital Gains Deduction of up to $375,000 (50% of $750,000 Exemption). Complete Form T657 to determine the amount of the deduction.

Line	Tax Tips for Double Checking Your Data Entries
255 Northern Residence Deductions	• If the taxpayer lives in a Prescribed Zone, they may be eligible to claim the Northern Residents Deduction. Calculate the amount on Form T2222. To qualify they must have lived in a Prescribed Zone for a period of at least six months beginning or ending in the taxation year. • The residency deduction is $8.25 per day for each day in the taxation year that the taxpayer resided in Zone A plus $4.125 per day that they resided in Zone B. The deduction is limited to 20% of their Net Income. • In addition, if the taxpayer received taxable travel benefits from their employer, which are reported in Box 32 of the T4 slip, they may be eligible for the travel deduction of up 100% of the travel benefit if they lived in Zone A and 50% of the taxable benefit if they lived in Zone B.
256 Additional Deductions	Additional deductions include: • income that is exempt under a tax treaty with a foreign country • the exempt portion of German social security pensions • 15% of reported U.S. Social Security benefits (50% if benefits were received in 1995) • employment income from the United Nations and its agencies • If the taxpayer has taken a vow of perpetual poverty, the amount of their earned income and pension benefits from the religious order.
260 Taxable Income	• This is the amount on which federal and provincial income tax is calculated.
Schedule 1 Federal Tax	• Schedule 1 is used to calculate federal tax, personal amounts and credits for foreign taxes paid. It is also used to claim the federal dividend tax credit, investment and the Overseas Employment Tax Credits and to report Tax on Split Income.
301 – 335 Personal Amounts	• The personal amounts claimed on these lines are multiplied by the lowest federal tax rate (15%) to calculate Personal Credits. These credits are non-refundable. That means they can be used to reduce federal taxes to zero, but any excess will not be refunded. Certain of the credits may be transferred to a supporting person if not needed by the taxpayer. • At the provincial level, a similar list of amounts is available. Each province sets their own level for these amounts and the tax rate that is used to convert the amounts to personal credits. These calculations are performed on the Form/Line 428 or 479 for the province or residence. Since the levels vary by province, so does the amount available to transfer to a supporting person.
300 Basic Personal Amount	• All full-time residents of Canada are eligible for the Basic Personal Amount ($10,822 for 2012). If the taxpayer immigrates or emigrates, their Basic Personal Amount must be pro-rated according to the portion of the year they were a Canadian resident.

Line	Tax Tips for Double Checking Your Data Entries
301 Age Amount	• If the taxpayer is 65 years or older, they are eligible for the Age Amount ($6,720 for 2012). • If their net income exceeds $33,884 for 2012, the age amount is reduced by 15% of the excess. • If the taxpayer is unable to use the age amount because their taxable income is too low, they may transfer the credit to their spouse or common-law partner. The spouse or partner should complete Schedule 2 to make the claim.
303 Spouse or Common-Law Partner Amount	• If the taxpayer supported a spouse or common-law partner in the year, the taxpayer may claim this credit. Beginning in 2012, the amount of this credit is higher if the dependant is infirm ($12,822 if infirm; $10,822 otherwise). • If their spouse has any net income it reduces this claim dollar for dollar.
305 Amount for an Eligible Dependant	• If the taxpayer maintained a dwelling in Canada, had no spouse or common-law partner, and supported a person related by blood, marriage or adoption who was under 18 who lived with them in that dwelling, they may claim the Amount for an Eligible Dependant. Beginning in 2012, the amount of this credit is higher if the dependant is infirm ($12,822 if infirm; $10,822 otherwise). • If the dependant has any net income it reduces this claim dollar for dollar. Complete Schedule 5 to calculate the claim.
306 Amount for Infirm Dependants	• If the taxpayer supported an infirm dependant who was 18 years or older, they may claim the Amount for Infirm Dependants. The claim is $6,402 for 2012. • If the dependant's net income exceeds ($6,420 for 2012), then the claim is reduced by their net income in excess of this amount and any claim made at Line 305 for them.
308 CPP Contributions Through Employment	• Canada Pension Plan contributions deducted by the employer may be claimed here. The amount is shown in Box 16 of the T4 slip. • If the taxpayer earns less than $3,500 from employment, they are not required to contribute to CPP. • The maximum deduction for $2,306.70 for 2012. If the taxpayer contributed more than that, claim the excess on Line 448. • If the taxpayer is both employed and self-employed, reduce the CPP payable on self-employment by twice the contributions through employment. Complete Schedule 8 in that case. • CPP contributions are prorated in the year the taxpayer turns 18 or 70, when begins to receive a CPP disability pension (and in the year of death). • Beginning in 2012, taxpayers under age 70 with CPP pensionable earnings will continue to contribute to CPP. For those under age 65, contributions are mandatory but after age 65, taxpayers may elect not to continue to contribute. Employees elect by filing Form CPT30 with their payroll department. • Overpayments of CPP will be calculated automatically by the CRA's computer or calculate them manually using Form T2204. Most tax software will perform these calculations automatically.

Line	Tax Tips for Double Checking Your Data Entries
310 CPP on Self-Employment	• If the taxpayer earns more than $3,500 from self-employment, they are required to contribute 9.9% of the profits to the Canada Pension Plan to a maximum of $4,613.40 for 2012. Calculate the required contribution on Schedule 8. • One-half of the required contribution is claimed on Line 310. The other half is deducted on Line 222. • If the taxpayer is both employed and self-employed, reduce the CPP payable on self-employment by twice the contributions through employment. • Beginning in 2012 taxpayers under age 70 with CPP pensionable earnings will continue to contribute to CPP. For those under age 65, contributions are mandatory but after age 65, taxpayers may elect not to continue to contribute. Self-employed individuals will elect on Schedule 8. • CPP contributions are prorated in the year the taxpayer turns 18 or 70, when begins to receive a CPP disability pension (and in the year of death).
312 Employment Insurance Premiums	• If the taxpayer earns more than $2,000 from employment, they are required to pay Employment Insurance premiums of 1.83% to a maximum of $839.97 for 2012. The amount deducted is shown in Box 18 of the T4 slips. • If the taxpayer contributes more than the maximum, claim the excess as a deduction on Line 450. • Overpayments of EI premiums are calculated automatically by the CRA's computer, or calculate them manually using Form T2204. Most tax software will perform this calculation automatically.
317 EI on Self-Employment	• Self-employed taxpayers may opt to participate in the EI program to be eligible for certain benefits. • Premiums are the same as for employees—1.83% to a maximum of $839.97 for 2012. • Premiums payable are calculated on Schedule 13. A credit is taken here (Line 317) and the premiums are added to taxes otherwise payable on Line 430.
363 Canada Employment Amount	• Taxpayers reporting employment income may claim an amount for the lesser of their employment income and $1,095 for 2012.
364 Amount for Public Transit Passes	• Taxpayers who purchased an eligible public transit pass for travel after July 1, 2006 are eligible to claim an amount for the cost of the pass(es). • This amount may be claimed by either spouse or common-law partner. • Passes for the taxpayer, spouse or common-law partner and dependant children may be claimed.
313 Adoption Expense Credit	• If the taxpayer finalized an adoption after 2004, certain expenses can be deducted from income up to a maximum of $11,440 for 2012. This amount can be shared by adopting taxpayers.

Line	Tax Tips for Double Checking Your Data Entries
314 Pension Income Amount	• If the taxpayer is age 65 or older and receiving pension income, or is receiving the pension as a result of their spouse's death, they may claim the lesser of $2,000 and the amount of eligible pension income (reported on Line 115).
315 Caregiver Amount	• If the taxpayer maintained a dwelling in Canada, and provided care in their home for a parent or grandparent, or another dependant who is over 18 and mentally or physically infirm, they may claim the Caregiver Amount ($4,402 for 2012) for that dependant. • If the dependant's net income exceeds $15,033 for 2012, then the claim is reduced by their net income in excess of this amount. The claim will also be reduced by any claim made for that dependant on Line 305. Complete Schedule 5 to calculate the claim. • Beginning in 2012, the amount of this credit is higher if the dependant is infirm ($6,402 if infirm; $4,402 otherwise).
316 Disability Amount	• If the taxpayer suffers from a severe mental or physical impairment that markedly restricts the basic activities of daily living, they are eligible to claim the disability amount. • A doctor must certify that they qualify by signing Form T2201. • The disability amount is $7,546 for 2012 plus a supplement of up to $4,402 for 2012, if the taxpayer is under 18 years of age. This supplement is reduced by any claims for Child Care or Disability Supports in excess of $2,578 for 2012. • If the taxpayer does not require the disability amount to reduce their taxes to zero, they may transfer this amount including the supplement, to their spouse or common-law partner (using Schedule 2) or to another supporting individual.
318 Disability Amount Transfer	• If the taxpayer supported a dependant who qualifies for the disability amount but does not need the credit because their income is too low, the disability amount may be transferred to the supporting individual. • If the taxpayer is the dependant's spouse or common-law partner, the transfer is performed on Schedule 2 and claimed on Line 326. • If the dependant does not have a spouse or common-law partner, the transfer is recorded on Line 318.
319 Student Loan Interest	• Interest paid on student loans in the current year, or unclaimed amounts carried forward may be claimed here. • If the taxpayer does not have enough taxable income to use the credit for student loan interest, the amount may be carried forward for up to five years.

Line	Tax Tips for Double Checking Your Data Entries
323 Tuition, Education and Textbook Amounts	• Tuition fees in excess of $100 paid to attend courses at a post-secondary level are generally eligible for the tuition amount. Qualifying tuition will be evidenced by official income tax receipts. • Students who attend a post-secondary institution on a full-time basis are also eligible for an Education Amount of $400 per month. • Students who attend a post-secondary institution on a part-time basis are eligible for an Education Amount of $120 per month. • Eligibility for the Education Amount will be shown on Form T2202 (or T2202A). • Students who qualify for the full-time education amount in a month also qualify for a textbook amount of $65 for that month. Students who qualify for the part-time education amount for a month also qualify for a textbook amount of $20 for that month. • There is no limit to the amount that the student may claim. However, if the student does not need the tuition, education and textbook amount to reduce their taxes to zero in the current year, they may either carry the unused amount forward to a future year, or transfer it to a spouse or common-law partner, or to their parents or grandparents (or those of their spouse or common-law partner). • The transfer of the Tuition, Education and Textbook Amount is limited to $5,000 less the amount claimed by the student. Thus, if the student claims $5,000 or more, no amount may be transferred regardless of the amount of Tuition, Education and Textbook Amount. • Complete Schedule 11 to determine the Tuition, Education and Textbook amount available and the amount eligible for transfer.
324 Tuition, Education and Textbook Amount Transfer	• If an individual qualifies for the Tuition, Education and Textbook Amount but does not need it to reduce their taxes to zero, they may transfer some of the unused amount to the taxpayer as a supporting person. If the student wishes to transfer to a spouse or common-law partner, the transfer must be done on Schedule 2 and claimed on Line 326. If the transfer is made to the student's parents or grandparents (or those of the student's spouse or common-law partner), record it here. • The transfer amount is calculated on Schedule 11 and is limited to the lesser of the unused Tuition, Education and Textbook Amount, and $5,000 less the Tuition, Education and Textbook Amount claimed by the student.
326 Amounts Transfer From Spouse Or Common-Law Partner	If the taxpayer has a spouse or common-law partner who qualifies for any of the following amounts but does not require them to reduce their taxes to zero, transfer them to the taxpayer using Schedule 2: • Age Amount • Amount for Children under 18 • Disability Amount • Pension Income Amount • Tuition, Education and Textbook Amount

Line	Tax Tips for Double Checking Your Data Entries
330 Medical Expenses	• Medical expenses may be claimed for any 12-month period ending in the taxation year. If the taxpayer doesn't have enough medical expenses to make a claim in one year, they may be pooled with medical expenses from the following year in a 12-month period ending next year. • Claims for medical expenses are reduced by 3% of the taxpayer's net income but never by more than $2,109 for 2012. • In addition to medical expenses paid, the taxpayer can claim private health care premiums such as Blue Cross that are deducted from their wages. • The taxpayer may claim medical expenses for themselves, their spouse or common-law partner, and for their dependent children.
331 Medical Expenses of Other Dependants	• Medical expenses of other dependants, such as parents, grandparents and adult children, who depend on the taxpayer for support may be claimed by the taxpayer if they paid them. These claims must be reduced by 3% of the dependant's net income. • Beginning in 2011 there is no maximum claim for medical expenses of other dependants.
335 Subtotal	• This subtotal multiplied by 15% to convert personal amounts to personal credits.
349 Donations & Gifts	• 15% on the first $200; 29% on donations over this. Aggregate donations by spouses on one return to get over this threshold or save for use next year. Unclaimed donations can be carried forward up to five years. • Dispositions after May 1, 2006 of eligible publicly traded securities to a charity will qualify for a capital gains inclusion rate of 0%. To claim this use *Form T1170 Capital Gains on gifts of Certain Capital Property.* Prior to May 2, the inclusion rate is 25%.
350 Total	• This is the sum of the personal credits plus the credit for Donations. If this figure exceeds basic federal tax, the taxpayer may be able to transfer some of their unused credits to their spouse or common-law partner or to another supporting individual.
362 Volunteer Firefighter Amount	• Volunteer firefighters may claim a credit of $3,000 if they volunteered for at least 250 hours in the tax year. • If this credit is claimed, any excluded income (Box 87 of the 4 slip) must be included in income on Line 101.
365 Children's Fitness Amount	• Eligible fees up to $500 paid for the enrolment of a child under the age of 16 in an eligible physical activity program. This will be calculated at 15% for a credit value of $75. • If more than $100 is spent for a disabled child, an additional amount of $500 may be claimed.

Line	Tax Tips for Double Checking Your Data Entries
367 Amount for children under 18	• Credit will be calculated on $2,191 for 2012. Add $2,000 if the child is infirm unless the child is also claimed as an eligible dependant. (Only one parent or guardian can claim this credit in that case). Otherwise this credit can be transferred to a spouse using Schedule 2.
369 Home Buyers' Amount	• Credit of up to $5,000 for first-time home buyers who purchase a home.
370 Children's Arts Amount	• Eligible fees up to $500 paid for the enrolment of a child under the age of 16 in an eligible RTS program. This will be calculated at 15% for a credit value of $75. • If more than $100 is spent for a disabled child, an additional amount of $500 may be claimed.
410 Federal Political Tax Credit	• If the taxpayer made a contribution to a registered federal political party in Canada, they may claim this non-refundable credit. The credit is three quarters of the first $400, plus one-half of the next $350, plus one-third of the rest of the contribution, to a maximum of $750. Receipts required.
412 Investment Tax Credit	• The Investment Tax Credit is available to purchasers of qualified property (in the Maritimes and the Gaspé Peninsula or who engaged in scientific research and experimental development. • Self-employed taxpayers who had qualifying apprenticeship job creation expenses may claim the Apprenticeship Job Creation Tax Credit on this line. File Form T2038.
414 Labour-Sponsored Funds Tax Credit	• Investments in Labour-Sponsored Funds are eligible for a tax credit of 15% of the investment to a maximum credit of $750. Certain provinces provide a matching or enhanced credit. • Investments within the taxpayer's RRSP also qualify for this credit so they may be able to "double-dip" and get both an RRSP deduction and a Labour-Sponsored Funds Tax Credit for the same investment. • Investments in the first 60 days of the tax year may be claimed on either the prior year's tax return or on the current year's return or the credit may be split between the two returns. However, credits may not be carried forward.
424 Tax On Split Income	• This special tax was introduced to stop taxpayers who own corporations from transferring income to their minor children in order to minimize their tax liability. • If a minor child received dividends or shareholder benefits from a private corporation, either directly or through a trust, this income is deducted on Line 232 but is subject to tax at the highest marginal rate (currently 29%). Calculate this tax on Form T1203. • Beginning in 2011, capital gains on the disposition by a minor of shares in a corporation owned by a relative are deemed to be dividends and subject to tax on split income.

Line	Tax Tips for Double Checking Your Data Entries
425 Dividend Tax Credit	• Canadian source dividends are eligible for the federal Dividend Tax Credit. For eligible dividends the credit is 15.02% of the amount reported on Line 120. For other dividends the credit is 13 1/3% of the amount reported on Line 120.
426 Overseas Employment Tax Credit	• The Overseas Employment Tax Credit is only available to residents of Canada who are employed overseas for a period of more than six consecutive months beginning or ending in the taxation year and who work for an employer resident in Canada or a Canadian owned foreign affiliate and perform services outside Canada in either the exploration for natural resources, or in any construction, installation, agricultural or engineering activity. • Complete for T626 to make this claim. Note: it will be phased out starting in 2013. This credit shelters up to 80% of the taxpayer's income while working overseas to a maximum of $219 per day.
427 Minimum Tax Carry Over	• If the taxpayer has a relatively high income and is eligible for a large deductions and/or credits, they may be subject to a different tax calculation called the Alternative Minimum Tax. This tax is calculated on Form T691. The amount by which the minimum tax exceeds the tax that would have been paid normally is carried forward to future years and may be claimed on this line. The maximum carry forward period is seven years.
Page 4	
421 CPP Payable Self	• See Line 310 for the calculation of this amount.
430 EI Payable on Self	• See Line 317 for details.
422 Social Benefits Repayment	• See Line 235 for the calculation of this amount. • Add the required repayment to taxes on this line.
428 Provincial Taxes	• In all provinces except Quebec, provincial taxes are calculated on Taxable Income as shown on Line 260. In Quebec, a separate provincial income tax return must be filed. • Outside of Quebec, calculate provincial taxes on Form 428 or 429 for the taxpayer's province of residence. In most provinces, the calculations are similar to the calculation of federal taxes on Schedule 1.

Line	Tax Tips for Double Checking Your Data Entries
431 Federal Foreign Tax Credit	• If the taxpayer earned foreign income, the country of origin often withholds income taxes on that income. Canada has tax treaties with most other governments to ensure that taxpayers are not taxed in both jurisdictions. To this end, they are given a credit for foreign taxes withheld. Calculate this credit on Schedule 1. • If the taxpayer earned foreign income from more than one jurisdiction, calculate foreign income, taxes and the FTC for each jurisdiction separately. Do this using Form T2209. To calculate the foreign tax credit against provincial taxes, use Form T2036. • Any foreign taxes paid that are not claimed as foreign tax credit may be deducted as carrying charges on Schedule 4. • If foreign business taxes exceeds the credit (because they are limited by income), unused taxes may be carried forward to next year and included on T2209 next year. If foreign non-business taxes exceed the credit, the excess cannot be carried forward.
435 Total Taxes Payable	• This is the sum of federal taxes, required contributions to CPP, repayment of social benefits and provincial taxes. To calculate the taxpayer's average tax rate, divide this number by Taxable Income.
437 Taxes Paid	• Claim all taxes deducted at source on this line. Taxes paid by instalment are claimed at Line 476.
457 GST/HST Rebate	• If Form GST/HST 370 was completed to claim the GST/HST rebate on union dues or employment expenses, reduce taxes payable by claiming the amount of the rebate here. • Remember that the rebate will have to be included in income (on Line 104) in the year received.
476 Instalments	• Claim all taxes paid by quarterly/annual instalments on this line.
484/ 485 Refund Or Balance Due	• A refund generally means that the taxpayer made an interest-free loan to the CRA during the taxation year. They should keep more of their own cash working for them by reducing the income tax withheld at source. To do so, complete Form T1213 *Request to Reduce Tax Deductions at Source.* The most advantageous situation to be in is to owe the CRA just less than $3,000 when the return is filed each year. • If this is a balance due, pay it by April 30 to avoid paying interest on this amount. • If the taxpayer owes more than $3,000 this year and in either of the prior two years, they may be required to pay taxes for next year by instalments. Your software will automatically calculate these payments.

Appendix 5. Additional Resources

Excellence in Financial Education from Knowledge Bureau Newsbooks

Managing the Bull: How to Detect and Deflect the Crap
by David Christianson

This is a must-read book for anyone who wants to develop the Winner's Mindset about money and is serious about financial freedom on his or her own terms. The book is inspiring, informative and impactful and, in some places, truly funny. Consumers need—more than ever—a proven path to follow. This book clears the roadblocks to smooth your financial journey. People are confronted today with confusion, noise and too much information. They want to cut through all of that bull, make the right decisions and take the right actions. *Managing the Bull* will empower you to embrace your successful financial future.

Also by Evelyn Jacks and co-authors Robert Ironside and Al Emid:
Financial Recovery in a Fragile World

Better understand market volatility and its effects on your long-term goals. This is the perfect book to calm jittery nerves? You can fortify your financial decision-marking with this comprehensive guide to the new world economy and your place in it, written by three of Canada's leading authorities in tax efficient wealth management.

A Canadian Bestseller Published by McGraw Hill

Make Sure It's Deductible by Evelyn Jacks
You earned it, now keep it! Maximize your profits by getting the most out of every tax deduction. No matter what kind of small business you have, you owe it to yourself to take advantage of every legitimate business deduction and personal tax planning benefit at tax time.

In the 4th Edition of *Make Sure It's Deductible*, one of Canada's most prolific authors, Knowledge Bureau president Evelyn Jacks provides the vital, practical information you need to increase your bottom line and run a tax-efficient and audit-proof small business.

The 4th Edition features a "help yourself" chapter summation and includes a handy "need to know" and "need to ask" guide to powerful, tax efficient decision making all year long.

This book is available on www.knowledgebureau.com.

Index

$1,000 Rule 183-184

Accounting fees 69, 207, 209, 305
Accrual accounting 205
Adjusted cost base 161, 178, 181-187, 189-190, 192, 197-198, 204, 261, 266, 270, 295, 297
Adoption expenses 127
Adventure or concern in the nature of trade 192
Advertising 206
Age Amount 37, 50-51, 60, 115, 164, 197, 221-222, 225, 236, 239, 240, 289, 290, 293, 296, 304, 307
Alternative Minimum Tax 173
Amount for an Eligible Dependant 51, 164, 165, 241, 307
Amount for Children Under 18 114, 115, 125, 135, 165
Amount for Infirm Adults Over 18 125, 147, 241
Amount for Interest Paid on Student Loans 133
Amount for public transit passes 95-96
Apprentice vehicle mechanics 72
Artists and musicians 71
Asset valuation on immigration 260-261
Assumption of debt 197
At-risk amount 179
Attribution Rules 112, 122, 131, 153-158
Auto expenses 206
Auto expenses—eligibility 75
Auto operating expenses 70
Auxiliary tax forms 13
Average cost 184
Average income down over time 235
Average life expectancy 221
Avoid lump sums 99

Babysitting 80
Bad debts 197
Balance due 278
Basic Personal Amount (BPA) 37
Blended families 120
Boarding school 80
Bonuses 103
Borrowing for exempt or registered

funds 210
Burden of proof 280
Business income and losses 123
Business Investment Losses (BIN) 195, 197
Business vs. personal driving 75

Calendar year 29, 205
Camps 80
Canada Child Tax Benefit 111
Canada Child Tax Credit 113
Canada Education Grants and Bonds 132
Canada Employment Amount 37, 50, 61, 72, 123, 308
Canada Pension Plan 53, 58, 98, 103, 111, 121, 124, 131, 144, 221, 226, 249, 261, 276, 302, 307, 308
Canada Savings Bond payroll deductions 209
Canada Student Loans Act 134
Canada-U.S. border 80
Canadian Controlled Private Corporations (CCPCs) 172
Canadian forces personnel and police 90-91, 105
Capital assets 270
Capital Cost Allowance (CCA) 15, 70, 74, 77-78, 161-162, 194, 204, 206, 297
Capital Dividends 174
Capital gain 33, 180
Capital gain on deemed disposition at departure 264
Capital Gains Deduction (CGD) 194-195
Capital Gains Dividends 174
Capital Gains Election 188, 203
Capital Gains Exemption (CGE) 194
Capital gains inclusion rate 181
Capital gains or losses 169
Capital loss carry back 183
Capital losses 123
Capital losses 270
Capital losses on departure 265
Caregiver amount 114, 126, 148, 241
Carry forward summaries 12, 287
Carrying charges 113
Carryover periods 85
Cash vs. accrual 29

CCA 204
CCTB and UCCB 156
Change in use of a principal residence 203
Change of use rules 78
Charitable donations 103
Charitable donations 149-152
Charitable donations 272
Charitable donations 97
Child care claims by higher earners 82
Child care claims by lower earners 82
Child care expenditures 80
Child care expenses 31, 79, 113, 124, 147, 162
Child support payments 162
Children's benefit 142
Children's Arts Amount 127
Children's Fitness Amount 126-127
Claiming deductions 112
Class 10 78
Class 10.1 78, 194
Classification of property 180
Clawbacks 40
Clearance certificates 272
Clergy residence deduction 103, 104
Combined retirement and survivor benefit 228
Commission sales 60, 69, 74
Commission sales employees 74
Commissions 105, 143, 182, 190, 210
Common errors 44-45
Common-law partner 110
Compounding vs. simple interest 178
Condominium fees 206
Conjugal relationship 110
Contributions to RRSPs and RESPs 156
CPP 103, 226-229
CPP death benefit 228
CPP premiums 47, 58-59, 142, 227
CPP proration 59
CPP/QPP death benefits 269
Credit filers 27, 39
Critical illness and long term care insurance 144
Cultural gifts 150
Cumulative Eligible Capital (CEC) Account 194
Cumulative Net Investment Losses

(CNIL) 195

Day trips 89
Daycare centre 80
Debentures 189-190
Debt forgiveness 197
Deceased contributor child benefit 228
Deductible rental expenses 206
Deductible sales expenses 71
Deductible travel expenses 70
Deductions 272
Deductions in the residency period 261
Deemed disposition 78, 181-182, 199, 203-204, 257, 263-265, 269-271
Deemed residents 259
Deferral to Actual Disposition (S. 45(2) Election) 203
Deferred Profit Sharing Plan 230
Deferred security options benefits 105
Departure taxes 262
Depreciable property 194
Detailed method 89
Director's fees 103
Disability Amount 37, 45, 47, 51-52, 60, 80-83, 115, 123, 125-126, 128, 135, 145, 146, 148, 165
Disability Amount for Children 128
Disability Amount Supplement 128
Disability amounts 83
Disability benefits 227
Disability pension 142, 227-228, 241, 307, 308
Disability supports deduction 113
Disability Tax Credit 21, 115, 123, 128, 132, 242
Disabled 141
Disabled contributor child benefit 227
Dividend Reinvestment Programs 174
Dividend Tax Credit (DTC) 171
Dividends 33
Divorce 159-165
Donations and gifts 116
Donation of non-qualifying securities 151
Donation of options 152
Donations of flow-through shares 151
Double-check my tax returns 276
Driving to and from work 61

Earned income for RRSP purposes 30
Earned income limitation 81
Ecological gifts 150
Education amounts 135
Educational Assistance Payments 132
Educational institution 80

Effective and marginal tax rates 31, 32
EFILE 7, 20, 22, 23
EI and the self employed 101
EI benefits 100, 143
EI compassionate care coverage 147
EI premiums and exemptions
EI repayments 82
Election to defer departure taxes 264
Elections 203
Eligible allowances 99
Eligible Capital Property 194
Eligible dividends 172
Eligible moving expenses 85
Emigration 12, 255-256, 259, 261-262, 264
Employee home-relocation loan deduction 104
Employee stock options 91
Employees 27, 74
Employees on salary 69
Employer-provided loans 09
Employer-provided loans 178
Employment expenses 69
Employment Insurance 65, 81, 85, 98, 103, 123, 131
Employment outside Canada 105
Excluded personal property 263
Exempt income 31
Exploration and development expenses 210

Factual residents 258
Fair Market Value (FMV) 78, 181, 260-261
Family business income and expense guide 117
Family member rentals 206
Farm property succession planning 196
Federal foreign tax credit 175
Federal refundable tax credits 35, 163
Filing due dates for final return 273
Firefighter's tax credit 103
Fishers 105-106
Fixed expenses 76
Foreign dividends 175
Foreign pension income 235
Foreign Tax Credit 175, 236
Forestry workers 72
Form RC Marital Status Change 41
Form RC66 Canada Child Tax Benefit Application 41
Form T1135 Foreign Asset Disclosure 14
Form T2200 Declaration of Conditions of Employment 75

Form T664 Capital Gains Election 204
Form T777 75
Formal Appeals 15
Full-time students 81, 83-84, 87
Funeral arrangements 272

Generating a pension from an RRSP 232
German Social Security 235
Gifts 187
Gross negligence 275, 278-279
Gross-up for eligible dividends 167, 171
Grossed-up dividends and net income 172
GST/HST credit: filing by 18 year olds 121
GST/HST credits 39, 42, 72, 133
GST/HST rebate 89
Guarantee at maturity 185-186
Guaranteed income supplement (GIS) 224

Half-year rule 78
Home and attendant care 146
Home Buyers' Plan 65, 67, 115, 251, 277, 294
Home modifications as medical expenses 139
Home relocation loans 86
Home workspace expenses 73
Honoraria 103

Identical property 184
Immigration 188
Improvement 207
Inadequate bookkeeping 279
Income 29
Income after death 272
Income bonds and debentures 175
Income definitions 31
Income from property 169
Income from property 191
Income in kind 29
Income inclusion rate 181
Income supplements 27
Ineligible allowances 99
Ineligible child care 80
Ineligible moving expenses 86
Infirmity 126
Insurance 206, 237
Inter-spousal loans 286
Interest costs 78
Interest-free and low-interest loan 104
Interest on investment loans 211
Interest Paid on Student Loans 133
Interest reporting methods 177

Interview checklist: finding a professional team 48-49
Inventory 192
Investment and other periodic income 269
Investment counsel fees 210
Investment, Revenue Property and Capital Gains Income 112
Investors 27
IRAs and Roth IRAs 235-236

Job termination 99
Joint accounts 170
Joint election to split pension income 232
Joint filing provisions 111

Kiddie tax 124, 155
Knowledge Bureau Newsbooks 315
Knowledge Bureau Report 223

Land 206
Landscaping 206
Lease cancellation payments by landlord 207
Leasing costs 78
Legal, accounting and other professional fees 207
Legal fees 70, 144
Legal fees on separation or divorce 163
Life insurance policy loans 211
Lifelong Learning Plan 65, 67, 131
Limited partnership losses 179
Line linking 27
Listed personal use properties 183-184
Live-in nanny 80
Lump sum payments 162
Luxury vehicles 77

Maintenance and repairs 206, 207
Making instalment remittances 160
Management and administration fees 207
Maximum child care claims 81
Maximum RRSP contributions
Meals 70
Medical expenses 115, 129, 146, 148, 272
Medical expenses for employees 96
Medical travel costs 140
Military pensions 31
Minimum tax 272
Mixed-use expenses 11, 76
Mortgage foreclosures and conditional sales repossessions 196
Mortgage interest 207

Mortgages 178
Motor vehicle expenses 70
Motor vehicles 77-78
Moves outside Canada 87
Moving and renting 203
Moving expenses 31, 84, 113, 122
Multiple owners 208
Mutual fund exchanges and switches 185

Net income 30
Net Research Grants 131
NETFILE 7-8, 17, 20-22, 145-146, 258, 268, 276
NETFILE restrictions 21
No attribution 204
No T-slips 170
Non-arm's length consideration 188
Non-capital loss 123
Non-refundable tax credits 288-291
Non-registered investment accounts 154
Non-residents 175, 259
Non-statutory deductions
Non-taxable income supplements 30
Northern residents deduction 92-93
Notice of Assessment 13, 15, 170
Nursery school 80

OAS 219, 223
OAS age eligibility deferral reforms 224
OAS clawback 82, 222, 235, 237
OAS pension benefit deferral reforms 223
Office and other supplies 207
Operating expenses 76
Options granted by a CCPC 91
Options granted by a public corporation 91
Ordinary income 32
Other deductions 175
Other employment income 130
Other property 161
Other taxable allowances 105
Other than eligible or ineligible dividends 171-172
Outlays and expenses 182
Overnight sports school 80
Overseas Employment Tax Credit 105, 259

Parking costs 70
Part-time students 82
Part-time worker 59
Part-year Residents 260
Passenger vehicles 77-78
Past service contributions 272, 303

Past service pension adjustment 64
Patronage dividends 176
Pension Adjustment 103
Pension adjustment 64, 66
Pension adjustment reversal 64
Pension income amount 60, 116, 231-235
Pension income splitting 111, 238, 272
Pensioners 27
Perks 93
Permission to destroy records 279
Permissive deductions 15
Personal amount 120, 272
Personal use 75-76
Personal use of employer's auto 104
Personal use properties 183, 201
Political contributions 116
Pooled Retirement Pension Plan 62, 226, 230
Post retirement benefit (PRB) 228
Pre-retirement counselling 232
Prescribed rate of interest 86
Primarily responsible 41
Principal residence 161, 200-203
Prior year returns 273
Private health care 115
Proceeds of disposition 181
Profits resulting from investments in a business 155
Prolonged impairment 145
Property taxes 207
Property transferred to adult children 156
Property transferred to minor children 155
Provincial Foreign Tax Credit 175
Provincial refundable tax credits 35
Provincial returns 13
Provincial tax adjustments 15
Public transit, fitness and arts amounts 165
Publicly traded shares, mutual funds and other shares 184

QPP 103
Qualified farming 196
Qualified fishing properties 196
Qualified SBC Shares
Qualifying donees 151
Quarterly instalment 286
Quebec 27, 59, 81, 92, 229

Reasonable expectation of profit 206
Recapture 78, 194, 206
Receipts for expenses 83
Record retention 279
Record retention period 12

Recovery tax 223
Refundable medical expense
    supplement 146
Refundable tax credits 288-291
Registered Disability Savings Plan
    (RDSP) contributions 154
Registered Disability Savings Plan
    income 144
Registered Education Savings Plan
    132, 134, 156, 157
RESP Income 132
Registered Pension Plan 62-63, 103,
    230
Registered Retirement Savings Plan
    62, 83, 230, 250, 263
Reimbursements by employers 87
Renovations for the disabled 207
Rent 191
Rental income 131, 204-205
Rental loss 206
Rental to Personal Residence (S. 45(3)
    Election) 204
Repayments of EI and CPP 143
Replacement properties 15, 195
Reportable property 263
Reserves 195
Residency deduction 93
Restoration 207
Restrictions for claiming meals 89
Retirement Compensation
    Arrangements 231
Retiring Allowances 99, 104, 231
Return of capital 187
Returning former resident 265
RPP past service contributions 272
RPP past service contributions while a
    contributor 105
RRSP accumulations 161
RRSP contribution room 64, 66, 99,
    121-122, 131-133
RRSP earned income 66
RRSP overcontributions 67
RRSP rollovers to RDSPs 271
RRSP withdrawals before maturity
    233
RRSPs and other pensions 271

Safety deposit box 113
Salaries paid to an assistant 70
Salary 103
Salary and commission 70
Schedule 4 Statement of Investment
    Income 169
Scholarships, Bursaries and
    Fellowships 131-132
Securities traders 189
Security options benefits 104
Security options deduction 104

Segregated funds 185
Self-employed 27, 73-75, 89, 101,
    103
Self-employment 32, 84, 132, 141
Self-employment income 112
Separated families 82
Separating assets 160
Severe impairment 145
Simple interest 178
Simplified method 87, 89, 140
Social Benefits Repayment 223
Social insurance numbers 41
Special averaging 143
Special needs persons 140
Special rules for students 86
Split child benefits 288
Splitting CPP income 227
Spousal Amount 110, 114, 164, 173
Spousal Income Transfer 173
Spousal RRSP 113, 160-161, 233-234
Spousal RRSP contributions 154
Spouse 110
Status Indian 105
Statute of limitations 15, 40
Statutory deductions 53
Stock dividends 176
Stock options deduction 91
Stock splits 176
Student loan interest 211
Student tax rebates 42
Students 81
Superannuation 232
Supplies 70
Support for children 160
Support for spouses 159-160
Support payments 162
Survivor's benefits 228

T1 line-by-line tax guide 292-314
T1213 Request to Reduce Tax
    Deductions at Source 60, 286
T3 slips 286
T4 slip 56-57
Tax credits 34
Tax credits on separation or divorce
    163
Tax evaders 279
Tax evasion 278, 280
Tax filer profiles 27, 28
Tax filing deadline 275
Tax filing milestones 286
Tax Free Savings Account 121, 131,
    263
Tax Free Savings Accounts at death
    270
Tax on split income 124
Tax professional 46, 48
Tax treaties 176

Tax withholdings 286
Taxable benefits 103
Taxable Canadian Property (TCP)
    260, 265
Taxable income 30
Taxpayer Relief Provisions 15
TD1 personal tax credits 60
Teenagers 39
Terminal loss 78
Textbook amounts 135
TFSA accumulations 161
Tips 103
Tips and Gratuities 130
Tools 70
Total income 30
Tradepersons 70
Transferred to a spouse 15, 240
Transfers of securities to charity 150
Transfers resulting from marriage
    breakdown 155
Travel deduction 93
Travel insurance 115
Travelling expenses 70
Treasury bills and T-bills 189
Truckers 88-90
T-slip guide for seniors 243
Tuition fees 135
Tuition, Education and Textbook
    Amount 115, 128, 132-135

U.S. Citizens residing in Canada 177
U.S. investment accounts 177
U.S. Social Security 235
Undeducted RRSP contributions 67,
    304
Undepreciated Capital Cost (UCC)
    78, 194
Universal Child Care Benefit 111, 163
Universities outside Canada 134
Untaxed retirement income room 224
Utilities 208

Valuation days 181
Van 115-116
Voluntary compliance 15, 280
Volunteer firefighter 103-104

Wages 103
Withholding taxes 175
Work crews 89
Workers' Compensation 105, 144
Working Income Tax Benefit (WITB)
    133